Encounters with Alphonso Lingis

Encounters with Alphonso Lingis

Edited by
Alexander E. Hooke
and Wolfgang W. Fuchs

LEXINGTON BOOKS
Lanham • Boulder • New York • Oxford

LEXINGTON BOOKS

Published in the United States of America
by Lexington Books
A Member of The Rowman & Littlefield Publishing Group
4501 Forbes Boulevard, Suite 200, Lanham, Maryland 20706

PO Box 317
Oxford
OX2 9RU, UK

Copyright © 2003 by Lexington Books

All rights reserved. No part of this publication may be reproduced, stored in a retrieval system, or transmitted in any form or by any means, electronic, mechanical, photocopying, recording, or otherwise, without the prior permission of the publisher.

British Library Cataloguing in Publication Information Available

Library of Congress Cataloging-in-Publication Data

Library of Congress Control Number: 2003107997

ISBN: 0-7391-0700-3 (cloth : alk. paper)
       0-7391-0701-1 (pbk. : alk. paper)

Printed in the United States of America

♾™ The paper used in this publication meets the minimum requirements of American National Standard for Information Sciences—Permanence of Paper for Printed Library Materials, ANSI/NISO Z39.48–1992.

DEDICATION

For my mother.

—Alex

ACKNOWLEDGMENTS

We want to thank our editor at Lexington, Jason Hallman, for his support of this project. Many thanks also to Alice Cherbonnier and Russell Henley of Allegro Communications, Inc. for their diligence in putting the manuscript in order, and Dorothea Thieleke-Fuchs for patiently transcribing our interview with Lingis. And special thanks to Nicole Reese for her administrative talents in keeping all the loose ends together.

Contents

Introduction ix

Section I: LOCATING LINGIS IN TRADITIONS OF THOUGHT

Chapter 1	David Farrell Krell *Far from the Pallid Float*	3
Chapter 2	Wolfgang W. Fuchs *Seeing the Named,* *Naming the Seen:* *Relations to the Tradition*	19
Chapter 3	Alexander E. Hooke and Wolfgang W. Fuchs *Reflections Since* Dangerous Emotions: *Interview with* *Alphonso Lingis, 2002*	35
Chapter 4	Thomas J. Altizer *The Sacred Vision of a* *Solitary Voyager*	43
Chapter 5	Janice McLane *Encounter the World, Keep a* *Clear Eye*	51
Chapter 6	Alexander E. Hooke *Silent Communities:* *Foucault and Lingis on the* *End of Philosophy*	63
Chapter 7	Mary Zournazi *Foreign Bodies: Interview with* *Alphonso Lingis (1996)*	83

Section II: DEPARTURES: SINGULAR AND COMMON REALITIES

Chapter 8	Jean-Luc Nancy *Limits, Borders,* *and Shores of Singularity*	101
Chapter 9	Gerald Majer *Dream of a Blind Sculptress*	109
Chapter 10	Elizabeth Grosz *Naked*	119
Chapter 11	David Karnos *There Is Always Another Island*	133
Chapter 12	Edward Casey *Mapping the Earth Otherwise*	147
Chapter 13	Thomas L. Dumm *Grief Suspended:* *Lingis, Cavell, Emerson*	165

Section III: THE RETURN HOME

Chapter 14	Alphonso Lingis *Trust*	175
Bibliography		187
Index		201
Contributors		205

Introduction

Alphonso Lingis has been one of the most significant contributors to building the bridge that connects Continental thought and American philosophy. As a translator, Lingis has made several major thinkers accessible to English speakers. As a commentator and professor, he has articulated for many audiences a rich understanding of seminal philosophers from modern and contemporary eras. And perhaps most compelling, as a traveler and author of ten books, Lingis has formulated philosophical perspectives that are gradually forming a distinct and intriguing way to investigate ideas and values central to Western beliefs and truths.

Responses to these perspectives have been varied. Many know Lingis as a dramatic and imaginative public lecturer. At conferences or invited colloquia throughout the world, he has been a major draw for philosophers and nonphilosophers alike. Within the rather staid climate of academe, a Lingis presentation can be something of a spectacle. Indeed, there are students and professors of philosophy whose knowledge of him is solely as a performer and not as a writer.

Many people have already been subtly influenced by Lingis in their discussions of two prominent philosophers—Merleau-Ponty and Levinas. When English speakers turn their scholarly attention to such important issues as alterity, embodiment, human nature, reason, and imperatives, they invariably rely on his translations. Check the footnotes of any volume discussing them, and the name most frequently appearing (aside from the featured philosopher) is invariably Lingis's.

This influence is also seen on others who know of Lingis as an interpreter, commentator, or teacher. The variety of his work devoted to either individual thinkers or topics is remarkable. If you wander through the library, for example, you can find his essay on Jean-Paul Sartre published in the *Journal of Philosophy*, on strange temples in *Soundings*, on savages in *SemioText(e)*, or on honor and street urchins in *Paragraph*. If your attention is turned to the thoughts of, say, George Bataille, Martin Heidegger, Michel Foucault, Michel de Certeau, Gilles Deleuze, Edmund Husserl, or Friedrich Nietzsche, there is a good chance you have seen in a book or journal a contributing essay from Lingis. If not, then at least there was probably a contribution from one of his many students who have been influenced by Lingis to examine and publish their reflections on ideas central to contemporary philosophy and thought.

Certainly, more formal acknowledgment of Lingis's writings occurs. Reviews in *Choice* have cited the remarkable imagery and mastery of philosophical discourse as reasons for recommending closer attention to his books. When they are discussed in more scholarly forums, such as journal reviews, a reader finds phrases such as "exquisite prose," "work of art," or "compelling descriptions."

And in a recent book devoted to some two dozen American philosophers who are part of the Continental tradition, the editors name Lingis as the "quintessential phenomenologist." Likening his writings to the paintings of Paul Gaugin, the editors add, "He [Lingis] has allowed the foreign and the native to gain their own unique, untranslated, expression and recognition in our language."

Curiously, these various encounters have not led to any sustained published discussion of Lingis's own thought as presented in his many writings. Aside from an occasional reference to his works, it would appear that readers, students, and teachers of philosophy and related fields in the humanities have considered but not yet had the chance to develop and articulate their encounters with Lingis's work. We suspect his readers, as well as those who have only attended his performances, will find it fruitful to be shown entrances to the work of Lingis that may provide them the opportunity to more easily pursue their own responses and thoughts regarding his work. This book intends to give this growing audience that opportunity.

As elaborated below, the contributors to this project invite us to consider numerous approaches to these aspects of Lingis's thought. Whether your orientation arises out of anthropology, cultural studies, political science, or your reading has been limited to some striking excerpts from *Abuses, Excesses*, or *The Imperative*, or your impression of him stems from a translation footnote to an essay on Merleau-Ponty or Levinas, or you recall an asterisk you highlighted as a promising session to attend during a conference, the selections here encourage you to develop these initial impressions by becoming open to the kinds of philosophical encounters one can have with Alphonso Lingis.

Background

As noted, these perspectives have often been introduced by way of performances and dramatics. Lingis's conference presentations are renowned for their dynamic tones and surprising shifts. It is no secret that even the most assured public speakers or lecturers have trepidation when giving a talk right after a Lingis presentation. "Anticlimactic" or "letdown" is how some sheepishly introduce themselves before they begin their talks. Compared to more conventional presentations, his are performances. He might appear in strange garb, with a light show of silhouettes dancing as backdrop; photos of unfamiliar faces and places, or the sounds of archaic voices chanting often accompany his own words. People who have never read his books can recall with vivid detail having been at his public presentations. "I remember he read a paper on mortality lying down in a casket," or "It was really weird, you never saw him; you just heard his vibrant voice, saw a flashlight to help his reading amid all these strange background noises," or "It was quite a song and dance," are some of the impressions reported by those who have attended Lingis's presentations. In any case, it is nearly always before a packed audience. Those in attendance might be reminded of the stories about thinkers of earlier generations—Heidegger, Marcuse, Sartre, or Foucault—whose public lectures were events.

Those who have experienced Lingis's presentations might be tempted to dismiss him as mere academic spectacle. This betrays a limited understanding of both spectacle and Lingis.

A spectacle is not only a popular and social event that somehow overstimulates one or more of the senses. It also stimulates one's own beliefs and attitudes. Many spectacles invite or challenge one to a kind of transformation. This transformation, however, is full of uncertainty, surprise, and chance. Historically, spectacles of one kind or another have a limited life span. The Romans from the early days of the Empire, for example, had trouble in continually funding gladiator battles and bestial executions of criminals and heretics so that the spectators would not become bored and unchanged. Europeans in the early days of Modernity were enticed with public executions of various sorts—from tortures to beheadings of heretics, thieves, and murderers. A presentation by Lingis is hardly so gruesome. But in the climate of academic life, his presentations breathe with surprise, passion, and intrigue to the point that many listeners are spellbound. Sometimes frustrated, other times fascinated, spectators are left unsure about themselves, curious about the images and scenes Lingis recounts with his philosophical reflections.

His presentations are, in any event, mostly works in progress. The more subtle components of his thought are better appreciated through his writings, which are quite varied. Lingis can interweave rather abstract reflections on the Athenian notion of friendship with experiences in leper colonies and Thai jail cells. He may juxtapose thoughtful accounts of Western values of beauty and moral goodness with the coming together of rebel fighters in Central American jungles or beggars in Southeast Asia. His descriptions of multiple realities are so lucid and compelling that the reader is often challenged to reconsider which value or truth he or she ultimately embraces. At the same time Lingis's own perspectives are drawn with a light hand, as if his writings were offering a means for challenging the values and truths he is expected to exemplify or espouse when he is teaching his university students.

In thematizing the challenges offered in studying Lingis, the sections outlined for this book intend to present three recurring concerns found in his work. One, what are the central issues of modern and contemporary philosophy that demand our attention? Two, which problems troubling current theoretical and moral disputes (on, for example, subjectivity, death, eroticism, beauty, justice, self/other) do Lingis's writings help us understand and analyze? And three, how do his writings prepare the stage for a kind of "conceptual lens" that offers direction to new kinds of inquiry, particularly with regards to alterity, imperatives, the body, and community?

These questions obviously do not exhaust the possible approaches to Alphonso Lingis's thought. We believe, however, that they can serve as pedagogical and philosophical tools to invite and direct readers to further study. They capture not only several features prominent in his work but also, in our view, necessary hallmarks of any innovative thinker.

Philosophy for Another Generation

Here we are reminded of the status of Michel Foucault a generation ago. Until the English translation of *Discipline and Punish* appeared in the mid-1970s, Foucault's work received little attention in the United States. He was rarely mentioned in philosophy courses, graduate seminars, or in journals. Since then, of course, Foucault has become something of a cottage industry. He has also become something more. Not only are major philosophy journals and books addressing the implications of his fertile research, but his seminal work has been the basis for ongoing research in a variety of fields.

In our view, Alphonso Lingis is one of the few American candidates with the potential to have such an impact on at least this and the next generation of readers in philosophy. His style of presentation, especially in his writings, invites fellow thinkers to reconsider those old age philosophical concerns: Who are we? What is true love, and how would I know? What is there? Is there any good amid so much despair and evil? Who offers joy or gives great beauty when we are surrounded by confusion, misery, and death? Lingis has his own insights to offer on contemporary life and its distinct values and methods of evaluation. His curiosity seeks out eye-opening encounters with a range of figures and phenomena such a Mishima, Michel Tournier, Gita, Augusto, the sacred statues of what we ineptly call Easter Island, the five-octave range of the Brazilian singer who in the pubs and bars is simply idolized as "The Voice," dancers in trance at Bali's the Temple of Death, among *so many others*.

These are among the ideas and experiences that Lingis discusses in his works in a distinct and provocative way. As the essays of this volume indicate, these discussions present the kind of reflection on experience worthy of yet further reflection by readers, critics, and scholars. They raise issues, possibilities, and vectored realities that need to be brought to our attention. These possibilities, however, do not resemble the far-fetched images analytic philosophers raise as weird counterexamples to weigh in with against any theory they do not like. Lingis's range of possibilities are not only earthly and embodied—they also speak of other realities in a positive or affirmative tone because they teach us new lessons about the good, truthful, and beautiful.

Describing and studying the exotic, the extraordinary, can shed light not only on these, but also bring more focused visibility to the ordinary, the common, and the taken-for-granted. Lingis admits that many of his essays begin as missives to friends. Hence his lucid, "as if you were there" accounts of hitchhiking in Iran, sleeping among the headhunters in Irian Java, embracing Gita in the dark night in India, following Augusto in the Nicaraguan jungles, scuba diving with Mario/Maria in the Philippine waters, spending the night with compassionate cellmates in a Bangkok jail, walking among the lepers in Calcutta, among *so many others*.

It is inadequate to call Lingis a postmodern. While his publications indicate he is quite conversant and sometimes sympathetic with thinkers who have been placed under the postmodern rubric, and Lingis has taken up some of their insights, frequently his descriptions celebrate much that is discounted or bypassed among the critics of this orientation and their cousins, the cynics. Even for those who find positive value in what is nowadays called genealogy, deconstruction, post-structuralism, there is the tendency to limit arguments and analyses to textual or historical anchors. Or they revive variations of the power/knowledge nexus that undermines or devalues human discourse and experience. Or they highlight the limits and dangers of a hegemonic discourse in the name of giving one's own group an identity in this discourse. But even in these circles there is still much that is clouded over. Even they still betray the many realities still eluding and awaiting us, observes Lingis.

To address these shortcomings Lingis provides a renewed support for the importance of phenomenology. To those who jumped on the bandwagon by dismissing phenomenology as merely an extension of the modern, Lingis holds that it is to a great extent with, and against, the great phenomenologists that one must still enter the activity of philosophy. And where he thinks against them, it is by the means of embracing the original phenomenological task of *description* in order to "*return to the things themselves.*" This undertaking is best understood, though, not in terms of self-consciousness but in terms of an encounter with an other.

As this encounter is sometimes most dramatically presented as vivid snapshots from his travels, it is tempting to conclude that the direction of Lingis's thought is primarily an extension of his translations of Levinas and Merleau-Ponty. Lingis is obviously indebted to Levinas's theories on alterity, the face and the elemental, joy, and singularity, and to Merleau-Ponty's ideas on the body, perception, and the imperative. But he is also much influenced by Nietzsche (and those influenced by him, such as Bataille and Deleuze) and his understanding of the tenuous self, the limitations of those who assert claims to universal truths and value, and the idea of excess or expenditure without recompense that Lingis finds expressed not only in the human world but also and sometimes more genuinely among animals and divine spirits.

Yet Lingis does not confine himself to the arena of inspirations and intellectual disputes within Continental philosophy. On the contrary, his sources are wide ranging. He will also call our attention to the writings of Hillary Putnam, Jaako Hintikka, Bernard Williams, Paul Feyerabend; he will cite the words of Marguerite Duras, Diane Ackerman, Montaigne; he will highlight the mastery of the stones at Machu Picchu, the temple Haggia Sophia in Istanbul, the erotic displays of Khajuraho; and more recently, he will interweave the findings of biologists and zoologists regarding the immense variety of life forms other than the human. In a word, it is his ability to wonder, that birth-moment of philosophy, that lets his and our eyes be opened.

In Foucault's case, recognition became more widespread as readers, critics, and scholars discussed his work in relation to tradition, the present, and how (with his archaeology and genealogy) he gives us conceptual apparatus to do further study. In Lingis's case, his relation to the masters of Western thought, his fascination with how human beings in the remotest regions of the world live today, and his phenomenology of perception and xenographic sketches all introduce a new conceptual apparatus and give access to worlds that need to be thought. This book hopes to give readers an appreciation and critical understanding of that apparatus and to the worlds that need to be thought.

The Contributions

The following essays are divided into two main sections. Section One, "Locating Lingis in Traditions of Thought," offers a variety of perspectives on how to understand his work with regard to many recent developments in philosophy and related fields, such as religion and political theory. In addition, they explore a variety of themes central to the history of modern Western philosophy, ranging from imperatives and space to rationality and the sacred. Section Two, "Departures: Singular and Common Realities," highlights different themes in Lingis's writings that encourage readers to pursue their own inquiries by using his distinctive approach to the varied issues related to alterity. Alert to the possibility that "otherness" has become something of a slogan or passing intellectual fashion, the contributors in this section discuss the other through perspectives featured by him. These include singularity, the body, and community, as well as experiences ranging from dreams to nakedness and grief. Interspersing these presentations are interviews with Lingis. Section Three, "The Return Home," closes the book with an essay by Lingis.

Section One begins with David Krell's reflections about Lingis as a human being, writer, and philosopher. His insightful and often humorous adventure begins with one of Lingis's innermost fantasies and ends with speculation that Lingis restores an American intellectual commitment previously embraced by Emerson, James, and du Bois. Drawing a parallel from D. H. Lawrence's rich and complex admiration of Walt Whitman, Krell presents a perspective that entices audiences reluctant to see Lingis other than as a translator or performer. It is in his written words that one becomes most moved by the ambivalent forces of his thought. According to Krell: "One comes away from the reading of this [Lingis's] writing sober but not clean, both elated and defeated, in love and in despondency at once. The despondency of love and of thinking: so *this* is what it would have been like to *live*."

For Wolfgang W. Fuchs, this ambivalence can also be a guide to comprehending Lingis's relation to ongoing intellectual controversies and thinkers of Modernity. Given that Lingis's publications on so many writers and issues are grouped under the postmodern rubric, there is the temptation to see him still as one more chisel chipping away at the edifice we call the Enlightenment. Fuchs believes this attitude is mistaken. The themes featured throughout Lingis's work—subjectivity, perception, imperative, alterity, embodiment, death, justice—are best appreciated in light of his ongoing dialogue with the masters of Western philosophy. Borrowing from Nietzsche, Fuchs further contends that to appreciate Lingis's originality we need to grasp how his books continually seek to name realities and truths glossed over or ignored by the masters. These points are especially useful in distinguishing how he is influenced by and departs from the philosophers whose works he has translated—Merleau-Ponty and Levinas.

In a recent interview Lingis elaborates on a more personal level on why he remains interested in philosophy and some of his enduring influences. Philosophy has the potential to help reveal or illuminate different worlds and realities. Thinkers such as Heidegger, Levinas, Nietzsche, Bataille, or Deleuze and Guattari provide us with new ways for crossing disciplines. Lingis confesses that he hardly feels bound by what academicians call Continental thought. Austin, Wittgenstein, and Bernard Williams are among the many philosophers who also demand attention, he observes, as well as researchers in other fields, including biology, astronomy, history, and anthropology. He then relates several experiences in which such commonplace notions as trust or honor take on new meaning.

Thomas Altizer proposes that Lingis can also be understood as a deeply religious thinker, in a quite unconventional way. It is no accident, observes Altizer, that many of Lingis's essays address temples, rituals, and sacrifices. Specifically, there is a recurring tension between Christianity (particularly in the Catholic Eucharist), its symbols, and Lingis's solitary voyages. Indeed, notes Altizer, these voyages introduce a paradox that celebrates ecstatic moments while these moments are often the result of violent acts that are ordinarily condemned. Here Lingis's work is important not only for philosophers but for anyone who is fascinated with and troubled by religious culture. Hence, according to Altizer, Lingis's ideas should be discussed in relation to the visions of Dante or Joyce, since they too spoke so intensely and poetically about God, the law of God, and the experiences of violence that test one's own beliefs.

According to Janice McLane, what Lingis does with these experiences makes him one of the most compelling philosophers among contemporary writers. In terms of teaching or explaining him, however, he also is one of the most challenging. Much of what he does requires both daring and discipline. Students might be tempted toward imitation or irritation, either write like he does or dismiss him because he is reluctant to spell out what he is doing and the arguments he is making. McLane proposes that students can miss out on how Lingis brings a new intensity to thought: "....the philosopher must approach his or her life," she writes, "with the same degree of ferocious and pitiless scrutiny a scientist might bring to dissecting an animal brain." This is philosophy as a purposeful "self-vivisection." Hence, she points out, much of Lingis's works can be read in the spirit one reads Augustine's *Autobiography*, Kierkegaard's *Either/Or*, or nearly any book of Nietzsche's.

Silence, often considered a religious idea, is discussed in Alexander Hooke's essay as central to Lingis's perspectives on politics and the tasks of philosophy. In his Preface to *Abuses*, Lingis evokes the importance of philosophy's capacity in speaking for those who are silent or silenced. This capacity is richly illustrated in many of his travels, from encountering the plight of the Bihari in northern India to the turmoil of street urchins in Brazil. Lingis's recent attention to what he calls technopoles highlights the immense increase of centers of communication (and power and money) while so many locales of the world—human and natural—barely survive in neglect and silence. To bring into focus the significance of Lingis's outlook, Hooke compares it to Foucault's thoughts on silence.

This section closes with an interview conducted by Mary Zournazi. She elicits from Lingis his observations about how he approaches his essays and some of the early formulations that have resulted in his remarkable ability to interweave his travels with philosophical discussions. Regarding the characteristic use of photographs, he relates to Zournazi how he first became interested in taking pictures of people and places he encountered, and how photographs complement his interest in describing surfaces, faces, and initial contacts. In addition, Lingis recalls some of the cultural inhibitions some people have with the camera, as well as how photographs make wonderful gifts to many who have never seen a picture of themselves or their friends and family members. Zournazi then encourages Lingis—well known for his rhetorical eloquence—to reflect on the significance and limitations of language. While words often express meanings and values that interlocutors have in common, initial contacts are often sparked by the tone of another's voice. Citing Jean-Luc Nancy, Lingis points out how the tonality communicates the singularity of another's appeal.

Section Two, "Departures: Singular and Common Realities," begins with Nancy's recent thoughts on singularity. While at initial glance singularity is the exception, it also is fundamental to understanding our sociality, our being-in-common. To clarify this paradoxical view, Nancy distinguishes three aspects or themes of singularity: as limit; as border; and as bank/shore. As with birth and death, the limit is essential to the singular but remains unaccomplished within it. Thus the limit is also an interval, giving rise to the importance of coexistence or what singularities have in common. Borders seem to mark the end of limits, yet they also function as a means by which singularities pass and establish contact, something like border crossings that nomads, travelers, and refugees know by experience. By the riverbank or ocean shore, things flow and the borders lose their recognizable edges and markers. There are only passages. Nancy closes the essay discussing the singular plural among existents just as we discuss the channel or rift of a river or other bodies of water.

With the ideas of Lingis and Nancy in mind, Gerald Majer turns to examine the singularity of one's dreams. A blind sculptress appears in the dark of night, and its source and status raise several disturbing questions that revolve around the relation of the dreamer to the dream. Is the dream about the dreamer's inner or unconscious self? Does he keep the dream secret? And does the very notion of "keeping the dream" already betray its own strange reality? Here Majer suspects that one does not possess a dream, no matter how vivid or personal it is. One is exposed to it. Moreover, there is an imperative that seems to belong to the dream itself, with its own appeals that are misleadingly described by analysts as a mirror of oneself. Instead, writes Majer, "In the mirror of these words, she is dreaming. Not of me, but only dreaming. Someone dreams: dreams of the world, the space of which one is the possession in a movement-with, a convulsion of the night."

Elizabeth Grosz shifts Lingis's ideas on the look and body to the political significance of contemporary art, especially with regard to the continuing debate about nudity, spectacle, and the pornographic image. There is something strange, according to Grosz, about how a culture carefully and imaginatively crafts its own ideal body types, yet exhibits so much shame in particular depictions of its bodies. This shame assumes that we know what the body means—whether in an erotic, utilitarian, reproductive, or biological sense. Yet, Grosz hypothesizes, we really do not know what our bodies are capable of. They are often going beyond themselves. At the same time there is something peculiar about the human body; it is, notes Lingis, anatomically ridiculous. "Can art," she asks, "be seen as a way of forcing this anatomical ridiculousness into productivity?" Efforts in making the naked body productive are often codified and organized, divided into acceptable or inappropriate, civil or offensive, intimate or public. Grosz concludes with proposals for resisting these social codes by envisioning one's own body as a work of art.

David Karnos examines a literary work that has compelled Lingis's attention, the novel by Michel Tournier, *Friday or the Other Island*. So intriguing is this novel that it has become something of a classic; there is even a version tailored for children. (With commentary on solar sexuality and abstractions on language, we caution the reader that the version being considered here is rated for mature audiences.) To account for its popularity, Karnos cites Simone Viernes's explanation: Tournier's *Friday* involves quests that go through three stages—separation from society, encounters with death, and rebirth into a cosmic harmony. Certainly such stages are discussed in many of Lingis's own writings, and most poignantly, regarding Tournier, in *Foreign Bodies*. Becoming naked with the elements, seeking solitude and freedom from social trappings, exposing oneself to alien forces, not to mention the sheer magic of it all, are the key features working through Karnos's discussion.

Edward Casey sees Lingis's work on the body as giving direction to a new kind of earth-mapping. To sketch out a map, however, involves much more than surveying locations that are relevant and putting things into proper scale. A map is also the work of our memories; try to make your own map of say, a campus, an airport, or a neighborhood, and you'll invariably distort the importance of your favorite hangout, the departure gate, or your house. A map is made in large part by the traces left on the earth's surface by the body—in its experiences, movements, creations, and thoughts. This creative aspect means, for Casey, that maps are cartographic but also artistic. Lingis's philosophical travelogues are intertwined with the work of contemporary artists Robert Smithson and Michelle Stuart to illustrate Casey's concept of earth-mapping.

Thomas Dumm reflects on another theme fundamental to Lingis's work—death. Not so much the traditional concern about human mortality as one's own, but the death that shadows one's encounters with others, either as anticipation or as remembrance of another. Grief, according to Dumm, is a passion that enlivens a community, such as the one he himself is presently discovering in light of a rare disease striking his wife. To understand this passion, Dumm finds a resonance with another important American philosopher, Ralph Waldo Emerson. While Lingis does not address Emerson's work, Dumm locates an essential link (via a contemporary American philosopher, Stanley Cavell) by recounting Emerson's meditations over the death of his young son. These meditations center on the notion of "caducous." Although many of us tend to associate grief with desolation or remorse, Dumm's insights to these three thinkers show that grief is also a source of goodness.

The book closes with an inquiry on trust by Lingis. He begins by relating an experience in Madagascar, where he had to rely on a young tour guide to lead him through the difficult terrain. The guide and Lingis shared no common language and, it turns out, the guide could easily have ran off with Lingis's camera or other valuables. He did not. The scene then shifts to the opulence of London, where the papers and television highlight the various skirmishes among local hate groups. This contrast sparks Lingis's reflections on the nature of trust. He sees it in relation to courage, laughter, and lust, while contrasting it with hate, fear, and suspicion.

I
LOCATING LINGIS IN TRADITIONS OF THOUGHT

Thoughts are gifts....thoughts are illuminations. They are things your mind retains above all as the most precious events in the stream of your consciousness. Unlike conceptual schemes produced in the culture and picked up by effort, you cannot recall these thoughts without feeling an upsurge of gratitude. Each of us treasures a thought someone gave us as a gift above all manner of material gifts.
—*"Gifts,"* Dangerous Emotions

The unlived life is not worth examining.
—*"Antarctic Summer,"* Abuses

Chapter One

Far from the Pallid Float

David Farrell Krell

Every philosopher has a closely guarded fantasy life. The more desiccated the philosopher, the more luxuriant the phantasm. However, what would be the fantasy life of a philosopher whose mind is awash with organs and glandular secretions? Alphonso Lingis once confessed to me his innermost fantasy—it was a moment of weakness, a confession over coffee—and I am going to betray it to my readers.

It is two o'clock on a chilly autumn morning in central Pennsylvania. The alarm clock shatters the night and Lingis struggles to his feet. They are well formed, they hold him steady, despite the hour. He performs his ablutions, affirms his reflection in the mirrors of his private *mise-en-abyme*, nothing helps an uncertain grace. He goes downstairs, feeds his birds, forgets about feeding himself, climbs into his car and begins driving west where one of the philosophy "circle" meetings is taking place—somewhere in the vicinity of Iowa, he isn't quite sure. His paper is scheduled for two o'clock; luckily, he does not forget the typescript as he walks out the door, clucking "*farewell! good-bye!*" to his birds.

Sometime that afternoon he arrives in a desolate midwestern town, locates the building, finds the room. There are tsk-tsks of impatience: he is ten minutes late. A dapper young colleague in a suit and tie, his commentator, is ready to make reply; the chair of the session, watch in hand and irritation on his face, is more than ready, and Lingis is as ready as he will ever be. The paper he will give is something he wrote in Papua New Guinea. Something on phenomenology. He reads his paper, an astonished and embarrassed silence ensues, the young commentator goes to the lectern and in fifteen minutes demonstrates that Lingis has gotten every detail about the master phenomenologist's doctrines wrong; what little he has gotten right the master anticipated decades before Lingis, having developed all his arguments and descriptions and reductions with relentless acumen and thoroughness. In short, while Lingis was traipsing about New Guinea he should have been in the archive doing his homework. The commentator smiles demurely, even forgivingly, and resumes his seat. The chair of the session, thinking of the second cup of coffee he hasn't had yet, invites Lingis to a *brief* rebuttal. Lingis rises, crawls to the lectern, his well-formed feet supporting him somewhat less steadily than they did at two in the morning or at the hour of that silky dawn in Papua. Tears well up in his eyes and course down his cheeks. Slowly he rips his paper in half from top to bottom and says, "I'm sorry—may I come back next year and try again?"

•

No philosopher will want to have been Lingis's commentator. No button-down academic will want to have been his moderator. He cannot be moderated, commentary seems graceless and pointless, and critique almost always misses the mark. Yet one cannot simply praise his work: as Heidegger once said when he heard a scholar praising Kant, "Praise from below is always an insult." To repeat, one cannot criticize his work, at least not in the usual ways, inasmuch as criticism from the sidelines is always a declaration of bankruptcy. Indeed, if one were to opt for criticism, it would have to be like D. H. Lawrence's criticism of Walt Whitman—at once scathing and helpless, apoplectic and worshipful. Lawrence roasts Whitman in the final chapter of his *Studies in Classic American Literature*, in passages such as the following:

> Post-mortem effects. Ghosts.
>
> A certain ghoulish insistency. A certain horrible pottage of human parts. A certain stridency and portentousness. A luridness about his beatitudes…
>
> Your self.
>
> Oh, Walter, Walter, what have you done with it? What have you done with yourself? With your own individual self? For it sounds as if it had all leaked out of you, leaked into the universe.
>
> Post-mortem effects. The individuality had leaked out of him.
>
> No, no, don't lay this down to poetry. These are post-mortem effects. And Walt's great poems are really huge fat tomb-plants, great rank graveyard growths.
>
> All that false exuberance. All those lists of things boiled in one pudding-cloth! No, no!
>
> (…) This awful Whitman. This post-mortem poet. This poet with the private soul leaking out of him all the time. All his privacy leaking out in a sort of dribble, oozing into the universe.[1]

Lawrence goes on like this for pages, not merely paragraphs: sardonic, acidic, merciless, accurate. One could imagine criticizing Lingis like that, for having let his soul bleed into every corner of the natural and cultural world, his body leak into every nook and cranny of the universe. One could do that. Lawrence does that to Whitman. But then comes a paragraph break in Lawrence's text, a simple paragraph

Section One: Locating Lingis in Traditions of Thought

break like all the others, giving not a hint or a warning sign of the shift that is imminent. Whereupon we read the following:

> Whitman, the great poet, has meant so much to me. Whitman, the one man breaking a way ahead. Whitman, the one pioneer. And only Whitman. No English pioneers, no French. No European pioneer-poets....Ahead of Whitman, nothing. Ahead of all poets, pioneering into the wilderness of unopened life, Whitman. Beyond him, none.

•

Farewell! Good-bye! Lingis is off again, devil knows where to, it will surely be south or east, though not to Europe, not anymore. Multiculturalism is one thing, but this is ridiculous. What would Christmas be without a Yuletide card from Al? One with seasons greetings scribbled on the back of a black and white snapshot of a man who looks as though he very much did not want his picture taken or a woman so beautiful that no pink and pinched Caucasian of either sex will ever forgive her. Farewell! Good-bye! He's off again.

Off again, on again. His boss complains he's always late with the paper flow. Mail from Jakarta is slow, rattlesnake jackets don't go well with suits and neckties, and silk shirts don't have button-down collars. He stopped going to departmental meetings and socials because he did not relish clots of processed cheese washed down with cheap wine, and because he could no longer bear either the pratings of boundless academic ambition and egotism or the snarls of academic rancor—all that teapotial tempestitude! Farewell! Good-bye to all that!

Those who are not insanely jealous of him, and they are not legion, worry that this time he will walk out into his death. Postmortem effects? He courts danger: witness "Matagalpa," discussed below. The Freudians and Lacanians worry about his drives, for they fear that the life and death drives may reduce to *one* drive. The Jungians worry about his literalness: they too believe in collecting exotic materials, but not hepatitis, not prison arrest, not inflammation and fevers—really, he goes too far in every direction in every sense. Always too far, and yet always farther and farther. He is wet for it and he makes the others wet for it.

•

London, at the Freud Museum and the *Alliance française*. All the fringe psychoanalytic groups and all the groups from beyond the fringe have gathered to hear some far-out "speculations" on Freud, the common enemy, the Father of the Horde, whom we never finish killing. It is a gala event. After it is over, the trustees of the Freud Museum will fire its entire staff for having sponsored it, for having invited strange persons to express strange views on Freud. All the freaks of British psychoanalysis are there, avid for Freud's undoing debunking deballing dephallustration. Lingis does not give them what they want. He reads a paper called "Lust." No, not merely *called* "Lust," but *producing* lust, evoking it, marinating the audience in it. Lingis in London reads a paper about Bangkok. Euphonious appellations all: Lingis, Bangkok, and lust, all agog in London. Lust of men for boys dressed as women, lust of women for women parading as boys, lust of all and everyone for girls for men for

goats
sheep
bushes
barbells
cheap hotel rooms
neon lights
outstretched hands
Lévinas
plastic

lust unlimited, it did not stop, Lingis's litany of lust in Bangkok in London, not even when his close-mouthed, teeth-clenched voice faded after the final period. The air in the hall was close and moist. All the fringe people were wet. And they were hopping mad.

They were not upset because he had exploited the Third World. Indeed, much of "Lust" was devoted to a Baudrillardian-Marxian meditation on the harsh realities of the international exportation and exploitation of pleasure—of imperialism by credit card, as Rotarianism goes on a holiday. They were not upset by his analysis of amorphous, polymorphous desires, an analysis as supple as it was relentless. They were upset because in a stuffy theater crammed with three hundred uncomfortable seats they found their pleasures provoked more powerfully than anywhere else out there on or beyond the fringe, the provocation carving out a certain hollow in the marrow of their bones, producing a rising in the gorge, a secretion in the groin, a helpless fury in the heart. This Colonial American was shameless: he had made the English feel what it might be like to be in a hotel room with a boy who proved that Madonna was a man dressed up as the Mother of a God who was himself in drag—he made them feel as though they were being crushed in a carnival crowd. It was a *carnaval* of masks and *carne*, a carnival of mask and meat, of carnality and juices decked out as harmless Bangkok sleaze and tease. The lusts of the London crowd were better provoked than they would have been in Bangkok. Each member of the crowd was left to cower in self-recognition and rage in a theater with two hundred and ninety-nine other anonymous victims who had thought that a scintillating intellect would distract and entertain them, would rescue them once again. It was clear to them now that he is wily and cruel, even in London, even at the Freud Museum, even when a Colonial speaks.

Afterwards, when the discussion period had allowed every representative of every fringe group to express a vapid view but vent a splendid spleen, after all the rage was spent—and it was quick to come but long in passing—Lingis limped off the stage like a wounded animal. He approached a group of American friends who were waiting in the crowd below, his brow furrowed in helpless, clueless consternation.

"They didn't like my paper," he mumbled.

•

I would like to comment briefly on two books by Alphonso Lingis: *Abuses*, published

Section One: Locating Lingis in Traditions of Thought 7

by the University of California Press in 1994, and *The Community of Those Who Have Nothing in Common*, published by Indiana University Press that same year. I want to try to trace the macrostructure, as it were, or to follow the basic rhythms of two chapters in *Abuses*: first, "Matagalpa," a chapter on Nicaragua and communication; second, "Lust," the paper just referred to, but this time in greater detail. I choose these two, and only these two, partly for economy's sake, and partly because I had the opportunity to read or hear earlier versions of them. After riding the larger waves of these *Abuses*, I would like to say a word about the entire project entitled *The Community of Those Who Have Nothing in Common*. Finally, I will ask Lingis himself to say or write a word or two from "Chichicastenango," the final chapter of *Abuses*.

•

"Matagalpa" is a brief chapter of *Abuses*, some sixteen pages in its line-and-a-half spaced typescript. It opens in Managua, Nicaragua, a scene of devastation after the 1972 earthquake. After eight years the downtown area is still more like a savannah than a city. The observer-narrator notes the cardboard shelters of the shanty town, the foraging pigs, the weeds, the bees, and army ants. He notes too the three buildings that survived the earthquake—Howard Hughes's Intercontinental Hotel, the Bank of America, and the Somoza bunker. He wanders to the shore of Lake Xolotán, looking for its freshwater sharks, which do not show themselves either.

On the third page of the chapter a space-break separates two paragraphs; the theme shifts, and so does the style of narration. A crisp expository style now informs the reader of communication systems among bees and ants and mammals that travel in packs—wolves, for instance. In the wolf pack, communication is almost always about relationships within the pack rather than about things in the world. Production of signs and communication among humans now come to occupy the chapter, with particular attention paid to body language and the implication or contestation of others in communication. Lingis emphasizes the subtlety and the hazards of human communication, the vulnerability, the things that could be the death of our meaning and of our selves.

By the eighth page of the chapter, halfway through the whole, it is the *look* of the other that dominates, although the particular charge of that look remains indeterminate, somewhere between the *regards* of Sartre and Merleau-Ponty, the *laughter* and *tears* of Nietzsche and Bataille, and the *desire* and the *saying* of Lacan and Lévinas. The look of the other is abashed but also disarming. It is cast by an eye that is both naked in its needs and clothed in the masks of gods. By the eleventh page, it is the imperative in the look of communication that rules the text, the imperative that rises out of a past we never inhabited and a future we will no longer inhabit, an imperative concerning that death which is not an obstacle but a medium.[2]

It is not clear what such a mortal medium could be, but by page twelve, three-quarters of the way through, another space-break separates two paragraphs; there is a change in verb tense and narrative style, and the observer of the opening pages returns. To close the frame of the chapter, perhaps? To categorialize the imperative? He or she, the observer, notes that the rainy season had come, the narrative voice reflects on the literacy campaign of the Sandinistas, reads their slogans posted on the ramshackle walls. Suddenly, the second-person-singular personal pronoun "you" interrupts the narrative, which now becomes direct address, or the simulation of direct address: an apostrophe to someone who is not there. The observer stops his car at a fork in the road, one branch of which leads to Matagalpa (a strange name: a conjunction of "hills" in Mayan and "murder" in Spanish). He stops in order to pick up a hitchhiker, now addressed as "you, Augusto." In an earlier version of the chapter, the dedication "to Augusto" enabled the reader to note the name's first appearance in the text proper as a singular sign, a sign of relationship. Now, the direct address "you" alone does that work.

The observer drives Augusto to Matagalpa and beyond. Augusto, in turn, directs the observer to a hotel outside of Matagalpa. In the middle of the night the observer is awakened: Augusto, with rifle. He says you must leave immediately, and the imperative word falls: *Contra*. You can read nothing in his eyes, no intention, neither menace nor solicitude, but you go with him, on foot, on faith, into the jungle. Occasionally he utters a monosyllabic word, but for the most part there is only his flashlight, the black hair on the back of his inscrutable head, his torso and arms, and his other two arms: the rifle and the machete. Under the Ceiba trees, at a site where, according to Augusto, Sandino himself once camped, he tells you to spend the night, and then disappears.

That is the end of the relationship, the end of all communication, except for the reader, who in the final lines of the final page of the chapter will catch one last glimpse of Augusto. Of what remains of Augusto.

Some six of the sixteen pages frame the philosophical discourse on communication with narrative or travelogue. The theses developed in that discourse, concerning signs, language, communication, relationships, and mortal imperatives, are both buttressed and buffeted by the narrative frame. For the frame, a perfect pavrergon, both enables the theoretical work to set itself to work in the text and frustrates that work forever. Precisely how this instauration *and* frustration of work, this encompassment *and* leakage occur, I leave to more careful future readers of Lingis's *Abuses*. All I can say here is that the relation of discursive to narrative text is like that of machete to serpent, except that the roles are interchangeable, and the very notion of frame is cut or struck dumb. Both the discursive and the narrative parts of the text are always doing more than they seem to be doing; they are working together, or dancing together, and the cumulative effect, the excess, can be *read*. It is as though reading were not inevitable blindness, nor insight either, but something with ballistic impact.

"Lust" works differently.[3] It opens onto the "Calypso Club" in Bangkok and the transvestite Show of Shows. "Lust" never seems to cross over definitively to the discursive text, at least, never with aplomb, never with ease and assurance. Freudian discourse on biological bisexuality, a chilly and chilling discourse, desperate in its appeal to an inexplicable (organic) "repression," scarcely distracts us from the blinding stage lights of "The Calypso." The two-page narrative of the opening gives way uncertainly to the discursive text on Freud and on a history of Indochinese low and high theater, and yet there is no diversion from the fast-moving show, no theoretical tease that the theatrical tease cannot top: the roar of greasepaint, the smell of the crowd. What the audience in "The Calypso" knows as a destiny and an obligation, to wit, their own singular sexual identity, the young men on the stage of the cabaret flaunt as ornament and accessory and merry-go-round. Even the apparatus of oppression appears to suffer a certain vertigo: the plastic-toting businessmen from Cincinnati and Tokyo are being served, and served so well that they become unsure of who they are and what they want. Even Baudrillard suffers a protracted evening's hesitation: the seduction can be readily condemned and despised, or simply ridiculed, but it cannot be so readily resisted, and it will not be understood.

And so this heady chapter goes round and round in a pirouette of attraction and repulsion, titillation and revulsion, distant analysis and close encounters of an utterly unsentimental kind. Harnesses and apparatuses of femininity and virility, parodies and gaudy aggressions, hostilities and negotiations of luxuriant, marbleized flesh: theater is the continuation of the war of the sexes by other means, and it is essentially transvestite. When the contrivance of narrative is stripped from the stage and only the costume of flesh remains—the lowest rung on the Aristotelian ladder being the only rung you have to reach in order to enter the splendor of the theater—all exposition is at its wit's end. Lingis's "Lust" provides Westerners with a brief history of Kabuki and Nô, as of low and high theater in China, Laos, and Thailand from the Middle Ages to Yul Brynner, from the warrior's court to the yuppie's R n' R heaven. Round and round the text goes, from the cool history of the theater to the hot retrospective anger over the way in which "The Calypso" and its flamboyant *symbolique*, so hungry for plastic, has demeaned you and culled your lust. One might also say, with Slavoj Zizek, that "The Calypso" has stolen your pleasure, the pleasure you never experienced, and run off to leave you hugging the big zero at the core of your being.

If theater is representation, and representation variously investiture and divestiture, but investiture and divestiture invariably transvestite, what binds it all to lust? What ties representation to the *production* of lust? For these Thai country boys are *producing* representations that both titillate and humiliate the Western men and women who know that precisely *they*, the Westerners, and not the poverty-stricken boys in their gay costumes, possess the *productive* bodies: the plastic in the Western wallet proves it. The representatives of the productive economies are here with their bodies toned by iron and by Nike Air; yet they are feeling vaguely "had," and by bodies that have precisely *nothing* to offer.

What is the relation of representation to libido and of carnality to production? How can a representation that is itself doubled and redoubled, done and undone at once, and always blatantly, as sheer comedy and satyr-play, evoke lust? How can it strike a target that is not only shifting with shame but also turning itself inside-out with overdetermined theoretical questions? It is one thing for the philosopher to track libido from Plato's drinking party to Freud's civilized discomfiture, another to be given horns by an outrageous, overblown, ostentatious parody. One tries to explain it in terms of those abject object-little-a's, or by the mechanics of bodies without organs, or by neon technoflash; one remains troubled nonetheless by a residue of flesh beneath the representation, flesh that touches by *actio in distans*. You went there for a giggle but it turned out to be "The Crying Game."

A space-break between paragraphs slightly more than halfway through the chapter is followed by the announcement that lust does not know what it is. News for the Delphic Oracle, translocated to Bangkok, delivered not only in London but also now to the American academy. Yet now the vague sensation begins to rise in the reader that he or she would like to know what it is like *to be* such a body of pure representation. The sensation becomes increasingly palpable as the turns of the chapter become less and less theoretical. Flannery O'Connor and Hieronymus Bosch enter on the scene, paralytic and bizarre, along with Dalí's oozing bodies, and suddenly there is talk of "transubstantiation." "Pornosophical philotheology," Lynch would mutter. "Metaphysics in Mecklenburg street."[4]

Hegel felt that there was a problem with the Last Supper because at a certain point the congregation would have to retransubstantiate bread and wine into something very much like divine waste, something that would discommode the divine and transfigure the human. Likewise the liquefaction of bone and muscle into borderless seamless gland and ceaseless secretion seems to challenge what others will have meant by the sacred, the totem, the Most High, and the Law. Lust is even a challenge to our secular cynicism: we can scorn Schwarzenegger's narcissism and hate his fascism and laugh at his ludicrous attempts to act and to speak lines, but he is counting on the fact that when he pops a bicep the reaction will always be somewhere *in between* laughter, loathing, and lust—and even if it is ninety-nine and forty-four one-hundredth's percent pure loathing, Arnold wins: he is the *Mittelwesen*, the daivmwn, taking you to heaven or hell on a brachial bulge. Revile him, vent your spleen, feel free, he will turn to you and in that absurd Austrian monotone utter an ancient line whose source he does not know. Dionysos to Pentheus: "Vould you like to *see* za vomen?"

Lust is radioactive. The Last Supper scene glows garishly in the dark. In "The Calypso" the yuppies from Singapore and New Orleans experience leakage and, as Lingis says, "intercontinental meltdown." Not that fission or transubstantiation leaves materiality behind, as Hegel will always have hoped. On the contrary, it extends the affliction and affection of bemused flesh over the entirety of human dwelling.

Lust is not appropriation, not intentionality as such. Its rhythms elaborate a time of their own, and Lingis's chapter spins toward its dénouement on periods and cadences of lust, transubstantiation, transaction, and transvestitism. The final words of the chapter are words of secrecy, of noncommunication within the psyche. Not the familiar "multiple personality disorder," but the inexplicable split in the cogito: the personal identity of even the most productive Westerner has room for secrets, for phantasms, for the sleek and slippery infinite and indefinite, *apeiron* in drag. Not the beast in the basement, not Mr. Hyde hiding, but the stranger who has been at home in us since the time before we were at home in ourselves, which, frankly, was at no time. One can *elect* to show astonishment in the face of these secrets—at least if one is Alphonso Lingis. The final sentence of this chapter, frameless and contentless (for costume cannot be content, surely) and intense, reads as follows: "One may want the enigmas and want the discomfiture within oneself." That reads like Lingis's autobiography.

Section One: Locating Lingis in Traditions of Thought

•

With his book, *The Community of Those Who Have Nothing in Common*, Lingis appears to be responding to the cry—ubiquitous in our time—for a politics, an ethico-politics, or a political ethics after the manner of Blanchot, Nancy, and so many others. All the requisite characters are there: the destitute, the prostitute, the street urchin, the torture victim, the pariah, the sex worker, the psychotic. Indeed, they are there in all their glory, which is to say, in no one else's reflected glory; they are there in all their stark differences and particularities, so that they cannot be *used* for anything, certainly not for banners and slogans, certainly not for charity or groveling or proselytizing, certainly not as balm for the wounded conscience of the West. Part of the *nothing* they have in common with us is the fact that Lingis's victims have nothing to do with our well-meaning clichés and our sentimentalities—our camouflaged power plays, our ways of always being our same old selves when we say we are open to the Other.

The book begins with the discourse of rationality. A stranger from points east asks the Greeks on the wharf why they do as they do, and the Greeks give *reasons*. To search for and to render reasons remains the Occidental way, and no Westerner heading east or south can jettison the cargo of reasons, reasons sought or reasons found, reasons offered or reasons foisted, reasons craved or reasons proclaimed. However, the imperative to seek reasons is both initiated and interrupted by the other human being. An archaeology of reasons eventually uncovers imperatives that reason does not know, imperatives of the *other* community, the community of those who have *nothing*, and who have it *in common*. How heed the imperative without translating it back into one's own homegrown reasonableness or domesticated irrationality? That is the question, and Lingis does not answer it. He lives it, in discomfort. Lingis's book is written on the frayed edges of communication, on the crumbling bark of face-to-face encounters and contestations, from the far corners of the globe and very close to home.

With regard to communication Lingis emphasizes the background noise, the static that systems of reason and meaning love to stifle—the murmur of the world, which is all-pervasive and thus a part of that nothing which joins us. In the face-to-face he stresses the nudity of the eye, which is both fragile and sovereign, appealing and imperious, destitute and impervious. Missing altogether from his descriptions is the pathos of pity, which, preaching the destitution of the Other, appropriates her or him in the name of an ethics, scarifying the face so that its otherness will be marked by those homegrown reasons or domesticated irrationalities that are always reassured of their righteousness, always most elated when they can grovel before that Other who lays low all the other others, who will not have strange others before it, stuffing their mouths with bread in order to muffle the voices. Lingis, by contrast, maintains the destitute in relation to the inscrutable and impervious, keeps the vulnerable in tension with the inviolate. Lingis offers us descriptions that are so true we do not know what to do with them.

In the fifth and seventh chapters, at the end of *The Community of Those Who*

Have Nothing in Common, he takes us to a deathbed, the deathbed of the mother, and to a companionability that has *nothing* to say to the imperative to say *something*. I, in turn, will say nothing about these remarkable chapters except perhaps this, that we thought that nothing more ever could or ever should be written about such a deathbed after Maurice Blanchot's *Arrêt de mort,* or after Derrida's *Circonfession,* but we were wrong. Something new has been written.

Yet there is something anomalous about this ethico-politics of Lingis's—if that is what it is. It seems to have forgotten why discourses on ethics and politics are so much in demand, namely, to serve as the final stratagems of the ascetic ideal for suppressing and obliterating the lived body and its discontinuous histories, for covering over all its imbroglios and boondoggles, for quelling the anxieties and the terrors of personal stories—the failed loves, the potentially infectious lusts, the timid and tepid emotions, the evidently irresistible desire to gossip and cavil and wound and drag down whatever is powerful and beautiful. Ethico-political discourses want to forget all this in the solace of a comforting, shared, legitimated, and appropriately impossible mission, a mission undertaken by these self-declared and self-defined victims, a mission unsullied by complicities and innocent of complexities, a mission to which one can submit oneself wholly and anonymously so that one's superfluousness will be overlooked by others and concealed from oneself. Lingis's politics fails to do this. In the end, the companion of the vulnerable one, the sovereign one, the dying one, *has no mission,* not even to assist the other into nothingness, because it isn't even *nothing.* The pain in the face of mortality does not edify and purify, it only hurts, and if one lingers in order to attend the deaths of others who are strangers it is not because of obligation or command or law or ethics or sanctity or even habit but because of a wretched predisposition or a contingent propinquity, neither of which offers consolation or comprehension.

Similarly, the joy is as rapturous and as bewildering as the misery is benumbing: when a seventeen-year-old Laotian boy dances on the table—if flaunting may be called dancing—he does so as irrefragable testimony to the nothing-in-common: one's own seventeenth year in the land of the Protestant work ethic was notably different. A serious reading of Alphonso Lingis's *Community* will, I suspect, leave the home community as unprepared for community as any work of philosophy inevitably leaves them. Unless the secret of community is reticence and a refusal to go the ways of power and scorn, piety and righteousness, a good-bye to the high moral ground and the high horse of victimization, a farewell to the oblivious who crave it, the memorious who fear it, and the obsessive who both fear and crave but who don't know where else to turn. Lingis won't stick around to direct the traffic, however, and for all those who will fall back on accountability, imputability, and the Kantian "intelligible character" that makes punishment possible and necessary, his book on the public realm will always already have been a failure. One comes away from *The Community of Those Who Have Nothing in Common* no clearer about either the community or the nothing; one is clearer only about the "Those," or at least *some* of "Those," namely, "Those" who in their irreducible and incommunicable differences defeat every ethico-political phrase.

Yet if phrases are defeated in Lingis's book, the writing itself, the narratives, dialogues, and portraits wrap around those they have contacted. There is no shaking Lingis, once one has been found. Would the point be, as Nietzsche wrote to Brandes, to try to lose him? Why try to lose what is most original and powerful in U.S.-American thinking? Alphonso Lingis seeks and often finds the word concerning which one knows neither why it needs saying nor how it came to be traced on the page, the word or words that to the religious will always seem blasphemous, to the political naive, to the wise foolish, to the desiccated lubricious. One comes away from the reading of this writing sober but not clean, both elated and defeated, in love and in despondency at once. The despondency of love and of thinking: so *this* is what it would have been like *to live*.

•

It seems important to reveal something about a philosophical production that is itself so revelatory. My remarks so far, which try to capture something of the macrorhythm of Lingis's texts, miss too much. Another word or series of words—not mine, Lingis's—are needed if my own text is to have any life at all. Aware of the dangers of citation, I am also aware of the folly of not citing the most quotable of writers and thinkers in my mother tongue. Allow me then to turn by way of conclusion to another chapter of *Abuses*, the final one, "Chichicastenango," in order to exhibit something more palpable about the revelations and concealments of Lingis's work.

In the arrival mode, the narrator is all eyes, ears, nose, and feet: he disappears somewhere in between the lines, and the reader finds himself or herself in a startling place:

> I went to Chichicastenango. By the entrance of the town there is a large billboard with the words *Dios Familia Patria* and *El Ejército es su Amigo*—"God, Family, Country" and "The Army is your Friend." Campesinos are still arriving, bent under huge baskets or heavy bundles of firewood. Many have walked the whole night. They are very small, with parched brown skin, the women dressed in extravagantly colored full skirts, the men in dust-clogged pants and wearing straw hats with the brims smartly turned up at the sides, down in front and back.
>
> Chichicastenango has hardly grown in five centuries; from the central plaza one can see the whole town, its streets stopped on all sides at the brink of gorges but four blocks away. The plaza is filled with stands. Down its narrow lanes blankets, hats, embroidered blouses and intricately woven skirts, iron picks and shovels and machetes, painted masks, fruits and vegetables, and salt are piled high. Tourists under broad cloth hats, enervated by the altitude, the sun, and the dust, are peering desultorily into the stands; occasionally one of them decides, after some confused bargaining, to buy something, and the others gather protectively as she or he extracts some quetzales from a moneybelt. Troops in combat dress carrying automatic rifles walk through the streets with impassive faces. In the center lanes of the plaza women are cooking pans of beans and corn, vegetables, stir-frying chicken, while conversing in their melodious tongue. Laughing children chase one another around the stands. The men, alone or in groups, are getting drunk on *chicha*. One walks the lanes

over the decaying husks of fruit, wrappings of leaves and twine, dirty plastic bags, broken bottles; in alleys and in doorways swept by the wind they pile up, splattered with urine and vomit, under swarming flies. (251-52)

The revelation is one of squalor: these late Mayans have been driven ever higher into the mountains of Guatemala by soldiers who are working for the wealthy ranchers. The ranchers have cleared the land and the people, cleared the people of the land off the land, in order to raise cattle for meat for hamburger—hamburger *al norte*, some of it destined for our own university food services, some for prisons, all supplied by the same giant firm.

Lingis now describes the Quiché rituals performed by the Mayan priests or shamans on the steps of the decrepit Colonial cathedral of Chichicastenango: sacrificial packets are burned to appease gods who, most of us suppose, must have fled the territory a millennium ago. The dilapidation and squalor trigger thoughts on the sacred and on the co-option of the sacred in religion:

> I was haunted all day by a sentiment I had felt nowhere in my country in neogothic cathedrals squeezed between high-rise buildings in cities or modernistic churches surrounded by spacious lawns and parking lots in the suburbs. The sacred hovered inconceivably in the charred hull of the once Catholic temple, in the broken idol in its circle of rough stones on the hill outside the town, in the grime of sacrificial stones and torn and bloodied chicken feathers, in the stunted bodies of Indians hunted down in these rocky heights by soldiers from the capital transported by helicopter. No, the sacred is this decomposition.
>
> Religion advances triumphantly over the decomposition of the sacred. From its turbid ambiguity, religion separates the covenant from the taboos; the celestial order from the intoxication with spilt blood, milk, and semen; the sublime from the excremental. Its intelligence separates a celestial and divine order from the—demoniacal—world of decomposition. It levitates the sacred into an extracosmic empyrean, where a reign of intelligible providence and a paternal image of a personalized deity function to foster in humans exalted phantasms of undecomposable sufficiency. It consecrates the profanation of the world, given over to industry, information processing, tourists bused to the market of Indians while soldiers tread through the lanes with Uzis. (257-58)

In the cemetery of Chichicastenango, Lingis locates the tomb of the German-American missionary who at first looked on helplessly as the religion he represented succumbed to the fits and starts, the substitutions, and the incorrigible promiscuity of the decomposing sacred, but then who, himself transformed, presided for decades over this resurgence of the sacred in Indio life. In locating that tomb, Lingis locates one of his own forebears:

> Germany was not sending Catholic missionaries to Central America; he must have been an American. I imagined a missionary order from a traditional

rural area settled by Bavarians, in Wisconsin or South Dakota. He came here to take over the Santo Tomás church, in a small town of Creole landowners and Chinese merchants and thousands of Indians come from the mountains on market day. He learned Quiché, discovered in the hamlets in the surrounding mountains their social order intact, the elected elders serving without salary, in fact having to expend all their resources to help in emergencies and to stage complex rituals. On market day they came to him with problems with the landowners and army. They brought offerings of corn and chickens, and sometimes old pottery they had had in their hamlets for generations. There was no money to paint the church, repair the altars. There were no nuns to run a school. The Cardinal Archbishop in Guatemala City did not visit outposts of foreign missionary orders. Little by little he let the Quiché people come in their own garb, which the Franciscans five centuries ago had forbidden, knowing that the apparently decorative patterns were so many woven amulets invoking Maya demons. He let the marimba players come in with their instruments, and when they began to play what were not hymns he did not stop them. He let them burn incense on the entrance steps, built over an ancient shrine. He himself took down altars which he was told were built over sacred stones. He ceased to demand that they consecrate their unions in matrimony. He ceased to demand that they come to tell him their sins in confessions. He let their officiants come with processions of flutes and drums into the sanctuary, the chuchqajaus to burn sacrifices in the center aisle. One day a delegation of *alcaldes*, village elders, showed him an ancient copy of the *Popoh Vul*, the great myth of the Quiché, which the world had believed lost irrevocably when Bishop Juan de Zumarranga in 1526 ordered all copies of the Maya sacred writings to be burnt. They let him come to their meeting house night after night to copy it. He learned the sacred script, and was spending more time studying it and pondering its meaning than reading his breviary. The Quiché brought their children for baptism; it was the only one of the seven sacraments that were still performed in the Santo Tomás church. He must have opened his door to women who brought him chicha for the long cold nights, and received them in his bed. How many children called him padre? His last trip back to the motherhouse in the North American midwest was before the war; his parents were gone and his relatives dispersed, and he found he had difficulty expressing simple things in English. He returned to the chuchqajaus he knew, who came with remedies and spells during his last illness. (259-61)

As the institutional power of religion flakes and crumbles like the whitewashed plaster of the cathedral walls, sudden revelations of the sacred shine through. A memory is kindled of something seen eight years before in the same village, a memory evoking tears and laughter: a funeral procession—with an Indio carrying his dead wife on his back—makes the narrator think that the German-American missionary too must have been borne to his crypt by such a procession.

And now, in dénouement, inasmuch as "Chichicastenango" is almost over, a revelation concerning the secular land of capital, the land to the north, to which the narrator himself will soon be borne:

> In a week I must leave, and return to the state university where big classrooms will be full of students preparing, with textbooks and computers, their futures in the gleaming technopoles of the First World. They are identifying and assimilating information. Their appetite is young and healthy, like their appetites in supermarkets big as warehouses piled with a half-dozen kinds of apples, oranges, cheeses, prepared meats, fish, dozens of kinds of wine and liquors, unloaded from tractor trailers from remote states and ships and jet airplanes from remote continents. Like the appetite they bring to shopping malls piled up with clothing, furniture, stereophonic sound systems, television sets and VCRs, computers, motorcycles, automobiles. The appetite they will bring to resorts selling snowmobiles, marinas selling yachts, real-estate agents selling condominiums and restaurant chains. (262)

Yet the revelation of this happy desolation in the north will not be the final flash of recognition. Self-recognition in the memory of a defunct missionary, the unlikely purveyor of the *Popoh Vul.* Who knows what economy of narration or thinking enjoins the final revelation and concealment? "Chichicastenango" concludes—that is to say, Lingis elects to conclude it, in an imperfect tense and in the subjunctive mood—as follows:

> The room was cold, there was nothing to do but take off my shoes and crawl under the blankets with my clothes on. I felt weary, and sleep, as for the old, came slow and fitful. From time to time I heard the slow steps of campesinos outside. Warmth finally came to fill my bed, the warmth of secretions and sweat, of ejaculations and stains.
>
> I would have liked one of them to come to me with chicha and to be received into my bed. Someone with face wrinkled by the mountain sun and hands gnarled by labor. (263)

•

The exquisite sense of the sacred and the profane, of decrepitude and exaltation, and the skills that underlie the descriptive prose as much as the discursive prose, the quiet erudition—these taken by themselves do not avail to make Lingis's work what it is. And what is that? A body of work that contrasts with our own, our own being so predictable and pusillanimous, so anemic and puffed up. Lingis's is a work that gently encourages us to go farther, to head elsewhere, to take a risk, to have a go at ruthless honesty. It is a body of work, and the work of a body, so powerful in its effects that many—perhaps most—will not forgive him for it, precisely because his voice reminds us of the fact that philosophy once upon a time, in the eras of Emerson and James and Du Bois, wanted to do something in these United States. Those who cannot forgive him fail to see that the man should be met by love alone and the work with respect and wonder. If one can ever succeed in meeting the man and the work at all. For they are always on the verge of departure.

•

Farewell! Good-bye! He's off again, his cargo concealed—that immense amount of learning which he carries so well, without ostentation, and that immense sensibility in the face of all those things which cannot be predicted and controlled. As he fades into the horizon, at some considerable distance down the road, he seems to have shrunk to our stature. That distance is the kindness he bestows on us, greeting in going, apparently as vulnerable and as fraught as any lump of life on its way. His destination? Exotic, no doubt; never exoteric. Reading him will *seem* easy, because he decides over and over again to make it that way, to wrap us round. He turns and waves. His grin is the song of unscrubbed children and the wingbeat of a thousand doves released over a temple roof.

Returning to his own birds that night, the night of the day of his ignominious defeat at the "circle" meeting, he strokes Love Junky all the way down to the human skin beneath the plumage. He plays with the thought of writing a book called *Plumage*. He feeds them all once again, again forgets himself, walks among them on his well-formed feet, bemused, exhausted, somnambulant, clairvoyant. He stands before his bookshelves, extracts a volume, opens it. To no one in particular he reads into the incessant murmur of the nocturnal world:

> There is no stoppage and never can be stoppage,
> If I, you, and the worlds, and all beneath or upon their surfaces,
>   were this moment reduced back to a pallid float, it would
>   not avail in the long run,
> We should surely bring up again where we now stand,
> And surely go as much farther, and then farther and farther.
>
> —Walt Whitman, "Song of Myself," ll. 1190-1193

Notes

1. D.H. Lawrence, *Studies in Classic American Literature* (Harmondsworth: Penguin, 1971), 171, 173-174, and 179.

2. Alphonso Lingis, *The Imperative* (Bloomington: Indiana University Press, 1998), sections 20-22.

3. Alphonso Lingis, "Beauty and Lust," in *Dangerous Emotions* (Berkeley and Los Angeles: University of California Press, 2000).

4. James Joyce, *Ulysses* (London: The Bodley Head, 1960), 564.

Chapter Two

Seeing the Named, Naming the Seen: Relations to the Tradition

Wolfgang W. Fuchs

Is it possible in the late twentieth century to be an original thinker in professional philosophy? In the very nature of things there is a great deal that speaks against the possibility of an affirmative answer. Already Alfred North Whitehead had posited that the entire history of Western philosophy was but a footnote to Plato.

Many a student of philosophy has been frustrated by finding that so much has already been said, and said so well, that there seems nothing new left to say. Some accept that with resignation, others declare that they will then simply write their own philosophy. But how? If one were to assert a new vocabulary, or a new method, wouldn't that simply be old wine in new bottles or the reverse? If the requirement for originality would be new "liquid" in new "containers," then it could not occur in the framework of loyalty and devotion to a discipline. So, the question remains, is it possible to be an original thinker? Nietzsche, who was certainly an original thinker, describes originality by way of the seeing of that which has not yet been named.[1] Alphonso Lingis has seen what has not been named by following the visions of those who have named what, by them, has been seen.

Philosophy as Discipline and Discourse

It belongs to the tradition of philosophical thought to locate itself in terms of its own tradition; no serious philosopher would write as though there had been no prior philosophical thought. Lingis submits himself to this discipline in that he responds to the voices that have spoken before him and uses the tools that have been evolved to distinguish good from bad thought: the distinction between intelligibility and unintelligibility, analysis, the examination and construction of argumentation, and, predominant in his own work, phenomenological description. It also belongs to this tradition that philosophy understands itself as reflective and reflexive thought.

Unlike the sciences, natural, social, or literary, philosophy is identified less through the object of its investigations than by its way of undertaking that investigation. To be sure, issues of method and orientation arise for the sciences, but rarely in the process of pursuing the science. Philosophy alone requires of its practitioners a continual justification of their activities, and one of the elements of such a calling itself into question is that the philosopher situates himself or herself for the reader by declaring the project at hand, referencing it to, and differentiating it from, similar projects in the history of philosophy. Further, the philosopher, at least within the continental tradition, clarifies matters of methodology and explicitly or implicitly acknowledges influences on his or her thought. In this way philosophy can be said to be cannibalistic in two senses: it is continually devouring its body, and it proceeds by stripping useful parts from older wracks.

The work of Alphonso Lingis can be situated as post-existential/phenomenological philosophy. But the hyphen is important here; his work is not just later than, but rooted in, existentialism and phenomenology. Except where scholarly considerations dictate otherwise, Lingis finds, for good reasons, these two schools of thought more or less interchangeable.[2] And because he has such a keen sense and powerful appreciation for the history of philosophy, he knows how to trace the themes and insights of twentieth-century philosophy to their origins, origins that are often still operative in determining our contemporary understanding of things. Lingis returns to Kant and Hegel in regard to those issues where their thought still dominates, and occasionally even to the Greeks. But his most immediate influences can be identified by just rounding up the usual suspects: Nietzsche, Freud, Lacan, Foucault, Husserl, Bataille, Deleuze, Sartre, Heidegger, Merleau-Ponty. Above all others, however, Emmanuel Levinas. It is a sign of Lingis's depth of comprehension of these thinkers that one does not need to have read any of them to gain a great deal of insight into their insights as these are presented or represented by Lingis. Because he has mastered their thought, he is able to escape their terminology and is able to render their thought in his own terms, in a language that is incredibly rich and that thus very rarely has to resort to technical terminology or the jargon invented by these sources for expressing their thoughts. It is not, however, Lingis's project to be a secondary source for the history of philosophy. Even those of his works that are primarily commentaries on other thinkers (*Libido, Phenomenological Explanations, Deathbound Subjectivity*) have as their purpose thinking through further some phenomena and issues that have been taken up by the thinkers whom Lingis presents, giving us a reading that is fruitful in a double sense.

Because they are what needs to be thought about, many of the same topics are approached again in the other sorts of books by Lingis, those books with photographs; books that do not proceed, first of all, by way of the history of philosophy. It is in the "assembled books" (a Lingis quip) with photographs, that Lingis's great skills and his philosophical originality come to the fore most clearly. Each book contains essays that speak to the theme announced by the book's title. Although each of the pieces can indeed be read without knowledge of the others, they are not groups of vaguely connected essays collected into books. Rather, each has a group of essays that make a book. Because of both themes and method a serial reading is a multiple enrichment; the understanding of, and reflection engendered by, the reading of one essay is deepened by reading the next ones. These, in turn, are approached in a kind of friendship because one has read the preceding one. *The Imperative* is the first of Lingis's books to break the pattern; it has a single theme *and* photographs.

Phenomenology can be encapsulated in Husserl's motto: "Return to the Things Themselves!" ("*Zurück zu den Sachen Selbst*"). It is a call for philosophy to be descriptive rather than constructive, to attend, through analysis, to how phenomena give themselves to be, both in the process of becoming known and in their being. The goal here is a double one; first, to not be prejudiced by preexisting theoretical structures in the approach to experiencing phenomena, and secondly to not be bound by one's own idiosyncrasies, the accidents of one's particular and peculiar psychology, self- interests, personal history, or modes of experiencing determined by one's culture, that is, by subjectivism. Knowledge of things is to be grounded in the evidence provided through unmediated and clear intuitions into the nature of the appearances. This, for Husserl, was the way to certainty in philosophy; this was the road to truth. But, how is this innocence to be won? Husserl and many of the phenomenologists who came after him wrestled repeatedly with trying to develop a methodology appropriate to attaining this end. But, as Lingis shows in *Phenomenological Explanations*, there is a tension in this phenomenological project that prevents it from giving an accurate account of how the perception of things, and even more, of other people, other subjects, occurs. It was giving up the attainment of complete innocence as a goal that characterized the existentialization of phenomenology by Heidegger and Merleau-Ponty.

Aristotle taught that philosophy begins in wonder. If it is not possible, methodologically, to establish innocence, is it still possible to wonder? Yes, but as Lingis shows us, not through a naivete, real or feigned, but by taking up an interrogative stance toward the world that first lays out what it is that we already know. Many of these chapter-essays follow the same format: a picture, then Lingis presents the conventional wisdom, the systematically organized knowledge that is part of our common discourse and provides for all of us the accepted manner for approaching phenomena, that allows us to give accounts, generate explanatory systems, articulate universal significance, in short, a rational understanding of experience and how things are. Lingis presents these dominating conceptions, these standard accounts with such simplicity, sympathy, and force that one is completely convinced by them; one reads what one has always known, and it is good. But, then he raises questions: is this how things really are? Is our established truth, our science that both fulfills and represents the standards for intelligibility sufficient? Can it really account for our experiences universally? He then goes on to describe experiences which cannot be accounted for by the theories which dominate our thinking. By means of his phenomenological descriptions he lets it be seen that the standard account is inadequate or at least needs to be supplemented, if it is to give an account of experience. It is this combination of powerful, succinct, respectful summaries of our conventional wisdom against which are set his bountiful, revealing and convincing descriptions of experiences and phenomena that lets his readers follow him into that condition where philosophy begins, into wonder.

The predominant themes that Lingis addresses are those that are central to the philosophical discourses of the continental thinkers of the twentieth century, particularly those who fall under the rubric of "postmodern." Subjectivity, existence and meaning, death, libidinal or erotic manifestations and forces, the body, perception, knowledge, intersubjective relations, the other.

It has been fairly conventional, at least since Freud, to take the extreme, even the pathological, instance to gain insight into the "normal" structures of what is being investigated. Lingis raises this to another level. The sources for his reflections are wide-ranging and unusual. They include not only the pathological instances, but also exotic places, faces, practices he has encountered in his travels. Also gratuitous or bizarre phenomena to be found in nature, as well as the, for us, unintelligible, customs, values, actions inscribed within exotic civilizations or cultures living and dead. Even within the commonplaces of experience Lingis focuses on the extremes as sources of the pathways to understanding. He is tremendously well informed about the things that interest him, the places he goes, the cultures he tries to understand, the experiences, common or uncommon, that he investigates. The resources he uses to attain wonder-beyond-naivete include many personal experiences, but also anthropological reports, scientific works, travelogues, works of literature. Lingis teaches us how to approach things in an informed way without the loss of wonder.

Nothing Human is Foreign to Me

It would seem that this claim, first made by the Roman dramatist Terence, could be taken as a motto and as an affirmation by everyone on whatever side of the "debates" about "cultural relativism," "multiculturalism," "diversity," or even "globalization." On the one hand it can be read as a formula expressing respect for persons, cultures, and practices that are dissimilar to what I know from my own experiences, and on the other hand it can be taken to mean that, in the end, there is similarity, there is a "standard" that allows for making judgements. That is exactly the problem. In philosophy what lies at the basis of this ambiguity has been formulated as the problem of the other. More strictly speaking, it is the otherness of the other that has presented itself as a paradox.

No philosopher has engaged himself with this problem more systematically than Emmanuel Levinas. It is from him that the contemporary discourse about this matter has its terminology, its parameters, its insistence. Because of how he analyses the relation of the self and the other, Levinas asserts, against the Heideggerian teaching, that ethics is prior to fundamental ontology. Being is relational, and the first, asymmetrical, relation is that of the self to the other. He calls this relation metaphysical. It is not as an addendum but as an originating impulse to existence that, according to Levinas, I encounter the other.

> A calling into question of the same—which cannot occur within the egoist spontaneity of the same—is brought about by the other. We name this calling into question of my spontaneity by the Other ethics. The strangeness of the Other, his irreducibility to the I, to my thoughts and my possessions, is precisely accomplished as a calling into question of my spontaneity, as ethics.

> Metaphysics, transcendence, the welcoming of the other by the same, of the Other by me, is concretely produced as the calling into question of the same by the other, that is, as the ethics that accomplishes the critical essence of knowledge.[3]

Levinas's influence on the work of Lingis has been profound, yet the movement of thought, the way each comes to articulate insights concerning otherness is quite different. Whereas Levinas provides fascinating, if short, analytic examples to break up the purely theoretical or even metatheoretical flow of his text, Lingis relies primarily upon the descriptions of experiences or phenomena, experiences we all could have had, phenomena we all could have become acquainted with, to bring us to see what can be seen and what needs to be understood if the other is to be encountered as other. Lingis has three other significant departures from Levinas; he does not insist along with Levinas that ethics is first philosophy, unlike Levinas he does not root the otherness of the other in God, and he lets the other be encountered in violation,[4] in lust, whereas for Levinas violence is the denial of the ethical.

In order to exploit the foundational certainty that the *cogito, ergo sum* delivers, Descartes first had to show, by means of the method of doubt, just how uncertain even our most mundane and unquestioned judgements of experience are. As one of his examples he cites the inference made while looking out the window and judging that it is men who are walking by on the basis of having seen hats and cloaks which may be covering robots. Although some ignore it, no thinker in Modernity overcomes this epistemological problem in regard to other subjects or agents. Even Husserl was not able to overcome this seeming inaccessibility of the other as a consciousness for my consciousness. In the conclusion of the chapter in *Phenomenological Explanations* where he has analyzed Husserl's attempt, Lingis moves the discussion away from Husserl's proposed solution, but also away from Descartes's position, by returning from induction to perception.

> We think then that there are forms of behavior that do not acquire their meaning for me by appearing synthetically associated with my behavior, appearing as a variant of my behavior....They are especially visible in the face of another—I see in his eyes that he addresses himself to me, invokes me, questions me, contests me.[5]

In no other aspect of his work is Lingis more in agreement with, or dependent on, the teachings of Levinas than in his insistence that the face-to-face is the primordial human encounter, the humanizing encounter, the origin for the possibilities of expression, communication, relation.[6] Yet, here too Lingis evokes the method that serves him so well. In most of the essays (and they are many) in which this becomes thematized, Lingis first falls back on the received wisdom, usually of Kant, Hegel, or Aristotle (which has the fascinating by-product of showing us how Aristotelean and Kantian our thinking really is) to allow the reader to see clearly that these profound teachings can be used to account for much in the way of human and humanizing relationships, but also that they fall short given certain kinds of experiences.

The Enlightenment, in giving claim to tolerance as a social goal presented us with our contemporary concept of the person, and no thinker articulated or justified this as well as Kant. We are obliged to treat the other with *respect,* for the other acts in obedience to the imperative of the law, the law of reason, the recognition of the sovereignty of the universal and the necessary, just as do I. What I feel in the sentiment of respect is the imperative force of what has the form of law.[7] But what Lingis, after Levinas, wants to emphasize, is that it is precisely *another* imperative, one not the same as my own that is encountered in the other, and first of all on the expressive face of the other. This expressiveness, this otherness, is encountered first of all as a call and as a command on the face of the other. Because this insight is so central to his philosophy, Lingis offers many descriptions of the face-to-face moment in its variations throughout his work. Lingis wants to guide our vision to what he has seen, so we too might see, might have revealed for us what he has seen. And what he has seen is the other, not only as Kant sees the other, as a fellow member of the kingdom of ends, but also the other as *other.*

> What initiates that other vision of him or her, that sense of his or her surfaces as commanded by another law—that represented by his or her own mind in obedience to its own imperative—is the immediate sense I have of the imperative in him or her.[8]

That I can also deny, reject, discount, kill the other is not an argument against this vision; they are secondary possibilities derived from it, just as lying is a possibility dependent upon true speech. And although this relation is asymmetrical and cannot be reversed upon my initiative or for purposes of my self-interest, it is also the case that there are those for whom I am the *other.* The test of this would be to be in a condition where I would be radically other, outside of all of the bonds that are normally in place in the interactions in which people treat each other with that everyday kind of respect for which Kant sought a transcendental foundation. This is one of the lessons Lingis draws from an experience he had, one which presented such a test case.

In "Community in Death," Lingis sets out from the conventional notion that society embodies the forms of commitment which we associate in the exchange of messages, resources, and services, and thus rests on a kind of kinship, that is, a recognition of obligation. In normal experience this kinship broadens beyond the family to include the various communities in which one participates on the basis of profession, language, race, nationality, and so on. Lingis reflects on the experience of having been helped, while helplessly ill in India, by someone he did not know, with whom he could not speak, with whom he had absolutely nothing in common, and to whom he could offer no reciprocity:

> One night, sick for weeks in a hut in Mahabalipuram in the south of India, I awoke out of the fevered stupor of days to find that the paralysis that had incapacitated my arms was working its way into my chest. I stumbled out into the starless darkness of the heavy monsoon night. On the shore, gasping for air, I felt someone grasp my arm. He was naked, save for a threadbare loincloth, and all I could understand was that he was from Nepal....He seemed to have nothing, sleeping on the sands, alone....[He] finally loaded me in an outrigger canoe to take me, I knew without understanding any of his words, through the monsoon seas to the hospital in Madras sixty-five miles away....

> We disembarked at a fishing port, where he put me first on a rickshaw and then on a bus for Madras, and then he disappeared without a word or a glance at me. He surely had no address but the sands; I would never see him again. I shall not cease seeing what it means to come to be bound with a bond that can never be broken or forgotten, what it means to become a brother.[9]

It is not only in the immediate encounter with the other that Lingis has found the conventional wisdom to be lacking. Examining the work of Aristotle, Marcel Mauss, and Lévi-Strauss in regard to social relations and circulation of goods in cultures, Lingis finds that thinking based upon these theories of calculation cannot offer an account of a social relation for which we have no better name than generosity. Phenomena of this sort had already been observed by Nietzsche—he mentions love and gratitude—who saw them as manifestations of what he described as "the solar economy," movements that out of overfullness wanted to discharge themselves, without recompense, without calculation.

Much in Lingis's thought revolves around the notion of the imperative as key to making human existence intelligible. The otherness of the other can be apprehended and thus sustained, only through the recognition that the actions, the very life of the other is guided by his or her own imperatives rather than by my imperatives. Already Kant, who first invokes the notion of the imperative in this extra-grammatical sense, clearly saw that. This is the source of the third formulation of the categorical imperative that requires recognizing the will of every rational being as a universally legislating will; that is, as that of a lawgiver, a sovereign, as well as a member of the kingdom of ends.[10]

On one level this is fairly easy to comprehend; since each person is the source of it, the imperative serves as the principle of uniqueness demarcating each person. Also, in a second sense, it allows us to account for different kinds of lives, and thus serves as a kind of principle of acceptance for differences in how people guide, lead, or live their own lives. What is at stake here then is the issue of sovereignty. As we will see, Lingis does not find sufficient Merleau-Ponty's account that bases all relations with the world on *praktognosis*, and this carries over to the way of being-in-the-world beyond that of the exigencies of practical tasks that orders lives. To cite a concrete instance:

> Beethoven and Mahler do not find that they have to let go of the order where things are imperative and contrive out of tones cut free from the resounding world willful constructions; they discover rigorous necessities and find the worlds of music imperative.[11]

Lingis, following Levinas, and in keeping with existential philosophy's revolt against classical thought, cannot be satisfied with a sovereignty that rests upon universality, since then *otherness* would be subsumed into universality.

> Existential philosophy formulates a refusal of the thought, proper to classicism, that equates the promotion in the subject of universality with the promotion to sovereignty. The existential protest is not a protest against the law. It is a protest against the universal form of the law.[12]

But the citation in regard to Beethoven and Mahler introduces, really, a second source, or at least a second relational term, of imperatives, the world. In one of his later books, *The Imperative*, Lingis takes up this reflection on the nature of the imperatives of the world as a central theme.

Finally, Lingis finds that there is also a third type or source of imperative operative in life, an imperative operative for everyone—death.

The Lived Body

The first generation of phenomenologists had already won the battle of the body by establishing, against Cartesianism and empiricism, against physiology and behaviorist psychology, that the objectified body is encountered secondarily, that our original encounter of our bodies, and the primordial requirement for giving an account of bodily experience, rests on what Merleau-Ponty came to call the "lived body."[13]

All scientific, dissecting, mechanized accounts are secondary elaborations that are based on the derived experience of knowing the body as an object, rather than as the locus of experience and action our body shows itself to be for each of us. In *Foreign Bodies* Lingis summarizes this line of phenomenological teaching as it reaches its apex in the work of Maurice Merleau-Ponty:

> Phenomenological methods, as elaborated by Maurice Merleau-Ponty, made it possible to understand the active forces of our bodies in a new way....Our bodies form within themselves postures and goal-oriented diagrams of movement, which address the layout of perceived obstacles and objectives. Phenomenology is the description of our perceptual and practical competence as we ourselves experience them.[14]

This understanding of the body, with which Lingis fundamentally agrees, he calls the competent body. This way of thinking the body has clearly become one of the conventional wisdoms. But, asks Lingis, does this experience of the competent body exhaust the ways in which we experience our bodies? Are there not also bodies foreign to this systematic explanation?

Lingis presents us with the phenomenon of the bodybuilder by bringing us to see that this practice, this cult way of living the body, is in conflict with practical competence and can be perhaps understood in light of the way that the techniques and instruments used for bodybuilding have had a kind of evolutionary feedback effect, one that is strangely incompetent and counterfunctional, and that is thus beyond the scope of explanation even of the contemporary phenomenological, let alone the older mechanistic, account of the body.

> But the human muscular system has taken on the second, expressive, role for which the other animals have evolved distinctive organs-to-be-seen. The human muscular system is not only the scaffolding that positions and turns the sense organs, the organs-for-apprehending; the vectors and surges of motor energy illuminate the muscular network itself and make its mesh and mounds snares for the eye. On human bodies muscle rettings are their peacock tails, curls worked on the lips their crests, biceps and pectorals their coiled horns, finger waverings their lustrous pelt.[15]

Lingis points to a clear distinction in contemporary culture between the cult of bodybuilding with its inherent goal of turning the substance of the body into a spectacle, and the fit, athletic body, the virtuous body attained through workouts in the gym. The first we find grotesque, the latter noble because still representative, heroic, ready to undertake tasks. This latter is the body that can be understood within the framework of Merleau-Ponty, the former not. As a second approach, Lingis interrogates what it means that our bodies are also substances that produce pain and pleasure in themselves and thus, reading with Foucault, become subjected to discipline, the occasion for the rise of practices and institutions.[16]

What he takes up in this work along the lines of Foucault's analyses of punishment, discipline, and sexuality, Lingis focuses into an analysis of contemporary torture where estranging the victim's body from truth and the established community is what is at issue:

> The torturer works to tear away at the victim's body and prove to him that he is a terrorist or psychotic and that what he believed in is delusions.... The torturer demands of the antisocial one that he confess that he is incapable of truth, that his bestial body is incapable of lucidity and discernment, that it is nothing but corruption and filth.... The confession uttered will be integrated into the common discourse that circulates in the community, and which each one joins whenever he speaks seriously. The cries and bestial moans out of which it came will be lost in the night and the fog.[17]

Death and Deaths

Deathbound Subjectivity is a book that "searches in the thought of six philosophers for the principle of subjectivity. It seeks to know the subject not so much as the generator of meaning but rather as a locus of order."[18] Central to the book is the theme of death, but it is approached quite indirectly over the idea of infinity as manifesting the theoretical attitude, the attitude which lies at the heart of the Western ideal of truth. So, against Husserl and Kant, who are in different ways adherents of this ideal, Nietzsche is read as contesting these ideals through his introduction of a different idea of infinity, one bound up with the ontological intensity of transitory moments (eternal recurrence of the same), rather than on a time infinite in extension. But, as Lingis sees it, this would leave Nietzsche's doctrine of sovereignty, based upon self-mastery, in the position of depending upon being ruled, or mastered by that which is outside oneself, death. It is Heidegger who, according to Lingis attempts to think a mortal sovereignty.[19]

Heidegger teaches that it is *temporality* as the transcendental horizon of existence that makes an existential interpretation of existence possible. Human existence is always a projection; thus to discover the essence of existence it is necessary to understand how the three dimension of time, past, present, future constitute existence. As living towards the future, human existence is, as part of its essence, also its possibilities. But, possibilities are both endless and anonymous—they are everyone's possibilities. Save one. Death. This possibility alone can be realized by no one else in my place; it is, says Heidegger, my "ownmost possibility." Thus, it is existence understood as the "being-towards-death" ("*zum Tode sein*") that my existence has as part of its structure and end or goal, that offers the basis for a modification of inauthentic or anonymous existence, the existence that could be that of anyone, into an existence of my own, authentic (*eigentlich*) existence. It is not the death of others, death as an event in the world, that can give me this insight, but only the confrontation with my own being toward death in the form of anxiety that makes possible that from now on I live possibilities as precisely *my* possibilities. That is, I live authentically, as an individual. As Lingis puts it:

> To my own potentialities for existence there would correspond, in the world, equally singular possibilities. We are to believe that the world is rich enough for that, that it harbors a set of tasks destined singularly for me alone, for this singular node of potentialities that has arisen in its midst. Opened to my death, I open to all that in the world lets me be, gives me the possibilities to be me, all that gives place for me to be. I am not then just thrown into a world where it is possible to operate as anyone operates; I am sent into a world for destined tasks, singular and finite.[20]

And yet, from the beginning of his analysis Heidegger has insisted that existence means being in the world with others, and others too are authentic (as well as not); they too live out their lives in taking up some of their possibilities and thus in leaving other possibilities unfulfilled. Heidegger sees that they leave me with their undone tasks also, leave me a heritage and a destiny. "Those who accomplish their own potentialities delineate what is possible; the effectuation of their own mortal itineraries destines potentialities for others."[21] But for Lingis this means much more than Heidegger can accept. It means that I substitute myself for the other in his dying.[22] Lingis finds that as rich as Heidegger's teaching on death is, it is fundamentally wrong.[23]

Levinas too had disagreed with Heidegger on this issue, but in the end roots the bond to the other, this irreversibility of the relation with the other, in God. Lingis would suggest that it is rooted in dying: "Yet this illeity, this God, this infinity, is perhaps that of dying, or at least its transcendence to the world is manifest in me as the unending departure of the other."[24]

In the concrete, Lingis works this out in three ways. He follows out Heidegger's notion that the others leave tasks for me that become my own, that become my imperatives; he examines what it means to accompany the other in his or her dying, an analysis impossible for Heidegger, and he locates experiences of dying elsewhere than in death. Every enjoyment is a death, a dissolution that traces for us the movement toward mortality and finality.[25]

Imperatives

In his contribution to *Portraits of American Continental Philosophers*, Alphonso Lingis concludes: "Vital tasks for philosophy: to recognize the multiple imperatives in the perceived landscape, in the elemental, in the night, in the abysses of death. To set forth the clairvoyance and decisiveness of joy as obedience to an imperative."[26]

David Hume, while in his skeptical empiricist mode, declared that it is impossible to derive "ought" from "is." This holds true not only in the sphere of values, of morals, but first of all, and originally more important for the history of philosophy, in the physical or natural world, where the issue at stake was labeled by Hume "necessity," or "necessary connection." Hume challenged us to identify the impression which could serve as the source, and thus as the legitimation, for this idea: that there are necessary connections that we must perceive. This challenge is what awoke Kant from his self-described "dogmatic slumber." In a sense, the whole of *The Critique of Pure Reason* is Kant's effort to respond to Hume's contention in a way that reveals that reason or thought or understanding has the power to apprehend and identify necessity, to make necessary connections appear to the knower.

From Kant's perspective, this alone could legitimize the sciences of nature, make them capable of asserting laws that do not have the status of just generally true but contingent observations. To accomplish this, Kant showed how a priori knowledge would be characterized by being both universal and necessary, and that there *is* such knowledge about nature in the phenomenal realm, that is, the realm of experience, because this is how we *have* to think to be in accordance with reason, with the categories imposed by reason, one of which is necessity. As Lingis so nicely puts it, "Thought is obedience."[27]

Kant grants Hume's point that necessity could never be the object contained in a simple impression in itself, but also maintains that nonetheless necessity rules in nature and can be known. Nature is to be understood as standing under the compulsion of necessity, and the human being, insofar as it belongs to this sphere as a physical being, also finds itself subject to the laws of nature.

Although in agreement with the phenomenological critique of Hume's empiricist's atomism, Lingis had already raised questions in *Sensations* about the existential-phenomenological accounts that had been given of sensation and sensuality. *The Imperative* takes up this critique again, but frames it within two larger theses. First, that neither the positivist physical determinist doctrines of causality, nor the existential assessment of perception as consisting of an exercise of freedom in the positing of perceptions, knowledge, and values are satisfactory accounts. Lingis wants rather to show that such interactions of humans with their environment are to be best understood as *responses* to the directions emanating from the environment, and are thus neither reactions (as in stimulus-response determinism), nor only intentional and teleological acts (as in the standard phenomenological doctrine of perception), for that recognizes only one kind of percept, things, figures against the background. The second thesis is that the standard account of sensibility and sensuality is also one of either affective reactions, of pleasure and pain, the determinist teaching, or the freely chosen positing of valuations, which "failed to recognize the obedience in sensibility and sensuality which every sensualist knows."[28]

Regarding perception, Lingis insists upon the pluralism given in experience: we do not perceive only figures against backgrounds, but also perceive the night, the elements, sensory levels, inhabited spaces. And these, which are not "things," are also not of only a single order; thus each requires its own description. Lingis is radically antireductionist. Certainly we, as phenomenologists who honor the call to "return to the things themselves," must attend to the claims put upon us by what is given to us in the living of perceptions. If these are indeed of multiple orders, then any attempt to find a least common denominator for the sake of a claim to universality or necessity, by way of a doctrine of sensations or anything else, is to look away from the phenomena. On the other hand, to simply assert that everything is "unique" or contingent, would be to look away from the logos.

Lingis supports his general theses by descriptive elaborations of, to mention just some topics, the night, sleep, the elements, the levels of the sensible, enjoyment, erotic sensuality, things. Lingis argues that a proper understanding of perceptions as responses, rather than as either physiological reactions or acts of intentional *Sinngebungen*, reveals that there are given within the world and its contents directives and imperatives that *appeal* to our sensibility. Responses, in this sense, cannot be categorized as either universal or contingent.

Even where Lingis is nearest to Merleau-Ponty's doctrine of perception, in the description of the perception of things, he would have us move our thinking in the direction of imperatives:

> The imperative in our environment is received, not on our understanding in conflict with our sensuality, but on our postural schema which integrates our sensibility and mobilizes our motor forces....This imperative weighs on us, finalizing our perception toward a perceiving of things and not of a medley of sense, toward a perceiving of the environment as a layout and not a chaos. The environment itself, the coherence and the consistency of reality, the style of all styles, weighs on us as an imperative. The environment is an imperative.[29]

It is here that Lingis applies his airbrush to the picture presented by Merleau-Ponty to which Lingis has previously given the name "the competent body."[30]

> When we go out for a walk, our look is not continually *interested*, surveying the environment for landmarks and objectives....The perception of things, the apprehension of their content and the circumscription of their forms, is not an appropriation of them, but an expropriation of our forces into them, and ends in enjoyment.[31]

If Lingis has finessed the necessity of Hume and Kant out of the perceptual environment in favor of imperativity, it seems to me that it was not only to be able to get to Merleau-Ponty, and then beyond to thinking imperativity in this arena; this was but the introduction to a more difficult philosophical task, the task of locating values.

The problematic of the "is" and the "ought" arises most obviously in the sphere of morality. Hume, being consistent, as an empiricist, if not as a skeptic, attributed the source of moral values to be a combination of sentiments (natural to humans) and collective experience, that is, custom or tradition. But Kant wanted more, and thus sought to ground morality in reason itself, a foundation that would thus have the characteristics of universality and necessity. The general expression of this is the categorical imperative, the command of reason that allows no exceptions. This command of morality comes from reason itself, since morality can only be acting in accordance with duty, that is, out of respect for the law (of reason). What I should do, if my actions are to have moral worth, is what duty demands every rational agent should do; circumstances do not alter cases, for this imperative does not stem from situations of the environment, nor from experience, but from reason alone. The moral agent is a universal agent and part of the kingdom of ends.

Section One: Locating Lingis in Traditions of Thought

Kant of course saw that there are actions I do that respond to the necessities imposed upon me by the structure of things—if I want to split a fire log I need to apply a combination of mass and velocity sufficient to provide the force necessary to split it—and named such imperatives hypothetical since they are determined by the objectives we are pursuing, objectives we could also not pursue. That which a rational agent, acting in the sphere of freedom rather than the sphere of nature, has to do falls for Kant under the rubric of the categorical imperative. This is the imperative of morality, the imperative "which declares an action to be objectively necessary in itself without reference to any purpose, that is, without any other end, is valid as an apodictic (practical) principle."[32]

Lingis finds that the clear distinction drawn in this manner between the imperatives is mistaken; it is a phenomenological misrepresentation to make the clear-cut distinction between means and ends that is essential to Kant's thesis. Lingis shows us how the distinction fails if we consider the urgency of action we are compelled to by hunger or thirst where the sequence of actions directed by this *urgency* are both a direct means to satisfy hunger or thirst *and* a good, an end that terminates them. How different this is from when we eat or drink in order to build up energy to engage in aerobic exercise or to stay awake to study for an exam, where it is not the force and urgency of hunger that now drive that further action.[33] As in the case of perception noted above, Lingis finds that there are pluralities in the realm of imperativity not acknowledged by traditional thought.

A second major break with Kant is to be found in Lingis's insistence, against Kant, that it is also the intrinsic importance of things, what is in danger and needs us in order to exist, and not a principle of duty, that determines what has to be done, even though this might conflict with my desires or needs.[34] Such a response could thus not be considered as subsumed under the hypothetical imperative, and yet should not, for Kant be seen as involving the categorical imperative either, since what impels me is not respect for the law of morality, the principle, nor wanting to do my duty, but is rather the response to the concrete specific need that determines what has to be done.

Lingis works out the way that Kant attempts to come to terms with how a thought becomes *my* thought, how an *I* that understands is constituted as subjected to respect for the imperative of the law, that is, to universal and necessary concepts. Then, drawing on Nietzsche and Heidegger, Lingis seeks not to dismiss, but to rectify Kant's notion, a notion which seems to exclude a genuine particularity, which sees the model for thought and moral action only as a universal one:

> Kant believed that all the cases where *what I have to do* is imposed independently of my wants and needs—is categorically imperative—can be identified with formal characteristics....Practical thought determines "what should I do about this?" by determining "What should anyone do about this?"[35]

Lingis responds, "What has to be done requires attention to the concrete particularities of this situation, and the thinking that recognizes *what I have to do* is ad hoc."[36]

We are not, however, left with having to assert an identity between being able to respond to imperatives addressing themselves to me (and thus the possibility of acting morally) with Heideggerian authenticity (*Eigenlichkeit*). One of the major themes of *The Imperative* is, after all, that response within and to the world is neither merely reaction determined by universal laws nor a free constitution by the individual. Lingis ends his book with the following sentence: "If in doing what I have to do, I do not act to actualize myself, neither do I act in order to actualize the universal agent."[37]

Lingis's descriptions have served to phenomenologically ground, in perception itself, the claims to *difference* that make possible an articulation of values outside of universality and a necessity nesting within universality, while also refusing the ambiguous comfort of grounding evaluation in mere mores, by showing that what needs to be accounted for is what makes them *mine*. This is what Lingis heads toward by refusing the false dichotomy of an imperative having to be either hypothetical *or* categorical.

Lingis has undertaken some of the tasks he calls for in the *Portraits* piece, and he did so by seeing, and listening to, what some of his great predecessors have seen and named. But he has also seen what had not been named. It may very well be that through his work he has provided us with the tools to take up some of those tasks ourselves, to do what needs to be done.

Notes

1. Friedrich Nietzsche, *The Gay Science*, #261, trans. W. Kaufmann (New York: Vintage Books, 1974).

2. See, for instance, the analysis of Merleau-Ponty's *embodiment* of Husserl's *intentionality* by way of Heidegger's *existence*. Alphonso Lingis, *Foreign Bodies* (New York, London: Routledge, 1994), chapter 1.

3. Emmanuel Levinas, *Totality and Infinity*, trans. A. Lingis (Pittsburgh: Duquesne University Press, 1969), 43.

4. Alphonso Lingis, *The Imperative* (Bloomington: Indiana University Press, 1998), 145.

5. Alphonso Lingis, *Phenomenological Explanations* (The Hague: Martinus Nijhoff Publishers, 1986), 89.

6. Emmanuel Levinas, *op. cit.*, 194-215.

7. Alphonso Lingis, *Sensations: Intelligibility in Sensibility* (Atlantic Highlands: Humanities Press, 1996), 100.

8. Alphonso Lingis, *The Community of Those Who Have Nothing in Common* (Bloomington: Indiana University Press, 1994), 29.

9. *Ibid.*, 158-159.

10. Immanuel Kant, *Fundamental Principles of the Metaphysic of Morals*, trans. T. K. Abbott (New York: Bobbs-Merrill,1949), 49-50.

11. *Foreign Bodies*, 22-23.

12. Alphonso Lingis, *Deathbound Subjectivity* (Bloomington: Indiana University Press, 1989), 56.

13. *Phenomenological Explanations*, 36-37.

14. *Foreign Bodies*, viii-ix.

15. *Ibid.*, 40-41.
16. *Ibid.*, 54-55.
17. Alphonso Lingis, *Abuses* (Berkeley, Los Angeles: University of California Press, 1994), 34. See also, "Carrion Body, Carrion Utterance," in *The Community of Those Who Have Nothing in Common.*
18. *Deathbound Subjectivity*, 1.
19. *Ibid.*, 106.
20. *Ibid.*, 115.
21. *Ibid.*, 124.
22. *Ibid.*, 184.
23. *The Imperative*, 16.
24. *Deathbound Subjectivity*, 189.
25. *The Imperative*, 22.
26. James Watson (ed.), *Portraits of American Continental Philosophers* (Bloomington: Indiana University Press, 1999), 124.
27. *The Imperative*, 11.
28. *Ibid.*, 13.
29. *Ibid.*, 67-68.
30. *Foreign Bodies*, ix.
31. *The Imperative*, 70.
32. Immanuel Kant, *op. cit.*, 32.
33. *The Imperative*, 290.
34. *Ibid.*, 219.
35. *Ibid.*
36. *Ibid.*, 220.
37. *Ibid.*, 222.

Chapter Three

Reflections Since *Dangerous Emotions*: Interview with Alphonso Lingis 2002

Alexander E. Hooke and Wolfgang W. Fuchs

Q.: *Why philosophy—and not something else?*

A.: Hmmm.

Q.: *Given that your interests are so varied.*

A.: I got fascinated with philosophy when I was a student. And I found that I have always experienced philosophy as a kind of revelation. I learned things from philosophy books. I learned to see things. I learned dimensions of reality in the world that I would not have noticed or found if I had not read books like *Phenomenology of Perception*, books of social philosophy, and so on. Phenomenology is to me a revealing of things, cultural things for example. One of the first things I wrote about was the Hagia Sophia. It was an essay completely derived from Heidegger, but Heidegger made me see this temple as a place where a world was revealed, where the Byzantine world was laid out, set forth, maintained, concentrated. If I hadn't gotten that kind of philosophical understanding of what a temple is I suppose I would have, like most tourists, or even art historians who specialize in medieval cathedrals, see them as just things that are agreeable and captivating to look at. They study them purely aesthetically or historically. So if I hadn't gotten that kind of Heideggerian understanding of temples I wouldn't have spent so many years unendingly fascinated by temples of different cultures. In books like *Excesses* and *Abuses* I wrote about things that moved me most profoundly in numerous places. I think in my life almost everything that counted was illuminated by philosophy.

Q.: *In* Abuses, *the preface, you said philosophy is something like the universal language because it is one's own words. You are familiar with positivism and all the other* *variations of philosophy where philosophy is supposed to clarify language and nothing more, where philosophy is to follow roughly the model of science in terms of sorting out what is certain or provable. What will be possible in philosophy for twenty-first-century students?*

A.: For me philosophy was really a revealing discourse and not simply a critical or secondary discourse that goes back over discourse to clarify concepts or criticize. When I lately went over once again Deleuze's *A Thousand Plateaus* I think both the students and I found so many things got illuminated. He crosses concepts from different disciplines and regions of the universe. It seems to me that in so many areas philosophy hasn't even begun to look at the things that science has uncovered. Ecology is a new area, and evolutionary biology; they have immense implications for the understanding of ourselves and our interrelationship with things. I think there will continue to be a kind of creative, illuminating work by philosophers.

Q.: *In all of your work you either implicitly or explicitly refer to philosophers, to some master thinkers. Who are they for you now in the last eight to ten years? Who are the thinkers that you still find fruitful to return to or that you discovered?*

A.: Deleuze and Guattari certainly, and Bataille. Nietzsche still, I think there are still things in Nietzsche that have not really been put to work. Someone just asked me to write something about Nietzsche's animals and it occurred to me that I did have some ideas about that. I think one of those things that science has given us in recent years is evolutionary biology and so much understanding of the other species. So there will be much room to rethink ourselves as a species of animal. I think certainly some language philosophers are of interest to me like Helmslef and also Lakoff. Like a lot of people nowadays, I think Bergson is another philosopher who still has much to be drawn from. One of the things that is most interesting to me now is biology and the philosophers who have tried to understand evolutionary biology and biological concepts. Lynn Margulis's *Symbiotic Planet* made such an impression on me. I think all creative philosophers have always recognized some books in other disciplines as really talking philosophically.

Q.: *Foucault once said in an interview that there are philosophers that he writes about and some philosophers he loves and doesn't write about. And then he said Heidegger and Nietzsche; he has one short essay on Nietzsche and he never wrote about Heidegger although he was a big influence. Is there any thinker—philosopher or non-philosopher—who has contributed a lot to your thought and yet you almost never talk about? A secret love that you don't want to make public—that's what Foucault mentioned.*

A.: Levinas is someone that I didn't write anything about for a very long time, and I haven't written much about him. But he was a very, very profound influence. In so many ways he illuminated things for me.

Q.: *How did you meet him?*

A.: Well I'm always shy about taking up the time of people I admire. I originally wrote him a letter with some questions about the translation of *Totality and Infinity* I was doing. And I phrased them in such a way that he could just tick off quickly the answers. But instead he invited me to come over to his place. That was the first meeting.

Q.: *So you had finished your studies then?*

A.: Yeah. *Totality and Infinity* was published the first year I was teaching, even before I had finished my dissertation. I undertook the translation almost at once.

Q.: *Are you surprised how popular Levinas has become?*

A.: Yes, especially in this country, since it is a very French writing. It's a very personal kind of philosophy, and not at all like the philosophers that had a big following in America, like Husserl and Heidegger.

Q.: *Are there philosophers that you use as touchstones in the sense that you can very clearly refer back to them, see them understood as sort of the common wisdom and then begin to think partially with them and partially against them? I am thinking of in* The Imperative, *for example Kant. But are there others, and what kind of relationship is there between you and those kinds of masters?*

A.: Yeah, there are certain philosophers that I simply found—what is the word exactly (laughingly)—*right*. Merleau-Ponty. Of all the things one knows or could know about perception, pretty much everything he said is pretty much right. When I was talking about Merleau-Ponty about a year ago in a course, I had long critical remarks. But, you know, the main body of it is like: *that is what we know* about this topic. I think what Nietzsche means by morality in *The Genealogy of Morals* is what we know about the origin of morality, about the concept of nobility. I like Bernard Williams enormously. There is so much of what he says I think is really correct. I think all the work of Austin had a great influence on me. I think of Austin as the truth of Wittgenstein. In fact in a certain way I read Heidegger with Austin's eyes. In a certain way you can consider Heidegger a philosopher of language.

Q.: *Some years ago you said: if only Nietzsche were as interesting as Heidegger's book on him makes him out to be. Have you rediscovered Nietzsche since making that statement?*

A.: I restudied Heidegger's *Nietzsche* and now I don't like it at all. For me the best thinkers on Nietzsche are Deleuze and Klossowski, especially Klossowski. These are the thinkers who found the ideas in Nietzsche that are not found anywhere else. But to go back to the philosophers for the future, I think Klossowski is one of those people. His book on Nietzsche is wonderful, and his book *Un si funeste désir*—a stunning title. Once I was saying how should we translate that—A so Baleful Desire....and Elizabeth Haar said "Oh no, it's much stronger than that: it's deathbound!"

Q.: *How do you pick the titles for your books? You have a penchant for one-word titles. Do you pick the title before you work on the book, or is it a collection of essays that sometimes gives you the title?*

A.: Titles are hard for me. *Abuses* was all written and I was with Karim Benammar in Guatemala, and every day we were thinking about a title for this book. Then he got very sick with dysentery, and he picked up the Spanish dictionary and opened the first page and was just reading over words, barely conscious, and he said *abusos*, and I suddenly stopped. I loved that word.

Q.: *In a recent lecture on trust you suggested that trust is almost presocial, precontractual. I was surprised that children are taught very quickly when they go to school not to trust strangers and they have a whole list for when a stranger comes to you and talks. And yet almost all the abuses that happen to children are from people they know, their families, their neighbors. And yet you said at the same time that trust is exhilarating, joyous. Is there something that children are deprived of by learning to fear and be suspicious of some people?*

A.: That's very striking; I didn't know what you just said. In the Third World that isn't true. One of the great pleasures of going to the Third World is that you have such friendships across age. So often I have been taken to places and shown them by children. I remember in Istanbul, I had explored the city with all the guidebooks there were. And then one day a kid showed me a passage underground that led to a three-story buried Byzantine palace. The kid took me down with a kerosene-bottle torch. At the bottom there lived a lunatic. I remember the very first summer I spent in Istanbul. There was a kid I met in a mosque. He was eleven or twelve, and he proposed showing me around. I thought he was proposing to be my guide, which I really didn't want. So I agreed to meet him once, and then I discovered he seemed not to want anything. Eventually I liked him so much that I met him every other afternoon. He would always pay the bus, and some days he wouldn't show up. Finally I figured out that it was because he didn't have that little money to pay the bus for both of us. If I proposed getting some ice cream some hot day, if he didn't have the money to pay for it he would pretend he didn't want any. At the end of the summer I asked him what I could send him from my country, and he said he would like a photograph of me. I have experienced so much trust in the Third World, children trusting. And of course they know so much, they know everything. I am really horrified by the thought that you presented that the first thing American children learn at school is to distrust all strangers. I want to say that it is natural thing to trust, and that children naturally trust others. And the thing that you said too is striking: that virtually all violence against children is done by their own intimates and not by outsiders.

Q.: *It seems to speak well for you and your experiences, but there is something that strikes your readers, most easily seen in* The Imperative, *where you speak of the directives that come from the environment and that's how one knows what one must do, but you don't address the same structure, or at least a similar structure of the compulsive, the person who is mad, the person who is acting out of orders from their dog or from god or whatever that are destructive. Is there a way to find a distinction between these two kinds of directives?*

A.: Here I'm afraid I feel very inadequate just now. I have a tendency—I think it is very Nietzschean, or at least I found something in Nietzsche akin to my own impulses—to put a fundamental primacy to the positive. To do an outrage to a human being seems to presuppose that you have a high vision of that human being. It would be hard to imagine getting into some sort of rage against someone that you consider just to be meat or a mechanism. Maybe we can take this example out of de Sade: in order to build up his rage he needs God. In order to be the absolute criminal he needs a kind of absolute to blaspheme against and spit on. I have always had the impression that the positive, like joy or health, is first. There is the Nietzschean idea that there is nothing more natural than to be healthy or joyous. Resentment is second; it's a kind of sickness, a secondary phenomenon. Just as soon as something is born it is happy. This is so visible in the animal kingdom. A colt that just dropped out of the womb of the horse is running around exuberant in the sunlight and radiant air. I think I have always tried to understand the primary phenomenon, the positive phenomenon. And I suppose that in most cases I never quite got around to understanding the negative or destructive phenomenon, the crime. In *The Imperative* I saw human life as directed by the light, the sun, the day, the night, living and non-living beings: and this seemed to me the primary phenomenon. I didn't get to really understand how a life could become hateful and destructive.

Q.: *You are also a political thinker. Do you think something like the modern state is simply unnatural?*

A.: Well I was just reading Benjamin Barber's *Jihad vs. McWorld*. The nation-state was the structure that built war machines, so my generation thought that the abolition of war depends on the overcoming of national sovereignty toward something like the world court and world government. Barber argues that the nation-state was the structure in which democracy developed. And that now there is this trivializing, commercializing globalism, and on the other hand Jihad particularism, in violent combat against it—which are also without boundaries. For him the structure that could anchor us in civil society and in democracy is the nation-state. This echoes thinkers in Europe who want to maintain something like a French identity against the universalizing and also trivializing European economic union.

Q.: *In* Dangerous Emotions *you raise and discuss and describe a variety of passions, emotions, imperatives. When it comes to these things I want to know what makes them dangerous? Would you agree that what makes them dangerous is that they either transgress or mock, laugh at or make sacred those experiences which civilization doesn't?*

A.: I am not sure I can answer that because I have not thought in terms of the notion of civilization.

Q.: *The dominant thinkers in political philosophy today are thinkers like Habermas, with rational communication, and John Rawls with contract theory...*

A.: Yeah, there is a big gap. There are a couple of ideas in Bataille I adhere to. There is the line where he says one does not encounter, one does not know the real if one does not know extreme pleasure and extreme pain. It seems to me that there is a destiny in emotions to go to extremes, breaking walls, and plunging into abysses. If you really want to make contact, plunge into reality, that is dangerous.

My book on emotions is very incomplete. I had this other idea that we do not have in philosophy, something like an emotional map of the territory. But that's what we have in literature. When you begin a novel by Faulkner you get a map of hatreds and jealousies and loyalties, conflicts between characters, families, dynasties. There is first an emotional map of this county and that will generate the plot. We don't have anything like that in social philosophy. We have the power map, the institutional structures that political and social philosophy study.

When I was in Palestine last summer, I was so struck by the thought that the horrors, crimes, tragedies that have been inflicted on these people since the beginning of the intifada are so terrible that it will take years, perhaps generations, to go beyond them. The other day Kissinger said that from here to peace will take a long time, that one has to think of incremental steps. So there is a recognition that one has to deal with the sorrow, despair, grief, anger that are real forces. And I don't think we really know how to map this out and see how it intersects with institutions and power relations.

Q.: *You began to answer a question I have not asked but I would like to ask now. In* Dangerous Emotions *you give a kind of list, a short list, of what are the fundamental forces. You added to that list last night when you talked about trust. Is that list finite first of all, or can one keep thinking new things to add to it, and, secondly, isn't that a project worth doing as a whole: making this map?*

A.: Yeah. Again I hadn't thought of that as a task. You are completely right. When I was writing that paper last night I connected trust with courage and laughter and lust. I stopped there because the paper was at a maximum length, but I did think that was a start. I wanted to start thinking about these things which I put under "immediacy."

Q.: *It seems to happen in almost every major culture, the kind of lingering memory of someone doing you wrong, even if it wasn't intentional or from a loved one. The best colleagues, you like them, and then you see them at a meeting and you wonder what happened to them: it is like all of a sudden they are transformed, and that is the image you start remembering of them. What happens?*

A.: You just raised a question as to whether it is universal in cultures. But maybe other cultures have ways to negotiate so that doesn't happen. I think for example of Myanmar: you never say "no" in Myanmar. It is considered impolite. If you ask "how can I get to the bus station?" and they don't know, they won't say "No." Outsiders very often don't understand this; they think that Burmese are devious. I thought the paper umbrellas that the monks carry were great and wanted one. I asked a Burmese friend if he could help me get one. He said "I'll try." The next day he returned and didn't have it. If you ask him "Did you find one in the market today?" he won't say "no"; he'll do some circumlocution. After awhile you catch one; you won't force him to a yes or no answer. This gives me a clue that maybe other cultures have some ways to negotiate to put an end to a lingering grief or resentment. I suspect they might.

Q.: *What occurs to me, though, is that cultures I will now call, just off the top of my head, "cultures of honor," honor in that sense where you don't allow yourself or your family or your clan to be insulted, that honor in that sense is entirely directed at slights and remembering those, and that that's the proof of honor.*

A.: In Albania they have a code, I think written in the fifteenth century but going back to pre-Christian times. Honor is extremely important in this society, but there is also a whole apparatus of reconciliation. Even if someone has killed someone, there is a way to reconcile the families, to put an end to vendetta.

Quite awhile ago, when you could still import birds, I needed a female Moluccan cockatoo for my male. So I went to the bird market in Jakarta. There an old man came up, apparently the only one in the market who spoke English. He didn't have a shop or birds, but he went to locate a female cockatoo for me. I gave him two hundred dollars for the bird, and—since I couldn't stay long enough to do it myself—another two hundred dollars to arrange the quarantine and get the documents and then ship the bird to me. At the time I thought if it were me I would probably not ship the bird and instead just keep those four hundred bucks and count on not seeing this foreigner again. But since at the time cockatoos were very expensive in the United States, and I really did want a female for my male, I thought it was worth taking the chance. As it happened, he did not ship the bird, and I wasn't surprised nor worked up any indignation over it.

The following year I happened to be back in Java, and headed off to the market, and the first guy I ran into was him. He looked upset and said "Come to the police station." He was perhaps afraid that I might be violent, and wanted the protection of the police. So we go to the police station, where some policemen bring tea and sweets and, like always in Java, there is a great deal of small talk before you get around to the issue. Finally the police captain asks me if I want him to arrest this man. Of course not. But I still want the cockatoo. Over the course of the whole morning little by little guessing how I feel about things this policeman—he really was very gracious—finally proposes this solution: this man will locate another female cockatoo and I'll give him again four hundred dollars. In terms of American justice, since I had given this man those four hundred bucks and he didn't ship me the bird, either he should return the four hundred bucks or now do what he had agreed to it. I saw that the police captain was searching for a solution both of us could agree to.

The idea was not to lay down some law but instead to make sure that neither party of a dispute are left with ill feeling. I agreed now, because this man has long since spent the four hundred dollars from last year to take care of his family, and so if I want a bird I have to put up four hundred dollars again. I can't find the bird I want by myself; they are not on display in the market. This man should be able to locate one because of all his network of acquaintances. I could see that the Indonesian notion of justice is that where there is a conflict, a breach in the community, it should be healed so that there is not any lingering indignation or resentment. The police captain asked me to come back two days later. When I did, again there is all the tea and sweets and conversation. Several hours passed, during which different policemen came in to chat awhile. I really didn't understand what on earth was going on. Finally I began to realize that the old man didn't show. And he didn't show because of course he didn't find such a bird. And since he had committed himself to the policeman to do this he lost face. And the police captain lost face because he had come up with a solution which now didn't work out. So what he had done is sent his men out to try to find the man. They didn't find him; he was lying low somewhere. The police captain was now talking about how fine the mountains are around Bogor, and told me I must come with him and his family for an outing in his car this weekend. I eventually understood that he felt he himself had to give me something, so that I would not harbor ill feelings about Indonesia. Instead of the old man finding me a bird I could not locate by myself, the police captain would give me a mountain trip I could never manage for myself. I could see that the whole concept of justice worked so that there isn't any lingering resentment in the community. Whereas in our system of course you just lay down the law, somebody would be punished and would sit in jail filled with anger and misery and resentment.

Chapter Four

The Sacred Vision of a Solitary Voyager

Thomas J. Altizer

Alphonso Lingis knows Catholic Christianity as a religion centered on sacrifice, for the Catholic Eucharist is not a commemoration but rather an actual reenactment of an ultimate and absolute sacrifice. As he declares in the opening chapter of *Abuses*, the Christian life can only consist in a real participation in the redemptive act of Christ, and to be a Christian is to make each moment, each act, each thought, and each perception of one's own existence, a sacrifice. Does such a sacrifice embody that core which is the very center of Lingis's own work and vision? Can his deeper work be understood as a continual and actual reenactment of that primordial sacrifice which is the Catholic sacrifice, and a uniquely Catholic sacrifice, even if, as he so fully demonstrates, this sacrifice is a truly universal sacrifice? While certainly a philosopher, and a genuinely radical one, are Lingis's voyages away from our uniquely modern Western philosophy, and genuine renewals or rebirths of a truly primordial or archaic philosophy, a philosophy inseparable from primordial sacrifice, a sacrifice which is at once both the creation and the ending of the world?

In the conclusion of *Abuses*, Lingis gives us perhaps his most self-revealing statement. Here, when confronting the charred hull of a once Catholic temple in Honduras, he can declare that the sacred is this decomposition, for the sacred is what repels our advance, and the sacred is not the salvific but the inapprehendable, the unconceptualizable, the inassimilable, the irrecuperable. Religion advances triumphantly over the decomposition of the sacred, separating the covenant from the taboos, the celestial order from the intoxication with sacrificial blood, the sublime from the excremental, and the celestial and divine order from the demoniacal world of decomposition. For by levitating the sacred into an extracosmic empyrean, where a providential reign of a personalized deity fosters in us exalted phantasms, religion consecrates the profanation of the world, finally giving us a world of total banality and emptiness, or, quite simply, a world which is our contemporary world.

This is the world that Lingis's voyages wholly leave behind, but is not this voyager a deeply Catholic voyager, one ever voyaging into the full actuality of sacrifice itself, and deriving from that very sacrifice his purest and most genuine thinking? Of course, what we know as Catholic theology is alien to this thinking, but this is a theology which cannot know the Crucified God, and thus cannot know what is here known as the absolute sacrifice of the Eucharist, or that absolute sacrifice which is inevitably embodied in our deepest acts. Lingis and other revolutionary Catholics can know the cosmos itself as the sacrifice of God, and one reenacted in every truly actual word and act, and if this Catholic vision is most luminously manifest in Dante and Joyce, it is certainly not absent in Lingis, and may well be his own deepest ground.

Already Dante was a deep Catholic heretic, and the first Christian visionary to know a Godhead inseparable from the very actuality of the world, and Dante is Joyce's primary precursor, that very Joyce who gave us our most visionary and comprehensive heresy, as here an absolute heterodoxy becomes reality itself, and the only reality which it is now possible actually and fully to speak. One can imagine Alphonso Lingis as a philosopher only made possible by *Finnegan's Wake*, and the *Wake* revolves about a continually reenacted primordial sacrifice, one here occurring in the fullness of language itself, and also occurring through that primordial sodomy or buggery which so fascinates Lingis, a sodomy issuing from what Lingis knows as an ultimate will to defy all law, and above all the absolute law of God the Father. Joyce follows Blake in knowing that Father as Satan, and while Lingis does not employ an explicit language of Satan, he goes beyond Lacan in understanding the Father as the absolute Phallus, the absolute imperative arising as a phantom of absence. For the phallus is initially constituted in repression, it is that which was first discovered as a lack, a lack opening the space beyond the immediately given, opening the way to the signification of civilization, and the objects open to civilized or castrated man are metaphors and metonymies of the phallus (*Excesses*, 92). This language of Lingis's is clearly in continuity with the language of *Finnegan's Wake*, and if only thereby this is a radically heterodox Catholic language, but a Catholic language which is a truly "catholic" language, and certainly so in our world.

Just as Levinas can understand the history of Western philosophy as an ever progressive profanation of God, Lingis can understand our Western history itself as such a profanation, one truly challenged only by our most revolutionary visionaries, and while these visionaries are all deeply heterodox, this is a heterodoxy making fully manifest the deep profanation of our orthodoxies. But here Catholic orthodoxy is inseparable from our positivistic and anthropocentric orthodoxies, and most clearly so in what it knows as Godhead itself, a Godhead ultimately sanctioning that which is most deeply given or at hand. For this is a Godhead which is not only absolutely beyond, but whose very beyondness is an absolute sanctioning of that which is most openly manifest or given, hence it can know a "natural law" which is the very Law of God, and a law embodied in everything which we can know as law, or everything which we can know as a pure imperative. Here, that imperative is ultimately the indicative itself, or is reality itself, a "reality" that Lingis can know as an absolutely repressive reality, and one that can only be transcended by an absolute sacrifice, and an absolute sacrifice of that very reality.

Hence the goal of Lingis's voyages would appear to be a continual reenactment of that sacrifice, and if this can occur only wholly beyond everything that we know as world, it also can occur only wholly beyond everything that we have known as God, as Being, as Logos, as Goodness, and as Truth, or, rather, it can occur only in the pure reversal or sacrifice of our deepest ground.

Now there can be no question that Lingis is deeply attracted by the language of violence, nothing so distinguishes him as a philosopher as does his own language of violence, and certainly his voyages are voyages into violence. This is just the very point at which Lingis is most offensive, but also the point at which he is most purely Catholic, and most purely Catholic in his continual reenactment of sacrifice, a sacrifice which is inevitably a violent sacrifice, and most violent in its sacrifice of God. Even if this is unknown to all our Catholic theologies, it is not unknown or unmanifest in the Eucharist itself, and if it is the Eucharist which is the deepest power of Catholicism, this is a power which thus far has been most unknown theologically, and surely unknown by that Catholic theology that cannot know the Crucified God. Nothing is more hidden in the cultic Eucharist than violence itself, and while the eucharistic breaking of bread is clearly a reenactment of the Crucifixion, it is nevertheless disguised as such, as now the Crucifixion is reenacted as a pure and sanitary act, and one wholly isolated from the brute actuality of the world. Lingis's voyages and thinking shatter that very isolation, unveiling the violence of the Crucifixion as the violence of actuality itself, this is the very actuality which is reenacted in genuine sacrifice, hence true sacrifice is necessarily a violent sacrifice, and can truly be reenacted only by violent words and acts.

Not until Nietzsche does violence fully enter our philosophical language, and if Nietzsche is our purest philosopher of sacrifice, this is most manifest in his continual proclamation of the death of God. But it is no less manifest in his revolutionary discovery of genealogy itself, a genealogy unveiling the advent of that absolute repression which is our interiority itself, and a repression that can only be ended by the death of God. This is the ending which Lingis knows as occurring in an absolute sacrifice, but that sacrifice must be every bit as violent as is the violence of repression, and if the violence of repression is most deeply an interior violence, and one wholly disguised by the signs and the semiotics of our civilizations, only a pure reversal of those signs can unveil the overwhelming and the comprehensive power of repression, and this is the reversal which most openly occurs in the rituals of sacrifice.

The Christian knows the blood of the Lamb as the one source of redemption, a blood which is renewed in the *anamnesis* of the Eucharist, and in Catholicism that *anamnesis* is not a remembrance or a commemoration, but rather an actual reenactment of the sacrifice of the Crucifixion, even if that reenactment is veiled or sanitized by a Catholic theology that cannot know the sacrifice of the Godhead itself. Lingis can only be heterodox, and profoundly heterodox, in his quest for that sacrifice, thereby he appears to be just as anti-Catholic as is Joyce himself. But Joyce's anti-Catholicism is a subversion of the established Catholic Church, and not a pagan or a secular subversion, but far rather a Catholic subversion, and a Catholic subversion employing a Catholic and a universal language, as most clearly manifest in the comprehensive reenactment of the mass itself in both the movement and the language of *Finnegan's Wake*.

Can we understand Lingis's voyages as reenactments of a cosmic and universal mass, voyages inevitably reversing both the Catholic liturgy and Catholic theology and authority, and voyages seeking that which is most deeply repressed in Catholicism itself? Here, a genuine paradox confronts us, for as Lingis's most radical thinking makes manifest, that which is most deeply repressed is simultaneously that which is most deeply celebrated, this is openly manifest in what Lingis continually calls forth as the violence of sacrifice, one reenacting our deepest repression in ecstatic moments of celebration, and here it is only the most violent acts that can embody that celebration. Hence they can occur only in the depths or in the abyss, an abyss unnamable by our Western philosophy, a philosophy whose very essence Lingis can understand as a pure sublimation, and a sublimation which could only be a repression of our original humanity, or of what Lingis frequently names as an original or primal society. Repudiating all our romantic notions of a primitive simplicity and a primitive cohesion, Lingis can speak of this society as a society of monsters: "as a multitude of essentially unsocialized, uncivilized individuals, not yet constituting a human species, spectacular, not recognizing any common humanity" (*Excesses*, 100). This is that original humanity which cannot be suppressed, but can only be repressed and driven underground, where it has become insatiable and infinite, leaving behind an unending field of symbols, symbols which are reversed in the languages and semiotics of our civilizations, civilizations whose members are stricken with an essential absence or emptiness, and who are subjected to the order of law.

Lingis can be understood as a radical Pauline thinker in his absolute opposition to the law, and, he too posits a pure opposition between law and grace, just as he celebrates a grace which is love itself, but this is a love which has never been understood by either our philosophies or our theologies. True, Lingis is deeply affected by psychoanalysis, but he nevertheless recognizes psychoanalysis as an instrument of sublimation, thereby disguising all genuine libido by sublimating all bodily libido. Lingis is in quest of the body plenum, or the body without organs, or the full body, a body constituting itself by incorporation, which he can speak of as the earth itself, but there is not an I at the center of this body, there is only Id, and certainly not the Id of Freud, but rather an Id that is a reversal of every psychoanalytic Id, for the Id which Lingis calls forth is not an original given, but rather the consequence of an ultimate excess or excitation, which he can speak of as "ipseity" itself (*Excesses*, 30). Perhaps this Id could be given the biblical name of Jerusalem, and not the old Jerusalem of monarchic and priestly Israel, but rather the new Jerusalem of prophetic and apocalyptic Israel, the new Jerusalem which Blake celebrated as the "Eternal Great Humanity Divine" and Joyce celebrated as "Here Comes Everybody" and "Anna Livia Plurabelle."

Blake, Nietzsche, and Joyce all share an ecstatic celebration of an ultimate and a cosmic sacrifice, a sacrifice which is a violent sacrifice, hence it is an assault upon civilization itself, but only Joyce among our visionaries knows this sacrifice as a liturgical sacrifice, and a liturgical sacrifice which is a cosmic and an historical mass at once. This is the mass which is the very plot or action of both *Ulysses* and *Finnegan's Wake*, and it is a mass revolving about a cosmic and an apocalyptic crucifixion, a crucifixion which is the death and resurrection of God at once. Is this a resurrection which Lingis finally envisions? First, we must note that Christian theology has been most pagan or most non-Christian in its dominant understanding of resurrection, a resurrection which is wholly a spiritual resurrection, even understanding the resurrected body as a spiritual body. So, too, this theology has understood the ascension into heaven as the true destiny of the incarnate and crucified Christ, a spiritual heaven which is the destiny of the redeemed, or the destiny of the predestined elect, and a destiny which is not ultimately challenged in Christianity until Dante himself.

While the Catholic Church has yet to canonize Dante, and initially condemned him as a heretic, virtually all Catholics accept Dante as their greatest visionary, and this despite the fact that his vision so profoundly transformed well over a millennium of Catholic history, and did so if only in so fully integrating the human, the cosmic, and the divine. One can only imagine the wrath with which an Augustine would have responded to Dante, but this does give us some sense of the deep transformations which have occurred in Catholic history, and if a Joyce can be understood as a visionary of the third millennium of Catholic history, could this be true of Lingis too? No doubt this baptized Catholic would repudiate such a suggestion, but he cannot deny the uniquely Catholic motifs in his own thinking, just as he cannot deny his ultimate fascination with the most radical vision. Is it an oxymoron to speak of a radical Catholic vision? Certainly Dante's was a radical vision in terms of the Catholic world which he inherited, and even if Catholic theologians are immune to this epic vision, that does not lessen its genuine Catholic ground, or lessen the challenge of a Catholic understanding of that ground. It is Dante's supreme theological challenge to us to understand that the genuinely Catholic is the truly catholic or the truly universal, a universality which Lingis again and again embraces, even if this is a universality demanding an ultimate reversal of our history, and an ultimate reversal of everything which we have known as both consciousness and thinking.

Clearly Lingis is reluctant to employ the word "God," a reluctance or withdrawal found throughout twentieth-century philosophy, yet he nevertheless again and again evokes God, and always negatively when speaking of "the father," a father who is the very source of repression, and above all so as the internalized, spiritualized, father. Indeed, Lingis can affirm that the binding power of socialization does not occur through the threat of an outside power, but rather through a universal eucharist by which the paternal reality, now vanquished and abolished, is constituted as an internal imperative that makes the libido speak, a speaking addressing itself to the demand of the other (*Excesses*, 98). Perhaps it is in speech itself that "the father" is most powerful, and most manifestly so in that speech which itself orders, an order occurring in that law which is the word of the father, and if it is only through speech that one comes into the presence of the other, Lingis can know genuine speech as revealing the truly or veritably other, a speech which is responsibility itself, and one inseparable from the alterity of the other. But is true alterity inseparable from the epiphany or the realization of "the father," at this point is Lingis bound to that Levinas whom he so brilliantly translated, or does he go beyond Levinas in understanding an absolute universality of "the father"?

For Lingis knows a universal eucharist which is alien to Levinas, a eucharist which is an absolute sacrifice, and therefore a sacrifice of "the father," a sacrifice by which "the father" is vanquished and abolished, even if the father continually returns in the actuality of speech. Is it the sacrifice of the father which makes possible the full actuality of speech, and is the genuine speech of responsibility itself a consequence of that sacrifice, one apart from which there could be no awareness of alterity or the truly other? This is a speech that Lingis can know as being most absent in the world of late capitalism, or in that world which we know as postmodernity. Is this also the world in which a universal eucharist is most invisible and unheard, a world in which genuine responsibility has vanished if only because there is no possibility of a eucharist for us? Is that why Lingis must continually voyage to the end of the world in search of such a eucharist? If nothing else, Lingis's work demonstrates that we have truly forgotten a universal eucharist, and therefore have forgotten sacrifice itself, or the depths of sacrifice.

Is this yet another consequence of the uniquely modern realization of the death of God, a truly ironic consequence, for those modern thinkers and visionaries who enacted the death of God precisely thereby called forth the absolute sacrifice of God, one luminously clear not only in Hegel and Nietzsche but also in Blake and Joyce, and is it this absolute sacrifice which Lingis understands as the Eucharist itself? And in understanding the Eucharist as a universal eucharist, is Lingis thereby an authentically Catholic thinker, a radical Catholic thinker, yes, but precisely thereby and only thereby a genuinely Catholic thinker? Nothing is more characteristic of modern theology, including Catholic theology, than its deep divorce between dogmatic theology and ethical theology, one broached only by Barth, who has given us the most paternalistic ethics thus far conceived, although his contemporary disciples are certainly striving to outdo him at this point.

Lingis would reverse every possible paternalistic ethics, but is this possible apart from an absolute sacrifice of God, or apart from the universal eucharist itself, a eucharist most openly refused by all of our contemporary dogmatic theology. Or can we understand Lingis as a dogmatic theologian at this crucial point? The fact that Lingis is a genuine philosopher does not foreclose this possibility, for Hegel, surely our greatest modern philosopher, was not only a dogmatic theologian, but one who revolutionized Christian dogmatics, and most clearly so by a philosophical and theological thinking centered upon the self-negation or the self-emptying of God. Is Lingis revolutionizing Catholic dogmatics by centering it upon that absolute sacrifice which is the Eucharist, and is this the recovery of a long forgotten Catholic ground, and not only a Catholic but a catholic or universal ground?

Yet Lingis would go beyond Hegel if not beyond Nietzsche in understanding absolute sacrifice as the final sacrifice of the Godhead itself. Does he thereby go beyond that radical Protestantism which so dominates modern philosophical thinking, and go beyond it by finally ending that absolute ego or that absolute "I" which even Husserl cannot escape? And is this possible only for a genuinely Catholic or catholic thinking, a Catholic thinking truly negated and eclipsed by modern philosophy, but which can return with the end of that philosophy itself? In this perspective, is it possible to understand that it is Godhead itself which modern philosophy cannot think, and cannot think it if only because it so absolutely thinks the absolute ego or the absolute "I," an "I" eclipsing that Godhead known by both a Catholic and a catholic humanity?

While Lingis is not alone in negating that "I," he is seemingly alone in effecting that negation by way of a calling forth of an absolute and universal sacrifice, one which is purely present in the Eucharist, and which can be understood only by understanding the full actuality of a universal reenactment of the absolute sacrifice of the Godhead itself. Orthodox theology refuses that sacrifice in its condemnation of Patripassionism, but Lingis joins Joyce in resurrecting Patripassionism, and it is only the sacrifice of "the father" which is finally the source of life and love, or finally the source of responsibility itself.

Chapter Five

Encounter the World, Keep a Clear Eye

Janice McLane

The words Alphonso Lingis writes can be unsettling to us. Not only is his subject matter unusual and even troubling, Lingis's style itself disconcerts the reader. But Lingis's work is too finely crafted for this to be accidental; the agitation he brings is clearly deliberate. Sometimes stringently formal, sometimes extravagantly lyric and personal, often almost simultaneously both, Lingis's work can leave the reader with a simple and heartfelt question: what is this man *doing*?

The present essay considers this question in a specific area: the form of Lingis's written work. I will contend that Lingis's strategies of composition are guided by his choice to live out a self-conscious philosophic encounter with the world. That is, Lingis continually repositions himself physically, intellectually, and linguistically to document the meeting between philosopher and world. Of course, the union of self and world is often a subject of philosophy, and indeed of life in general. Yet few philosophers write or live in the extremity Lingis regularly chooses. For him, not simply academic matters but how to live and act, what people, places, and things to approach, all become choices to examine and live out philosophically. One might say that Lingis's life itself has become a phenomenology.

To succeed, an undertaking such as his requires both chutzpah and discipline. Chutzpah, because it takes as meaningful not just philosophic life in general, but the encounter between the particular philosopher—Lingis—and the world.[1] At the same time, this philosophizing requires great discipline. To be done well, the philosopher must approach his or her life with the same degree of ferocious and pitiless scrutiny a scientist might bring to dissecting an animal brain. This is philosophy as purposeful self-vivisection.

Phenomenology

We may understand Lingis's work better if we briefly consider the philosophic tradition of phenomenology. Alphonso Lingis is steeped in this tradition; his work is an outgrowth of it. Phenomenology proper began in the early twentieth century with Edmund Husserl. Husserl attempted to achieve accuracy in philosophy by analyzing phenomena as they were directly present to the conscious mind, prior to bias, culture, or theory. Since these analyses would be nothing but *descriptions of things themselves*—i.e., would not contain the personality or assumptions of the describing philosopher—Husserl intended them to achieve universal certainty.

Claims to universal knowledge were implicitly or explicitly continued in the work of later phenomenologists: in Heidegger's understanding of all human life as what he called Dasein; in Sartre's claim that all people are defined by their freedom; in Merleau-Ponty's analysis of the commonalities of embodied perception. But this desire for universality was undermined by phenomenology's very methods. First, phenomenology analyzed the phenomenologist's conscious experience. But though the aim was to describe things purely in and of themselves, it eventually became clear that *a description of the contents of consciousness* could not be separated from *the specific character of a person's consciousness*. That is, people are unavoidably structured by their cultural context, personal history, gender, class, physical uniqueness, etc. The unique aspects of a person therefore cannot be ignored in a description of the contents of her or his mind; they rather become part of what is analyzed. Second, and correlatively, the *relation* between phenomenologist and phenomenon (the experiencer and thing experienced, perceiver and thing perceived) emerged as a crucial component of such descriptions, and became an explicit theme of phenomenology. Thus over time, phenomenology has tended to bring to the fore precisely those elements Husserl in his early works thought he had bracketed out—the relational and personal components of things.

What Lingis has done is take the presence of the philosopher in phenomenological descriptions, and the relationship between experiencer and thing experienced, to a new level of self-consciousness. His concerns are not random, but a logical outgrowth of phenomenology; in Lingis's work, the specific, personal, and relational elements which in other philosophers were covert become part of the very method of philosophizing. Furthermore, not simply the content but the form of his writing reflect this determination to take phenomenology to its limits.

First-Person Chronicling

From his earliest efforts on, we can see Lingis's preoccupation with how human beings encounter the world. For example, his major translations are of Merleau-Ponty's *The Visible and the Invisible*, which proposes that all experience manifests the reciprocity of living flesh, and of Emmanuel Levinas, who defines the most fundamental human experience as facing another person. However, it is with *Excesses: Eros and Culture* that Lingis's distinctive approach to philosophic writing emerges. In this book we see the peripatetic philosopher in the Third World, reporting as it were from the front, describing and analyzing his experiences as a work of philosophy and plunging us into embodied face-to-face encounters. Let us then examine one essay in *Excesses*—"Cargo Cult"—to see the philosophic function of writing in the first person.

"Cargo Cult" contains minute summaries of Aristotle and Kant, interleaved

Section One: Locating Lingis in Traditions of Thought

with described encounters between Lingis and persons he met in India and New Guinea. The juxtapositions of these two forms—summary, description, summary, description, etc.—are not haphazard; they follow what we might call a philosophical narrative. That is, the theoretical point of the essay is made not only through argument, but by the movement between these contrasting sections, which movement makes a sort of conceptual "story" with a claim to philosophic truth.

A closer look at the article will show how this method works. The essay's theme is the impossibility of Western rational analyses to encompass what truth, friendship, or generosity can most deeply be. Thus in one subsection, Lingis summarizes Aristotle's view of friendship as the equalized exchange of money, honor, and noble actions. This account is immediately followed by a description of Lingis's friendship in Calcutta with a young man named Arun. While walking through Calcutta streets, Lingis is overwhelmed by the immensity of the suffering he sees.

> I used to think that there was a proportion, that the pain was human, that if there was pain there was also a capacity to measure the pain....In a half hour I was back, trembling, in my room. How could one look at, how could one comprehend the pain of that dreadful night? It was beyond all proportion, an abyss; now, here, five thousand miles away, Arun, I find I cannot even imagine what I felt and saw that night; in fact a week after I left Calcutta I could no longer remember or imagine. (1983: 141-42)

Arun is one of the crowd who, when Lingis walks through Calcutta streets, seeks to sell Lingis something, to pry away some of his Western money. Arun and Lingis give various things to one another—companionship, money, goods, words, a massage. Yet there can be no equal exchange between these two men; their lives are so incommensurate that this is impossible. Nevertheless, as Lingis's description makes clear, for that brief time they are truly friends.

Structurally, we see it is the juxtaposition of the Aristotelian summary with a description of Arun and Lingis's friendship which reveals the inadequacy of Aristotle's theory. That is, in reporting a friendship between a man who exists in the "abyss" of pain Lingis describes, and one who is a comfortably-off Westerner, Aristotle could see only an unequal relationship. Arun certainly could never "repay" Lingis in money, and social honor would have to go to the man with more access to public acclaim—again, Lingis. As for nobility—what nobility could there be for a petty street hustler? Any "friendship" between these two would, for Aristotle, necessarily be like that of god for man, or master and slave—i.e., no real friendship at all, or one in only the feeblest of senses. But Lingis's encounter with Arun reveals that there must be a serious, perhaps even a fatal flaw in Aristotle's theory.

Well, then, why not simply say this? After all, I just did. Why not argue: "Contrary to Aristotle's contention, real friendships exist between people so socially disparate that truly equal exchange between them is impossible. Aristotle's theory of friendship is thereby seriously damaged or even disproved." This would be the sort of counterfactual argument a professional philosopher like Lingis could make with one hand tied behind his back.

One reason not to use traditional argument alone is that the essay's subject militates against it. "Cargo Cult" is about the impossibility of confining friendship, truth, and generosity within a closed rational system. To only *argue* this point might be then to *miss* the point, since argument itself functions according to the rules of a closed rational system. This is not to say that Lingis's writing is irrational gibberish. It is to say that because Lingis is attempting to utter philosophic truths about phenomena that go beyond the rational, the phenomena themselves invite us to use comprehensible methods other than rational argument. The counterpoint between the descriptions and the traditional philosophic sections is thus not purposeless; it rather highlights and clarifies the essay's philosophic point about the limitations of rationality.[2]

Lingis uses these methods to overcome the limitations of philosophical argument not only in "Cargo Cult" but in many other books and essays. Again, this strategy can be linked to elements of phenomenology. Since descriptive accuracy is key in phenomenology, any phenomenon that argument cannot adequately describe calls for forms of writing other than or in addition to argument. And indeed, the structure of argument does work against some forms of description. In argument, each piece of reasoning must fit into and support the next, ideally without gap, break, or inconsistency. But this implies that experiences to which gaps, breaks, inconsistency are central, phenomena not containable by closed rational systems, may call for first-person chronicling and description in addition to argument. I will examine in turn three such phenomena in Lingis's later work—discontinuity, responsibility, and violation—in order to suggest how each of these elicits his strategies of composition.

Discontinuity

In *Sensation: Intelligibility in Sensibility*, Lingis points out that phenomenology traditionally presupposes that we experience phenomena and the world itself only as integrated wholes. (1996: ix-xiii, 13, 31) That is, we experience a hammer as one object; the task of hammering as unified by our intention to build a house; the world in which we hammer as a single world connected without gaps all its parts. But Lingis claims that, while in some ways unified and unifying, our experience is also radically discontinuous. We do not simply experience objects as wholes, or engage in actions with a unifying beginning, middle, and end, or even find ourselves located within only one world. We also find ourselves drawn into experiences that sink into themselves, that have no task at hand, and that are discontinuous with one another. Attending those who are dying, when nothing more can keep them alive; the way our eyes sink into color or are lifted by light; the languor of erotic longing and sensation; all these and more are examples of the discontinuity of human experience. (1996: 10, 26-29, 63-65) Even task-oriented perceptions are often disconnected from one another. The technology by which a scientist perceives traces of elementary particles and the senses by which she perceives her ordinary world are, for example, radically different, giving her an almost nonhuman as well as a human body.[3]

If it is true that experience occurs in discontinuity as well as unity, then discontinuity must also be communicated by philosophic writing. We have already addressed this in considering the use of argument in "Cargo Cult." A more general way to reflect on the same issue might be to consider dialectic and rhetoric. Since ancient times, philosophy has been based upon dialectic—i.e., uncovering the hidden relations between concepts, and showing how one concept arises from another. But Lingis's phenomenology requires him to attend to human experiences which are unrelated and nonunified as well as related. If, then, philosophy is not simply dialectical, if philosophy is also an uncovering the *non-* and even *anti*dialectical elements of human existence, then philosophical writing must also in part be non-dialectical. It is for this reason that Lingis's writing often depends on something usually judged inappropriate for philosophy: rhetoric. What we have been calling the descriptive or "literary" elements of his writing are in fact attempts to reintegrate rhetorical persuasion within the body of philosophy.

Responsibility

While discussing this subject, it is important to note that discontinuity does not occur only for or within individual persons; there is also radical discontinuity *between* human beings. This brings us to the second theme we will consider: responsibility. Responsibility is usually thought of as a moral connection between human beings. Lingis does not deny this, but emphasizes that such connection only occurs because human beings confront one another in their differences, as well as their similarities. Human difference is not necessarily alienation or a struggle for mastery, although of course these can occur. Instead, Lingis finds the presence of another person something that: "(C)alls upon me, and requires something of me. He or she requires that I respond, requires that I respond in my own name. Facing me, the other singles me out." (1996: 70)

Facing another human being and our divergence from him or her reveals the responsibility we have toward that person. The face of another provokes us to ask: who is the other? What does her or his existence call me to do, or not do? How does connection with him or her happen, how does it fail to happen, what is the aftermath of such meetings? These are the questions of ethics, although Lingis, naturally, is not a traditional ethicist. Nevertheless, we find him grappling over and over with what it means to face another person bravely, with cowardice, with concern, with cruelty. Lingis's work underlines our constant capacity to *respond* to the other—in fact, our necessity to do so. For him, the face-to-face encounter, not an abstract principle of universal respect or rights, is the governing ethical imperative.

Since the fact of encountering others is examined in a serious way, it makes sense that the "others" Lingis considers are not simply from the Western world, or even those facing us across time from the past or future. To come face-to-face with other human beings most deeply, Lingis travels to those our culture shunts aside, whether within itself or in non-Western, nonindustrialized countries. Lingis's writings on Third World cultures and on those marginalized in the West can be seen as a necessary outgrowth of his attention to the connection and separation between human beings in general.

A further extension of Lingis's preoccupation with the responsibility of facing another is a profound concern with animals and landscape. He shows that the embodiment and sensation we face are not confined to human beings, but exist in animals, plants, and even the landscape itself.[4]

> To speak is to respond to someone who has presented himself or herself. We catch up the tone of his address, her question, his voice resounds in our own, we answer in the words and forms of speech which are hers. We catch on to the urgent, the frantic, the panicky, the exultant, the astonished tone. We catch on to the level of the purring kitten, the frantic cries of the bird, the snorting of the distrustful horse, the complaint of the caged puma. We catch on to the tone of the blackbird marsh, the hamlet meditating in the Himalayan mountainscape, the shifting dunes under twilight skies. (1998: 136-37)

The ethic we are called to is thus larger than one concerning other human beings alone. By Lingis's thought, we are called to the connection to, discontinuity from, and responsibility toward all beings we face and which face us.

What, then, does this have to do with the structure of writing? When Lingis sees the face of another and finds there an imperative to respond, the experience cannot be encapsulated within an abstract principle. The encounter is by definition more than rational; the other is not subsumed by our understanding, but remains stubbornly and ineradicably other. For Lingis, then, the best way to write the ethical responsibility such a presence elicits is *to write itself the experience of being face-to-face with another*. Although such a description will be imperfect, and although it may be facilitated by theory and argument, argument and theory alone are crippled by the absence in writing of the face-to-face. Thus Lingis uses more than argument and dialectic; he uses rhetoric. Vivid, often first-person description is a means to bring not only himself, but the reader into a relationship of responsibility with human and nonhuman beings.[5] In eliciting the flavor, texture, smell, sight, and emotional content of others, Lingis illuminates the concrete meaning of responsibility—the concreteness which he holds as responsibility's fundament. In fact, it may be that Lingis must write in this way or fail his own responsibilities. For in encountering the world, the world makes a call upon Lingis himself—a call to which he must respond in *his* own name, as a philosopher, a particular philosopher, and a philosopher who writes. He must not only show the face of the world and of other people as he finds them, but show his *own* face, or be guilty of moral cowardice.

Violation

All this talk about letting the other be other, obeying their imperative, and respecting the discontinuities of experience is all very well, but what then of truth? As a philosopher, Lingis must (however ambivalently) be concerned with truth. What kind of truth does his philosophy then appeal to? If accurate description is what he values, why shouldn't he just write novels or poetry?

We may find a way to answer these questions through examining the essay "Violations," from *Dangerous Emotions*. There, Lingis considers human communication. Communication, he points out, relies on *commonality*, on sensing that we are enough like each other to share a world, our thoughts, and our feelings. People—especially philosophers—often assume that this sharing is chiefly verbal. By this assumption, true human communication must be linguistic and rational, and must respect

Section One: Locating Lingis in Traditions of Thought

the rational boundaries of those involved. That is, all beings (and *only* beings) with rational minds are deserving of our respect, precisely due to their capacity to think. Thus the rights of rational beings as rational must never be trampled on; acting ethically means never to violate such rights, but bear them constantly in mind.

Lingis, however, disputes this assumption. In fact, he implies that defining rationality as the basic commonality between human beings makes it almost impossible to recognize other people *as* human. (85) He argues instead that connection most fundamentally takes place when human beings share laughter, grief, and erotic feelings. In laughter, for example, the boundaries between one person and another break up and dissolve: we laugh because the unexpected happens, because dignity is punctured, because we are simply happy and overflowing. Yet it is precisely laughing together that we recognize one another as human, as the same kind as ourselves, as *kindred*. In similar ways, we know one another as human through our tears, and through the sexual pull of one person on another.

Yet these sorts of sharing—laughter, grief, the erotic—are quite opposite from maintaining respect for another's rational boundaries. In fact, they violate such boundaries, creating a "vortex" of "surplus energy" (2000: 92, 101) that passes around, through, and between human beings. Human commonality, the basis of communication, occurs when we join one another in such a vortex. And because communication founds truth, truth is only possible by entering into the swirl of connection which violates and sustains us at the same time.

> Truth begins in conversations, shared laughter, friendship, and eroticism. But other people are not just other perspectives, other points of view, bearers of other data. How reckless and violent is the will to open one's eyes and face what happens, what is, among them! It is this reckless and violent will we seek in contact with them. We would not know what happens among them, if, exposing ourselves to what happens, what is, we did not know extreme pleasure, if we did not know extreme pain! (101)

This article elucidates how Lingis's conceptual and compositional approaches are intertwined. First, the "reckless and violent will we seek in contact with them" is our *own* will—the will of the philosophic investigator. It is the recklessness and violence, the surplus energy of our *own* lives that we search for in contact with others. Thus it is not disinterestedness that draws us outward, but possible extremities of pleasure and pain, intensities of connection we may find, that impel us to "open our eyes and face what happens."

The extreme experiences Lingis so valorizes are not (only) ends in themselves. If truth is seeing and articulating the world well and accurately, and if these accuracies in turn depend on contact with the world and others, then the best, the most faithful works of truth, come from a life lived seeking "reckless and violent" contact with other people and the world. Truth comes from connection, not isolation. But Lingis points out that connection is not "respectful" and "rational"; it is a violent dissolution of the boundaries between oneself and the world. As he states, "The tone of the one who addresses me does not respect but pervades my inner space." (2000: 100) Hence for Lingis, a philosophical life is one in which the philosopher experiences "extreme pleasure" and "extreme pain" because those pleasures and pains are themselves the union by which he or she sees the world faithfully and well. In other words, a life of considered extremity is one which sees the world as truly as possible.

The search for truth therefore has its own imperative with regard to the philosophic thinker/writer. For if communication arises in experiences through which one's boundaries are violated, then that search for truth itself pushes the phenomenologist into more and more intense experiences, experiences which show the world in highest relief possible. Not simply intellectual inspection, but what one does, the choices one makes, become part of the phenomenological life. A paragraph from the essay "Blessings and Curses" in *Dangerous Emotions* might be taken as a watchword for this approach to philosophy.

> Philosophers have described truth-seeking as a breaking into, a taking apart of things, a violation of the taboos with which ancient reverence had surrounded them. But to seek contact with reality is to expose ourselves not only to the hard-edged resistance of things but to be pained and exhausted by them....It is because we sense that the only way to know what we are capable of, what we care about, what we fear, is to plunge into insecurity, loneliness, hunger, and cold, that we leave home to hitchhike across the country. We go live in such wretched placed—Haiti, Bolivia, Salvador in Brazil, Congo, Bangladesh—places whose culture is in ruins, whose people are destitute, diseased, despairing—because just staying in the safe and comfortable places, at home or in the developed countries, is to skim over reality. (79)

And when it comes time to write philosophy as well as privately experience truths, a philosopher must connect with a reader the same way that he connected with the world. If the philosopher's truth begins in his experiences of laughter, grief, and the erotic, then it is legitimate—perhaps even necessary—to write philosophic truth by evoking these same experiences in the reader.[6] Lingis intends that the reader enter an encounter he (Lingis) describes, or recall a similar encounter, in order that author and reader might enter a community of philosophical experience and thought.[7] (Cf. 2000: 99) This community is what Lingis's more "literary" writing seeks to make. Of course, there must be disciplined conceptual analyses alongside, interleaved with, and (most artfully) as counterpoints emerging from and supporting such evocations. Were such analyses not there, Lingis's work would indeed be memoir and nothing more. But to spark in the reader laughter, anger, outrage, sexual feelings, sadness, delight, and wonder, is not philosophically empty. Done skillfully, it is a form of philosophical community from which truth can arise.

However, it is worth remembering that along with the choice of extreme encounter with the world comes disappointment with and contempt for those who choose otherwise. Thus in the essay "Gifts" in *Dangerous Emotions*, Lingis lambastes systems of moneyed security and those who partake in them:

> Such a system seeks to constrict us within every grubby act of will. The goal of such a system is to ensure that someone who thinks, "Well I do like this town and this cushy job gives me security," should understand that his decision also means, "I am deciding never to go spend twenty-four hours and see

dawn, high noon, and midnight in the sequoia forest! I am deciding never to climb to Machu Picchu! I am deciding to die without even once seeing the coral reefs of tropical oceans! I am deciding now never to hurl a rock at a riot squad protecting the oligarchy! (181)

This quotation is a good example of the way Lingis not only disturbs and decenters the reader, but takes pride in so doing. In addressing us philosophically, Lingis self-consciously pervades our inner space to connect with us and evoke revelatory experiences he himself has had. The writer experienced pleasure and pain; the reader feels pain and pleasure in the act of reading. The reader may not appreciate being brought into community in this way; the reader may feel that writers should take care of how and why they violate one's inner space. Nevertheless, one need not agree with Lingis on all points or all approaches to have profound respect for the dedication with which he has lived out a project of philosophically uniting with the world.

One might argue that the very act of being in a world one struggles to describe truthfully is an act of extremity. Thus in order not to skim over reality and be existentially and philosophically shallow, Lingis exhorts himself and us to unite with its sinews and bones. Whether we agree with this exhortation or not, it is not a random or unmindful act. Rather, it is precisely a call to be mindful in the face of so much that induces mindlessness.

Performance and Imitation

I will close with some thoughts concerning Lingis's work as a performer, and the imitation of his philosophical content and style. As Alexander Hooke and Wolfgang Fuchs point out in their introduction, Lingis's spoken presentations are "spectacles" rather than traditional philosophic lectures. Further, it is implicit in the analysis I make that Lingis's written work is often a sort of performance: a presentation of the philosopher's self and experiences formally offered as the basis of philosophical communication. This is a sort of recreation of self through philosophic voice: Lingis the philosopher and writer as "spectacle"—literally, that which is seen. What then does it mean to "perform" philosophy? Who is the audience? And what is the relation of the performer/philosopher to this audience?

While recognizing the possibility of discussing Lingis's work via recent analyses of self as performance, I will focus here on the continuities between Lingis and the philosophic tradition. For example, it might be noted that in Plato himself there is precedent for philosophy as dramatic narrative, and for including a philosopher's personality in both the narrative and philosophic structure of a work. And although this tradition has not been continuous or even predominant in philosophy, its presence is felt in such diverse works as Descartes' *Meditations*, Augustine's *Autobiography*, Kierkegaard's *Either/Or*, and most of Nietzsche's oeuvre. Thus the written or spoken presence of the individual philosopher is not automatically an illegitimate inclusion, and might even be said to have a fine pedigree.

Finally, we began this essay asking of Lingis, "What is this man doing?" Now that we have an idea of what he does and why, we can ask another question, namely: should we do it ourselves? Should we position ourselves to encounter the world in extremity? Should we as philosophers write in the first person, or descriptively? Are our lives, too, phenomenologies?

Imitation is of course necessary in any process of learning. Nevertheless, imitation of Lingis ultimately misses the point of his work. For if, as I argue, Lingis seeks to examine in a radical and disciplined way his encounter with the world, then the point is most emphatically not to examine *Lingis's* encounter with the world, but our own. And our own encounter with the world may be quite different than his. It may eschew extremity, and value the ordinary; it may find extremity in places other than the top of Machu Picchu. This gives rise to a dilemma. On the one hand, as long as the encounters we philosophically explore are our own, and as long as we follow them through, then we have faced the world responsibly and well on Lingis's terms. However, Lingis also makes it clear that to eschew risk-taking is to be found in some way lacking. Is this the exhortation of one world-traveler to another, whatever "world" we hope to travel in? Or is it philosophical romanticism?

Given the prickly possibilities of this dilemma, it is not surprising that some readers of Lingis fall prey to the fear of being judged philosophically or personally inadequate because of a failure to be sufficiently "violating" and extreme. In what is in fact a move into intimidation, they seek an imitation of Lingis's style and subject matter. Such imitation by intimidation is, without doubt, what Lingis would most truly reject. For if we take the form of his writing as the best exemplar of his thought, it is only when we immerse ourselves in our own process of writing, our own urge and imperative to communicate, that we enter as equals into his work.

Bibliography

Emmanuel Levinas, *Existence and Existents*, Trans. Alphonso Lingis (Boston: Kluwer Academic Publishing, Inc., 1978).

Emmanuel Levinas, *Totality and Infinity*, Trans. Alphonso Lingis (Pittsburgh: Dusquesne University Press, 1969).

Emmanuel Levinas, *Collected Philosophical Papers*, Trans. Alphonso Lingis (Pittsburgh: Dusquesne University Press, 1998).

Emmanuel Levinas, *Otherwise Than Being: Or Beyond Essence*, Trans. Alphonso Lingis (Pittsburgh: Dusquesne University Press, 1998).

Alphonso Lingis, *Excesses: Eros and Culture*. (Albany: State University of New York Press, 1983).

Alphonso Lingis, *Libido: The French Existentialist Theories*. (Bloomington: Indiana University Press, 1985).

Alphonso Lingis, *Deathbound Subjectivity*. (Bloomington: Indiana University Press, 1989).

Alphonso Lingis, *Foreign Bodies*. (New York: Routledge, 1994).

Alphonso Lingis, *Abuses*. (Berkeley: University of California Press, 1994).

Alphonso Lingis, *The Community of Those Who Have Nothing in Common*. (Bloomington: Indiana University Press, 1994).

Alphonso Lingis, *Sensation: Intelligibility in Sensibility*. (New Jersey: Humanities Press, 1996).

Alphonso Lingis, *The Imperative*. (Bloomington: Indiana University Press, 1998).

Alphonso Lingis, *Dangerous Emotions*. (Berkeley: University of California Press, 2000).

Maurice Merleau-Ponty, *The Visible and the Invisible*, Trans. Alphonso Lingis (Evanston: Northwestern University Press, 1968).

Notes

1. As will be made clear later, this is also Lingis's way of asking the reader to pay philosophical attention to his or her own life.

2. We might say first that, even when a specific philosopher is not referred to in the text, Lingis implicitly relies on the tradition of philosophy as counterpoint, as implicit point of reference and respondent. However, one does not need to have read widely in the philosophic tradition to understand Lingis. It is not unlike reading Nietzsche, in which the remarks and allusions may address the philosophic tradition. Yet *The Gay Science* can be picked up and read fruitfully by anyone with a desire to grapple with the text.

3. The prostheses-equipped competencies of scientific observers become those of the eyes of eagles and wasps, of the sonar echolocation of bats and the sixth sense of fish, of the magnetic or cosmic sense of migratory birds and insects, of the sensitivity of single cells or single electrons in those bats and fish. The imperatives that scientists find in the micro- and macrocosmic theaters they enter are no longer the imperatives the natural perception of our species found in things. These imperatives are recognized and obeyed with other competencies than those which enable our bodies to perceive things. (1996: 49)

4. Thus Lingis writes in "Bestiality" of the unbroken line between our embodiment and that of animals, plants, and the inorganic world:

> The form and the substance of our bodies are not clay shaped by Jehovah and then driven by his breath; they are coral reefs full of polyps, sponges, gorgonians, and free-swimming macrophages continually stirred by monsoon climates of moist air, blood, and biles....What is fascinating is the multiplicity in us—the human form and the nonhuman, vertebrate and invertebrate, animal and vegetable, the conscious and unconscious movements and intensities....What is mesmerized in us are the pulses of solar energy momentarily held and refracted in our crystalline cells, the microorganic movements and intensities in the currents of our inner coral reefs.

See also chapter 5, "Things" and chapter 13, "Face to Face," in *The Imperative*.

5. Here one might note that the photographs which accompany Lingis's texts are thus part of both uniting with the world and showing one's discontinuities with it. How can we look at the picture of the woman whose portrait heads the essay "Face to Face" without considering what it means for our shielded and distant eyes to look at her photographed face; for her eyes to have looked directly into Lingis's; for him to look at her and to photograph her? We are reminded both of our connection to her and our estrangement.

6. I severely doubt Lingis would claim that the only way to do philosophy is by first-person narration, or that all philosophers must spend their time traveling around the world. However, I do argue that by Lingis's understanding, only passionate involvement of both philosopher and reader in the world and the act of doing philosophy can produce truth.

Exactly what form this involvement takes would probably be something judged on a case-by-case basis. Whether the passion of this involvement is self-conscious on the part of either philosopher or his or her reader is a side issue.

7. Such community is not a rarified artifact of the late twentieth and early twenty-first centuries. It is what is and always has been required for more traditional understandings of philosophy to be possible—for anything to be seen, to communicate rational reasons why what we see is accurate. One might note that this realization is evident in the work of the most antirhetorical of rhetorical philosophers: Plato. For it is in Plato's best work that we see the community of truth arising in grief, laughter, and the erotic—in the *Apology* and *Crito*, the *Republic*, the *Symposium*. Where would Plato be without the erotic longing and disappointment of Alcibiades and Socrates?

Chapter Six

Silent Communities: Foucault and Lingis on the End of Philosophy

Alexander E. Hooke

As for a common language, there is no such thing; or rather, there is no such thing any longer.... The language of psychiatry, which is a monologue of reason about madness, has been established only on a basis of such a silence. I have not tried to write the history of that language, but rather the archaeology of that silence.
—Michel Foucault, Preface, Madness and Civilization[1]

Then what is distinctive about philosophy is not a certain vocabulary and grammar of dead metaphors and empirically unverifiable generalizations. One's own words become philosophy, and not the operative paradigms of a culture of which one is practitioner, in the measure that the voices of those silenced by one's culture and its practices are heard in them.
—Alphonso Lingis, Foreword, Abuses[2]

Chance Meetings

Whether in the dusty archives of the national library in Paris or in strange locales quite remote from the sources of Western philosophy, Michel Foucault and Alphonso Lingis have featured a variety of curious figures in their work. Herculine Barbin, nineteenth-century hermaphrodite, Maria/Mario, Philippine transsexual, the regicide Damiens, subject to public torture, two rebel South American women, subject to private torture, the legendary ship of fools, the abandoned Bihari of India, obscure vagabonds and street urchins, are among the highlights of their writings.

Rhetorical gimmicks? Stylistic ploys? To those used to and expecting more conventional presentations—ones that declare their premises and conclusions outright, ones that articulate their hypotheses and discuss the pertinent proofs or counterarguments—the sundry individuals enlisted by Foucault and Lingis might seem little more than efforts to poke fun at more earnest and rational forms of philosophical discourse. Hence the frequent designation of Foucault and Lingis as postmodern, implying that they too have joined the bandwagon that seeks to undermine the foundations of all that is positive in philosophy.

Such objections can be and have been raised for any number of thinkers. What distinguishes Foucault and Lingis lay in their responses to such accusations. They acknowledge frequently how much they are representatives and participants in conventional discourses. Their respect for modern thought, after all, is readily noted in their work. Foucault edited a volume on Kant for a French-speaking audience, and Lingis translated major works of Merleau-Ponty and Levinas for an English-speaking audience.

Each also has an uncanny knack for finding the shortcomings and oversights of philosophical discourse. Yet this knack should not be construed as negative or pessimistic. Each endorses a philosophical approach that is affirmative and constructive. Foucault and Lingis are interested in conventional forms of thought, reality, and truth but more as stepping-stones towards finding new forms of reality and the truths they reveal. They help us explore the many experiences and beliefs that give rise to realities escaping and eluding our conventions. What more is there to know, how are other values embraced, is there something one could or should do to change things, are themes underscoring their various projects. In studying these issues, Foucault and Lingis seldom set out to verify or demonstrate their own assumptions or premises. More often they entice their readers by sustaining an element of surprise, as if they too are unsure where their exploring and thinking are leading them.

Many of the surprises are chance meetings that invoke a sense of silent communities. Moved by stories appearing in neglected texts or in the faces of unfamiliar peoples, Foucault and Lingis see different kinds of silence as positive forces in formulating their respective philosophical outlooks. That is, silence is not only a break in language or an indicator that reason or communication has failed. Silence also is able to bring about recognition, social contact, and directives to further inquiry. These directives are outlined in their respective projects. In Foucault's case, his use of archaeology and genealogy bring to the forefront what he calls "subjugated knowledges." In Lingis's case, his use of xenography and a revived art of phenomenology present to audiences the silent truths passed over by our conventions and habits.

The following three sections elaborate these points. "Shared Passions and Knowledge" highlights forms of recognition that are initiated more by passions than by use of a common language. Contrary to the tenets of moralists and psychologists, passions are not only the stuff of corrupt desires and unconscious needs; frequently, they present elements of knowledge. Nor are passions solely individual experiences whose reality is internal. We talk about inner feelings or hidden emotions, but many passions arise from unpredictable encounters with another. The section "Insights of the Silenced: Collaborators and Accomplices" emphasizes this point by discussing the social and political implications of silent contacts. Foucault's attentiveness to madmen locked up in asylums, patients in clinics, and miscreants in the penitentiary is legendary, and deservedly the source of lively disputes about his political convictions. Lingis, perhaps more than Foucault, is alert to the guerillas hunted down by military thugs, prostitutes offering their bodies as coals of fire, and emaciated children dying blocks from lavish palaces and temples that attract tourists and Western scholars. The last section "Readerships" outlines a two-fold relation between a philosopher and an audience comprised mostly of readers: the thinker engages in dissemination as a mode of communication and provocation to what social scientists call schools of thought.

Shared Passions and Knowledge

This book first arose out of a passage in Borges, out of the laughter that shattered, as I read the passage, all the familiar landmarks of my thought—our thought, the thought that bears the stamp of our age and our geography—breaking up all the ordered surfaces and all the planes with which we are accustomed to tame the wild profusion of existing things.
—Foucault, Preface to The Order of Things[3]

Prior to the speech that informs and the speech that directs and orders, there is the speech that articulates for those who were not there, and articulates further for those who were, what we laugh and weep over, what we bless and curse. Our speech is polarized by the grand things, the blessed events that come as surprises and accidents from the outside, and by the sinister things.
—Lingis, "Violations," Dangerous Emotions[4]

Consider a class in college as a model of social life. For over three months, or forty-five contact hours as administrators prefer to call them, students meet two or three times a week. Regardless of their divergent interests or diverse backgrounds, the students are periodically with one another. As implied by the root meanings of college (to assemble together) and university (to turn into one), a course promises to be an experience of and participation in an intellectual community. Under the guidance of the assigned texts, a rigorous syllabus, and dutiful professor, students gain a sense of what counts as a life of reason. Dialogue, opinions supported by arguments, and respect for one another's points of view guide students toward realizing the objectives of the class. What students share is a language and domain of knowledge by which to pursue the objectives. Despite the occasional malcontent and the possibility that most students are required to take the course, professors and administrators like to uphold the classroom as a microcosm of democratic society. After all, isn't the mission of many institutions to prepare students not only for careers but responsible citizenship?

For Foucault and Lingis this model is inadequate.

In Foucault's case, the serenity of a seminar dialogue betrays the reality of the dynamics of power that underscores social (and academic) life. Institutions are more than places and organizations. They also "institute"—to make stand, to put something into place. As Foucault's own studies of asylums, clinics, and prisons point out, what is instituted are codes of conduct, rules and guides for controlling or defining oneself, levels of authority, and forms of knowledge. Education systems are institutions, then, insofar as they help students conduct and define themselves, encourage them to recognize proper forms of authority and expertise, and encourage them to immerse themselves in their fields of knowledge by distinguishing serious and credible insights from superficial or unverifiable notions. In short, an institution involves power, but also meaning, value, and truth.

Laughter, as a kind of silence, has the potential to strike at the core of an institution's domain or an established truth. Two examples illustrate this potential. In a study of changes in juridical trials, Foucault recounts a 1975 scene in which the judge asks an accused rapist if he can explain his behavior. Three times the accused says nothing. Finally, an exasperated juror shouts, "For heaven's sake, defend yourself!"[5] In the early part of the eighteenth century this inquiry would have been irrelevant. Then, determining innocence or guilt was the primary task of the courtroom, hence making a defendant's self-examination largely irrelevant. Now, the accused's silence upsets the legal proceedings, for a third component has become essential: who is the accused? The defendant's accounts are not to be taken entirely at face value, of course. But when completed by psychologists, criminologists, and doctors who testify to defendant's pathologies, in Foucault's account, the defendant's own reports are integral to understanding—and judging—the nature of the crime and the penalty for the offender. Still today the media report on whether a convicted murderer expresses remorse or offers a motive to the criminal deeds. Be it Timothy McVeigh, the Unabomber, or a mother drowning her five children in Texas, attention is devoted to whether and what the accused has to say, and to what extent his or her account matches up with either a rationale or plausible explanation. Whereas in earlier times what the guilty person said only mattered between him and God, today silence disrupts our sense of criminal justice that is not content to punish only, but also wants to understand or explain the object of its punishment.

A second example appears in *The Order of Things*. The passage from Borges lists the different accounts of "animal" according to a Chinese encyclopedia. Included among the items: embalmed, sucking pigs, fabulous, frenzied, drawn with a very fine camelhair brush, having just broken the water pitcher, and "that from a long way off look like flies."[6] Contrast this with an American Heritage Illustrated Encyclopedia, which lists: any organism of the kingdom Animalia; distinguished from plants by locomotion, growth, cell walls, sense organs, metabolism; an organism other than a human being; a person who is bestial or brutish. The second seems more sensible or familiar. Yet, given the range of encounters people have had with animals, the Chinese version has its merits. Animals, we learn, can be discussed through all sorts of categories. Anyone who has attended dog-training classes is hardly surprised. The range of terms owners employ to describe their pets can be daunting. For they are more than just beagles, retrievers, poodles, or mutts—they are also sensitive, lacking self-esteem, jealous of the cats, anxiety-ridden, eager to mount the other dogs, ill tempered, adorable, passive/aggressive, to name a few.

In any event, this laughter of Foucault's is revived when he closes the famous section, "Man and His Doubles." Tracing the events or works that ushered in the studies of human beings were gradually accorded the status of science (that is, how what is said or known about humans is more than anecdote or literature, but becomes a discourse about human nature and of truth and falsehood), Foucault points out how the birth of anthropology coincides with the question raised by thinkers of Enlightenment. In addition to what can I know, hope for, or do, a fourth issue is introduced: What is mankind? Foucault undercuts the drama and importance of this question by highlighting its temporary life. It is only for a couple of centuries—a relative drop in the bucket of human knowledge—that the science of human nature gained any following. Soon something else will come along to compel our curiosity. Many of us understandably would be either squeamish or horrified by the possible disintegration of this kind of knowledge. Foucault is not one of us. Instead, he admonishes us: "To all those who still wish to talk about man...in his essence...as their starting-point...who refuse to think without immediately thinking that it is man thinking...we can only answer with a philosophical laugh—which means, to a certain extent, a silent one."[7] Foucault does not say whether this silent laughter is the kind most students experience during the doldrums of college semester.

There is more to Foucault's writings than laughter. In an interview conducted during his stay at the University of Vermont in 1982, Rex Martin notes, "Your writings carry profound emotion, undercurrents unusual in scholarly analyses: anguish in *Discipline and Punish*, scorn and hope in *The Order of Things*, outrage and sadness in *Madness and Civilization*." Foucault responds that there is a biographical component to most of his works. "For one or another reason I had the occasion to feel and live those things," he observes.[8] Whatever passions sparked Foucault's inquiries, they are in any event components of an experience that arises in and from a social institution. They are, as he tends to put it, part of the games of truth and struggles for freedom that lend themselves to genealogical and archaeological studies.

Lingis, albeit intrigued by the dynamics of power and knowledge, is not convinced that Foucault exhausts the range of passions and their relation to truth. Laughter and other passions are more than indicators or responses to the aporias and frailties of human knowledge that become established in social institutions. Often the passions lie at the root of much of what we believe is true and with whom we connect. "There is a fundamental good conscience in us," observes Lingis, "whenever we laugh over things in our environment; we believe the truth of what laughter, and what tears, have seen."[9] The passions are frequently more than effects of or responses to relations of power. They can be found at the origins of encounter.

For example, picture, as Lingis does, an American waiting in a Japanese airport the day after sarin gas was planted in a Tokyo subway. Everyone is suspicious and guarded. A Buddhist priest walks through. He does not notice and trips over the American's stretched out leg. The priest falls, and from his robes crash onto the floor two bottles of Chivas Regal. For a moment everyone in the corridor freezes, silent in possible panic. Then, as they see what happened, reports Lingis, "laughter breaks out, spreading wider as people get up to see what is going on...In each individual, the laughter is now no longer pleasure over the unexpected...but pleasure over the dissolution of boundaries...It makes the object or event that unleashed laughter slip from attention and sets into motion an intense communication."[10]

This is not the kind of communication that serves as a benchmark for pursuing a fruitful dialogue that represents the ideals of a college seminar or civic meeting. To be civil we learn that emotions need to be curtailed, properly framed, or first interpreted in light of a given text or reflected experience. Borrowing from Nietzsche,

Lingis distinguishes the strong from the weak or reactive emotions. The latter tend to be guarded and cautious. They accompany our moral judgements and rational decisions. Reminding us that everyone pursues his or her own interests, the weak emotions are best appreciated in and help sustain the moral community. Feeling safe, having assurance, and wanting respect are among the emotions that maintain the system of expectations and negotiations that comprise ordinary social interactions. This system, whether in a classroom or in a neighborhood meeting, flourishes as participants confirm themselves and identify with one another by using a common language. Pledging allegiance to this system, we value weak emotions while strong ones are consigned to the domain of personal privacy or social danger.

Such a system of communication overlooks the original force of strong passions such as eroticism, anger, awe, courage, grief, and compassion. They thrive not as private or internal feelings but as forces of communication. Nor are they a social danger, but rather the originating motives for becoming sociable, thus spawning the urge to establish words, language, and the conventions of a moral community.

Lingis elaborates:

> The grief that opens to the pain of an accident victim in a foreign land communicates its compassion to any bystander. The fear and pain of the marchers attacked by the police spread like a wave to the ranks behind and to the people watching from windows. Acts of courage strengthen the hearts of everyone who witnesses them. Joyous exhilaration demonstrates its evidence like a comet flaring in the sparkling night. Deeds of heroism communicate as no clear and distinct explanations ever could....It is laughter and tears, euphoria and torment, sensuality and terror that give rise to language, where whatever we say we say for others, where what we say we put in the words and grammar of the one to whom we say it, where what we say seeks to clarify a world and his own feelings for himself.[11]

Where Lingis diverges from Foucault involves their respective views of Nietzsche. For Foucault, the issue of power is ineluctable. That is not to say, as critics have sometimes contended, that his analyses are reducible to who wields power and how. Foucault joked that he wished things were that simple. Instead, his analyses focus on how power intersects with truth, freedom, and modes of subjectivity. Lingis, on the other hand, finds that the link between power and subjectivity is overstated. It ignores that humans—indeed, every organism in nature—also live in symbiotic relation with all sorts of life forms. According to him, "The relationship of an individual with other individuals of its species, and with individuals of other species, is not one of domination and subjugation."[12]

Passions can bring disparate individuals in contact with one another. In anger, for example, one finds the force that brings recognition to those who have been silenced and glossed over. Echoing Foucault's notion of the disciplinary archipelago, Lingis describes a technological-economic archipelago that thrives not only by the power of normalization but also by the power to subordinate and exclude. The distress and anger move many to pursue or create another kind of community, one that might arise "when we come into the presence of singular lives in the outer zone, and the significance of their singular and communal forms of life."[13]

The results often show up as communities that are symbiotic. Momentary creations, they are rich in what they have to offer us. Symbiotic experiences stretch from the erotic to the sacred. They are often unpredictable and spectacular. To approach them in a laboratory experiment or through coverage of the secondary literature only takes us so far. For these approaches still bypass or overlook much of what is real and what is true. Lingis'ss writings, highlighted by gripping descriptions juxtaposed with philosophical reflections, focus on the creative elements of symbiosis that Foucault mostly ignored or held to be suspicious. That the story of Herculine Barbin is essential for modern thought Lingis grants Foucault. But do not her early years of joy and laughter count for something, too? In Lingis'ss case, then, experiences in which various lives give so much of themselves without self-regard should also be central to our reflections on human or social life. For example, he likes to observe, is the female angel fish that is some thirty-five times larger than a male angel fish and thus keeps him around only long enough to either receive his sperm or eat him, any possible social or political model for us contemporaries? And, less remote, are orphan children in Calcutta, volunteers in American hospices, performers in Brazil's Carnival, also possible models? Their joy and laughter, and their capacity for expenditure without recompense, is daunting. Maybe there is no paradigm or rule of thumb to explain sufficiently these phenomena without diminishing their singular intrigue and existence.

Despite this contrast on the relative significance of power and symbiosis, Foucault and Lingis are two of the few philosophers who take silence as integral to emotions and passions. Moreover, this relation deserves substantive attention for those who love or seek the truth. Substantive in two senses: first, the relation between silence and emotions is by its very nature full of ambiguity and mystery, inviting various observations and speculations; and second, substance implies empirical and practical support, so that some sensible reasons make this relation credible. At the same time, both are aware of a paradox raised by one of their mutual influences, Georges Bataille. In his view silence can be thought about but not spoken. For once uttered, of course, the speaker has betrayed the reality and experience of silence. To fully address this paradox something more than the rules of logic are needed—it requires a sense of transgression.

To transgress means to recognize and dare certain limits or boundaries. Yet transgressing also requires more than a careful reflection or intellectual grasp. It is fueled by passions that make one moved by or toward another. Insofar as this movement circumvents the demand to verbalize one's reasons, there is a silent component central to transgression. Yet this silence is hardly negative, for it presents the moment when collaborations and associations are developed, when other possibilities of social and political life are created or risked.

Insights of the Silenced: Witnesses and Collaborators

Forgotten Voices

In a 1976 lecture Foucault introduced another way of describing his philosophical tasks. It consists of bringing to life again what he calls "subjugated knowledges."[14] They refer to historical realities that have been buried or silenced by the prevailing fields or systems of thought. These realities were more than idiosyncratic lives of so-called oddballs or recluses—they were lives in which human beings experienced a range of emotions, ideas, and beliefs with other humans. The knowledge that gave sense and meaning to their lives, however, was relegated to, say, madness, sickness, or criminality, by more authoritative and systematic forms of thought. Eccentrics were found to be insane by psychology; deviants were detected by doctors as suffering a pathology; vagabonds who relished the freedom in having no home were designated as vagrants and threats to social well-being. Hence the knowledge these various figures had of their own lives was subjugated as irrational, immoral, and not deserving of serious attention and unqualified to claim any truth. In a word, they were silenced.

Foucault does not take their being silenced as a cue to idealize their lives. Contrary to some critics, he does not romanticize their lives and portray them as exemplars. While he does find them fascinating, they are especially noteworthy because they present lessons on the powers that subjugate. These powers were not always expressly political—i.e., laws and governments. The subjugation frequently came at the hands of seemingly more benevolent types—scientists, counselors, doctors, humanitarians. Moreover, their benevolence is not strictly a matter of having a beneficent will: it stems from what they embrace as the truths of the world.

The story of Herculine Barbin and Foucault's resurrection of her or his life has special intrigue for Foucault. Alexina's/Herculine's memoirs span the mundane and sensational. Her life in the religious girl's school is striking. It is both ritualistic and full of little surprises. There is an order to all the members' lives while they nevertheless dare to challenge or transgress various components of the order. Mocking the annoying teacher, forming and changing ranks among residents, much cherished holiday visits back home, and unpredictable passions and friendships, all provided their dramas, pleasures, and worries. For Alexina all this changed when, after a late puberty and physiological confusion, she visited a doctor who, astonished, declared that she was wrongly identified at birth and should instead be classified as a male.

While the doctor's counsel to Alexina's mother is memorable—"It's true that you've lost your daughter, but you've found a son whom you were not expecting"[15]—for Foucault the shift in identity to Herculine speaks enormously of the growing power of medicine and the emerging sciences of psychology and sexology. His subsequent suicide is only a part of the larger dynamic that consigned the memoirs to silence until Foucault gave voice to it again. This voice, according to Foucault, demands we rethink the nature of personal identity, love, sexual identity, the relation between biological and cultural properties, as the scope of the law when it requires official gender designations. From this perspective we can see how Foucault's quip about genealogy and archaeology is both playful and daring. Asserting them to be "anti-sciences," he points out that genealogy's task is to raise the silence of subjugated knowledges to a political level. He explains:

> The silence, or rather the prudence, with which the unitary theories avoid the genealogy of knowledges might therefore be a good reason to continue to pursue it. Then at least one could proceed to multiply the genealogical frag-

ments in the form of so many traps, demands, and challenges, what you will.... Our task, on the contrary, will be to expose and specify the issue at stake in this opposition, this struggle, this insurrection of knowledges against the institutions and against effects of the knowledge and power that invests scientific discourse.[16]

In sum, Foucault takes the insights of the silenced as directives to articulating and challenging dominant forms of knowledge as well as their relation to different kinds of power. At the same time, he acknowledges the ends of his own philosophical endeavors. His work can be construed as a witness or tool whose uses he cannot fully dictate. This is more than an issue of interpretation or systematic completeness. For Foucault, the tasks of intellectual work come to end when the questions he raises are finally answered only in some nonintellectual form—that is, no reasons, no justifications, and no words. As he puts it, "I dream of an intellectual...who, wherever he moves, contributes to posing the question of knowing whether the revolution is worth the trouble, and what kind...it being understood that the question can be answered only by those who are willing to risk their lives to bring it about."[17]

Mute Bodies

Lingis presents a less historical focus. He acknowledges and often endorses the basic thesis of Foucault's regarding the subjugation of minor and transient realities by more formal and systematic fields of knowledge. Lingis abbreviates these under the rubric of the "rational community"—the work aimed at establishing a language that articulates values, explanations, and reasons whose purpose is to reach and include a universal humanity.[18] Whereas Foucault undermines the rational community by looking into its own archives to detect so many forgotten voices that reflect the realities and truths of silent communities, Lingis looks to those who are still forgotten. For him, one finds other truths not only by genealogy and archaeology of past and current discourses, but by exposure to mute bodies.

This exposure takes numerous forms. It might arise through intense moments brought on, say, by a good-spirited friend, seductive office mate, troubled neighbor, maybe even a grieving or cheerful stranger. It could also appear in responding to the marvelous stories one has heard or read about. Third, this exposure often demands that one be so committed to the other that his or her own self is dissolved. Or is prepared to dissolve, such as in love, courage, joy, or death. This last form, however, is for a very logical reason difficult to recognize or admit. Oftentimes people, contrary to what logical positivists and rational communication theorists claim, do not have equal ability to match what they say with what they do. However, this does not mean there was a lack of thought. To describe the thought of others—how it drives or justifies ones deeds and decisions as compelling, real, and deserving of our attention to what is true or good, illustrates what we might call Lingis'ss version of xenography. It involves a philosophical sketch of aliens or others that addresses conventional truths—the ones we believe and the ones we live by.

In Lingis'ss frame of reference, this exposure tends to be of encounters that address what is joyous, cruel, unpredictable, laughable, tragic, disturbing, erotic, or hopeless. As theorized in his more technical writings and elucidated in his more descriptive works, exposure can push one to silence oneself. This does not prevent one from being alert.

While Foucault was remarkably alert to the philosophical importance of such unfamiliar figures as vagabonds and hermaphrodites of previous centuries, Lingis encourages attention to today's forgotten realities and neglected lives that have the potential for new insights. They are especially occluded in light of the emerging proliferation of technopoles. These are locales such as London, New York, Singapore, Paris, Hong Kong, Sao Paulo, and some other two dozen centers of mass communication. Transcending more old-fashioned divisions of people by class or race, even national boundaries, technopoles drive free-market economies and militaries with the promise that a global village lies in the near future. Instant and long distance exchange of information, however, serves a consumer economy and military arsenal that can only flourish by hushing up the many voices trying to resist or contest it.

A strange logic ensues. First, these voices do not have the vocabulary; if they have the vocabulary then they lack an audience; if they find an audience then they lack the means to present their own beliefs and commitments to influential members of the technopoles. Or their voices are co-opted by the technology of image making. Like it or not, most of us have a hand in this development. According to Lingis, corporate funding for anthropological research does not seek to record and understand the experiences of people in preliterate cultures, but "to convert the subject of research into images that can be reproduced, edited, transformed, and technologically disseminated. Not the deaths of thousands of marginals, homosexuals and Haitians, but appearances by Elizabeth Taylor and Princess Diana make funds available for AIDS research."[19]

To contest this imposition of silence sometimes requires an even more forceful exposition of silence. Lingis presents such an exposition in an essay called "Coals of Fire." It begins with a woman, probably a nurse, attending to someone very ill. Then we are taken to Dhaka, Bangladesh, to meet some nasty security guards at a fancy hotel, and a string of natives directing a traveler to a taxi or rickshaw. The driver then offers to take the traveler to a lodging not listed in the tour guides, or to visit other natives who can charm the traveler with a delicious meal or a companion for the night.

The natives wind up bringing the traveler—and Lingis's readers—to the story of the Bihar. Émigrés from East Pakistan, some 800,000 Biharis live in virtually unlivable camps. From the fallout of British colonialism and decades of political turmoil among Bengal, Pakistan, and India, among Muslims, Hindus, and members of the United Nations, the Biharis are the losers: no member of the community of nations is willing to find a hospitable land for them. Instead it offers them a worse fate. What in earlier times was considered the worst kind of death—dying alone—modern civilization has now consigned to the Biharis. Lingis writes, "Humankind is silent about the Biharis, waiting. All the others, the men and women organized into the community of nations which have taken possession of the earth, demand of the Biharis that they do this—die."[20]

No match for the intellectual and political sophistication of the rational community, they respond with something other than paid consultants, sound bites, and relentless chatter from the warring parties. The Biharis instead prepare for their own demise. Daily they practice getting ready, as witnessed by their compatriots and occasional visitors, including Lingis, "to pour kerosene over themselves and die in the flames." As a silent community they will transform their bodies into coals of fire.

Interspersed with this report are notes about a night of erotic pleasure that results from several local men bringing a foreigner to a young woman. Brief moments and glimpses are described. Between the couple there is the heat of passion, twisted bellies, vibrant muscles, but no words are exchanged. Finally, the man asks her name. Silence. How is it, he asks, do these men own you? Again, silence. Perhaps exasperated or bemused by his insatiable curiosity, she soon whispers, "Gita." But that, the man recalls, is the name of the temple prostitute. And when he asks again, she responds only with a pressing kiss, "her hair shimmering over your chest like fire." Like the Biharis, her mute body too becomes coals of fire.

These experiences are more than isolated events. They are done before witnesses and among collaborators. In practicing the procedures for self-immolation, the Biharis are saying something to themselves and to anyone who has been with them. It is in their silenced bodies that their truth is expressed. Moreover, Lingis observes, so often the efforts of collaborators are enlivened without a word of exchange. The courage and beauty of their efforts does not lie in whether they succeed or how history judges them. This is exemplified in a story of guerillas seeking refuge in a farmhouse. Bringing to them a bottle of rum, the farmer and guerrillas say nothing, not a word about ideology or economic warfare or the government thugs who are trying to capture them. Something more impressive happens, he concludes: "All that they have thought about, labored over, fought for, was that men, even in the most remote and most destitute corners of the land, partake together of the fruits of the earth. Here, this night, the revolution, the utopia, is there."[21]

Readerships

In the Shadows of Masters

I admire the courage and wisdom of Socrates in everything he did, said—and did not say.
—Nietzsche, The Gay Science[22]

We know of Socrates mostly through the written word of Plato. His understanding of Socrates came from being his student and friend, hearing about or participating in the numerous discussions when Socrates examined, speculated, and contested the various opinions and thoughts held by the thinkers and experts of ancient Athens. The forums of these discussions could be quite diverse. Certainly more so than today's institutions, for Plato presents Socrates's philosophical pursuits in the courtroom, at a dinner and drinking party, in jail, at a scene of dying, among the markets, with naïve servants and dim-witted lawyers as well as desperate friends and public charmers such as the poets and orators. Given the intimate, unpredictable, and agonistic qualities of the Socratic dialogues, do they represent the ideal of communication, and hence the model of community?

Plato's knowledge of Socrates is based on dialogue not only because Socrates did not, as far as we can tell, leave any writings, but because there was in their time a fundamental controversy about the nature of writing and its potential to displace dialogue as a genuine form of communication. As John Peters points out in his recent historical study on the idea of communication, this controversy raises issues that still elude satisfactory answers, even today with e-mail and the Internet becoming so much a part of everyday life. In grasping the truth, what is the relation between presenter and audience? Love, mutual respect, expertise-to-novice, or hired hand, are among the candidates for expressing an ideal situation. Does the face-to-face encounter represent or distort the ideal? If so, then how should we regard the various and intense efforts of those who seek the truth offered by the gods or spirits, messages from prophets or dead ancestors, or signals etched in artifacts or works of nature? In a word, what counts as understanding?

Historians of reading point out that when written words were introduced as new forms of communication, the words themselves had no spacing or punctuation. The letters were simply strung together. Since writers then expected that their audiences read aloud, usually to someone else but also to themselves. Imagine how laborious it would be to always read out loud an essay or book of a favorite writer. To facilitate the growing numbers who wanted to read only to themselves while ensuring that their own intentions and meanings were not dismissed, authors began inserting commas, periods, dashes, and spaces. They acted as the pauses, hesitations, voice fluctuations, and stops that indicate moments of silence. So punctuation made silent reading a much richer experience while the separation of words also makes catching the author's key points more likely.[23] A richer experience because the reader had so many ways and so much time, if chosen, to read at his or own pace and as many times as desired, since no speaker was there to protest. At the same time the author had to keep an invisible audience in mind, one for whom the written word was no longer a transcription from or interpretation of the spoken word. The word achieves a different status. Being read rather than heard, the word reaches an audience less compelled by the mastery of the speaker and more by the mastery of the author.

This sense of mastery certainly compelled much of the work of Foucault and Lingis. As thinkers renown for their engaging public presentations and dramatic and idiosyncratic ways of writing, they both know that reading involves a sense of working in the shadows of the masters. For in only reading about and learning from someone's thoughts, we can never reciprocate in any dialogic fashion. We do not applaud, drop some money into a bucket, or immediately request the thinker to write again or to propose what we should do.

The contact between a writer and reader forms a silent community. It presents an ambivalent relation. On the one hand, the written word is stable, almost eternally fixed when compared to the spoken word. It sounds quaint to ridicule teachers who expect us to capture the author's voice, but they raise an important point. An interpretation is based on what appears in the text; it does not change and is there for everyone to read. Hence the use of quotation marks and footnotes. On the other hand, with the written word the author loses control or authority. Mastery shifts to the reader. He or she has time to ruminate, apply the words to different places and

Section One: Locating Lingis in Traditions of Thought 75

times, compare it to what has been written since, or check records and texts never available to the writer.

How Foucault and Lingis address this ambivalence is striking. In Foucault's case, it leads to what he calls a study of "problematization."[24] Though formalized toward the end of his life, it is a central feature to his project on the history of thought. Unlike a history of ideas, which studies the development and shifts in theories and basic truths, a history of thought attempts to pinpoint how certain experiences and ideas at a particular juncture in our past led well-known thinkers to problematize a belief, attitude, or practice, that had previously not been a problem. The relation between concepts of crime and justice, the point when truths about sexual behavior shifted from a religious and moral discourse to a scientific and psychological one, under which conditions are claims about human nature, silly or serious, are among the many examples highlighting his work.

In other words, what has been problematized as free, virtuous, rational, just—standard themes in philosophy—is for Foucault another way of reading the thought of others while understanding ourselves. What the ancients or the moderns have problematized often remains part of or still directs our controversies and critiques, though with different twists and details. Those who we know only through the written word still deserve credit—or blame—for contributing to an intellectual, political, or moral problem that did not have to exist. After reading the first volume of *The History of Sexuality*, many readers, myself included, were surprised when Foucault deviated from his original plan and turned to the texts of ancient Greece and Rome. But Foucault was not disappointed. In these ancient texts one found a silent community—those under the sway of certain problematizations.

His caustic remark in the introduction to the much-delayed second volume to *The History of Sexuality* is worth repeating. He reminds readers of the chance meetings with unsuspected masters and how they altered his own directions and projects. The original plan to study modern sexual deviancies needs postponing. Still, to return to two-thousand-year-old texts in their original language for which Foucault has little training involves considerable risk. Alas, he confesses to being vulnerable to the powers of curiosity, but confident that the results of his work will help Foucault to think differently, to "get free of oneself." To those for whom "work in the midst of uncertainty and apprehension is tantamount to failure," he writes, "all I can say is that clearly we are not from the same planet."[25]

In Lingis's case, the ambivalence in reading and hearing the word leads to a different kind of silent community. One recognizes not so much a common or recurring problematization in our ideas but an ongoing expenditure of another's thoughts. Words and ideas also act as insights and gifts. As beneficiaries of these gifts, however, we are tempted to think we have grasped the thinker. "I got it!" we tend to proclaim. That is, we know what he or she really meant, we can formulate an essay or paper on the thinker's key points, or, at least, we can defend the thinker's more seminal views. In a word, the reader is understandably tempted to conclude that he or she has understood the thinker.

Any understanding, cautions Lingis, can also imply a misunderstanding. By asking whether language itself is a medium of misunderstanding as well as understanding, he emphasizes the fact that the enigma or mystery that compels the writer can overshadow the lucidity with which he or she writes for a readership. Encountering the wonders of Inca architecture or the intricate lines drawn over two hundred kilometers in the deserts of Peru by the ancient Nazca civilization, for example, the writer winds up leaving much of the truth simply unstated. For the communication in the encounter with a distant voice or figure is only partially communicated to others. "Trafficking in thoughts is so like trafficking with prostitutes," he notes, not because there is negotiated exchange of services but because there is a common but often unspoken expropriation of one's energies, resources, and personal reserves.

This expropriation forms a silent community among writers and readers. Nietzsche is an example of a bond that extends across the ages. According to Lingis:

> To those who, before his explanations of Sophocles or Jesus, asked, "what new philological or historical scholarship, what corrected translations of the texts, justify your explanations?" Nietzsche's answer is: "I have the instincts of Aeschylus, of Jesus, they are my blood brothers!" The protestant, gentle, yuppie, the socialist, fascist, or liberal Nietzscheans of his and our day do not, could not produce anything but misunderstanding of his writings.[26]

Yet this ambivalent force of the word is also manifest in the most immediate forms of contact. In a recent essay, "Word of Honor," Lingis describes the significance of a person declaring such mundane phrases as "I tell you," "I am going to do this and not that," "I will help you," by emphasizing how listeners assume them to be true. Their truth-value, however, is not verified by an independent source or disproved by a far-fetched counterexample. Instead, another's words have truth-value because they are spoken from the heart. It takes guts to tell the truth, it requires some nerve to be fully candid, and sometimes we just have to bite the bullet to tell what we know. Scientists have recently discovered that the Pinocchio myth—that a liar's nose betrays him by growing larger—actually has some concrete evidence to support it. When former President William Clinton appeared on television so often during his impeachment debacle, careful viewers could detect that on certain subjects his nose actually inflated. In fact, most of our noses undergo minute inflammation of the nostrils due to the pressure of trying to get away with telling a lie. (Not as much as Pinocchio's of course, since the fairy-tale version typically embellishes or exaggerates an important point, in order to convey a valuable insight—that parts of our body change according to how or whether we speak truthfully or falsely.)

What often brings us to recognizing the truth-value of another's word, then, lies in a relation to his or her body. Emotions such as laughter, sorrow, joy, anger, and others described by Lingis have a truthfulness about them. A surprise visit from a relative, a numbing story from a colleague, a stricken or joyous encounter with a stranger, all remind us how certain we can be that something is true before we ever subject it to independent verification. As Lingis puts it, it is clear that many times we are convinced of the truthfulness of another's words not out of understanding but out of honor.

With honor also comes dishonor. Words of another are invariably distinguished between those we find credible or valuable and those found incredulous or meaningless. Echoing Foucault's earlier studies, Lingis observes how established discourses—in universities, governments, research institutes, or entertainment industries—effectively exclude or elide the words of those considered irrational, mad, fervid, or fanatical. In shifting direction from Foucault's genealogy and archaeology, however, Lingis adds a significant philosophical dimension to Foucault's masterful inquiries. Relying on a descriptive phenomenology that is more anchored by exposition and expenditure to others as a substantive force, Lingis charges "that our society maintains a discourse of dishonor over their memories. At the same time an ever expanding global media industry feeds on them....By night our citizens feed their imaginations and instincts on the decapitated, dismembered bodies of fanatics and terrorists. Strange cannibal Eucharist!"[27] What we glean from the words of documents and historical texts can be found still today through other means.

This other means is for Lingis an inquiry into the value of words uttered by those with whom we often do not even have a language or culture in common. Terrorists, freaks, fundamentalists, guerrillas, geeks, nomads, the sedentary or solitary ones, are among many current illustrations of how tempting it is for any seeker of truth to not only neglect other seekers but also denigrate them as evil, mad, dangerous, or savage. Yet if we could learn in their words the importance of what they said but also admire the truth in what they did not say, we might be able, according to Lingis, to consecrate the honor of savages. Found among militants who carry vials of deadly poison in case they are captured and among those captured who invoke silence to protect their comrades, this honor oftentimes escapes meaningful words. It can also be found, observes Lingis, in rituals such as the dreadful mystic banquet of old Tibet in which ascetic but ecstatic dancers, trumpets made of human bones, decapitations performed by feminine deities, and visions of demons and ghouls, lead to the celebrant's own recognition that he or she is part of the sacrifice.

Whereas Foucault often enlists ancient texts and historical records to help us engage the thoughts of masters, Lingis entices us with insights from the shadows of the masters of those who, he reflects, "spoke to me." They include political enemies, animal passions, departed gods, sacred temples, and, he notes, "people my nation and my culture have conquered and silenced said to me with their mute bodies....I understood that what they said to me they were saying to you."[28]

Schools of Thought

Another type of mastery shows itself in how a thinker's ideas are disseminated. While individuals who know the thinker sometimes may turn the ideas into something of a legacy, more often readers whom the author may never meet or know attend to and sustain his or her influences. By contributing their own research, interpretation, and commentary the readers form another kind of silent community—a school of thought.

Here we loosely borrow from the work of social theorists Edward Tiryakian and Richard Monk. According to them a school of thought emerges when there is a theoretical crisis in a field of knowledge and a thinker formulates both a philosophical solution to the crisis while also initiating new ways of conducting research. To emphasize the aspect of a school's dynamics, the traditional focus on a solitary thinker needs to shift to the proliferation of intellectual work that reflects the thinker's own innovations. According to Tiryakian, the school is "an actual socio-historical community of professional scholars, brought together by a charismatic intellectual leader. The key function of this figure is to formulate...a scientific research program."[29]

A school's development is analogous to conception of a fetus or the nurturing of a plant. There is an incubation period, when the thinker begins working out the various disputes dominating the field of inquiry. As a kind of cross-fertilization of ideas, the thinker then turns to other disciplines to expand the theoretical and empirical directions that are neglected by his own field. At first this sort of work seems unorthodox. Specialists in the field are tempted to scoff at these initial efforts— that's not what, say, true historians or sociologists or philosophers are supposed to be doing. Here the institutional component is integral. For the thinker who launches a school of thought has a geographic setting in which to teach, present papers, and help their students whom they have mentored to find positions elsewhere. To continue with the organic metaphor, they spawn minischools or, in Tiryakian's terms, "auxiliaries." The eventual outcome, observes Monk, is at least a "generation of important insights into the growth of scientific disciplines and knowledge systems."[30]

For sociologists the classic examples are Max Weber, Emile Durkheim, Talcott Parsons, and Robert Park. Each devised a conceptual apparatus that directed a variety of research programs by subsequent generations of students and scholars. A classic example for philosophy is Immanuel Kant's concept of autonomy. According to J. B. Schneewind,[31] Kant recognized that the ethical disputes of his time were unsolvable given that the principles and values moral philosophers were working with invariably led to problems about the status of God, voluntarism, social benefits, and natural law. To work out a rational and universal ethic that overcomes these problems, Kant comes up with the idea of autonomy. As Schneewind points out, however, Kant was alert to the context of his times from philosophers and non-philosophers alike. His sense of autonomy, then, was more than a response to his philosophical predecessors. It was also a response to the scientific, political, and religious disputes of his time. Since then every moral dispute—be it normative or practical—must address the issue of autonomy. It seems impossible to discuss issues such as responsibility, free will, adulthood, enlightenment, citizenship, euthanasia, and medical experimentation without directly or indirectly invoking some sense of autonomy.

Is Michel Foucault a recent example of an emerging school of thought? In a rough approximation of the model set out by social theorists, Foucault satisfies the four basic criteria. He was, by any account, an engaging, complex, and unpredictable individual. Yet his seminars, attended by the likes of Gilles Deleuze, Jacques Donzelot, and Jacques Derrida, spawned a variety of debates about the implications of his central ideas. Third, journals such as *The History of Sexuality* and volumes such as the *History of the Private Life* or *Fragments on the History of the Body* testify to the Foucault's remarkable influence. They show how our ongoing debates about, say, sexuality, the body, and the political force of ideas remain indebted to Foucault's insights on archaeology and genealogy. Fourth, his work has spawned auxiliaries or minischools. Scholars as diverse as sociologist Richard Sennett, literary critic Edward Said, anthropologist Clifford Geertz, and historians Peter Brown and Linda Gordon have relied on key components of his thought. Ian Hacking's studies of abuse, multiple personality, and social construction exemplify unique ways of employing Foucault's perspective on the history of systems of thought. And William Connolly, as editor of the journal *Political Theory* and as professor in political science, anticipated long before his many colleagues in philosophy that Foucault could enrich the intellectual possibilities for American audiences. His writings and those of his students signal a minischool insofar as they rework new possibilities for using Foucault's seminal ideas.

It is perhaps too early to predict any of these options regarding Alphonso Lingis. While students and conference attendees might verify the charismatic aspects of Lingis, this feature is probably less important in light of the possible formation of silent communities. Still, there is not yet any evident formation of a school. As yet, no journals or institutional forums are prepared to establish projects or research programs with the expressed intentions of utilizing components of Lingis's thought. Despite his presentations to a variety of audiences including many outside philosophy, there is no sign yet that his revived senses of phenomenology and philosophical approaches to xenography have sufficiently addressed the philosophical controversies of our time. These are matters awaiting debate. For the present, his approach can readily seem unorthodox and not the way earnest philosophers go about their business. To them this might seem an end to philosophy that for Lingis is only a momentary pause that philosophy can illuminate.

It is the power of this unorthodoxy that makes Lingis's work to be one of the few candidates today with the potential to inaugurate a school of thought that can complement the ongoing contributions of someone like Foucault. In a recent meditation on an ancient Javanese stone axe given to him by a farmer near Jogjakarta, Lingis wonders if one can ever find some contact with the emotions, rituals, stories, and thoughts that gave life to the stone axe thousands of years ago. Historians, archaeologists, psychologists, and anthropologists can provide some contextual insights, but often at the cost of diminishing or sterilizing the complexity and intensity of the stone axe. Citing Nietzsche, Lingis speculates that modern thinkers tend to eliminate the savage element from the stone's life. But this element is not decadent or debased. It is noble. For the life of the axe testifies or communicates a courage and honor that is more than utilitarian or symbolic—it communicates by overflowing, by dissemination.

From the chance encounter with a stone axe or a historical figure found in a discarded text, Lingis and Foucault present their readers with new ways of understanding and making contact with the most unfamiliar realities. As Lingis concludes from a visit to a church built inside a mountain rock, "In fact wherever you wander from then on, across Ethiopia, across Africa, across oceans and continents, there will be something in you that has become, ineradicably, a pilgrim, who, God willing, will return to Lalibela. From time to time, from his cell carved in the rock walls beside a church, a hermit greets you like a brother."[32]

In such chance meetings one encounters the greetings of passions, of knowledge, of silent communities.

Notes

1. Michel Foucault, *Madness and Civilization*, trans. Richard Howard (New York: Vintage, 1973), viii.

2. Alphonso Lingis, *Abuses* (Berkeley: University of California Press, 1994), ix.

3. Michel Foucault, *The Order of Things*, trans. A. Sheridan (New York: Vintage, 1973), xv.

4. Alphonso Lingis, *Dangerous Emotions* (Berkeley: University of California Press, 2000), 98.

5. Michel Foucault, "About the Concept of the 'Dangerous Individual' in 19th Century Legal Psychiatry," *International Journal of Law and Psychiatry* 1 (1978), 1.

6. Foucault, *The Order of Things*, xv.

7. *Ibid.*, 342-343.

8. Rex Martin, "Truth, Power, Self: An Interview with Michel Foucault," in *Technologies of the Self*, ed. Luther Martin, Huck Gutman, and Patrick Hutton (Amherst: University of Massachusetts Press, 1988), 11.

9. Alphonso Lingis, "The Misunderstanding," (*Parallax* 1999).

10. Alphonso Lingis, *Dangerous Emotions*, 92.

11. Alphonso Lingis, *The Imperative* (Bloomington: Indiana University Press, 1998), 127-128.

12. Alphonso Lingis, "Satyrs and Centaurs," in *Why Nietzsche Still?* ed. Alan D. Schrift (Berkeley: University of California Press, 2000), 166.

13. Alphonso Lingis, "Anger," in *On Jean-Luc Nancy: The Sense of Philosophy*, ed. Darren Sheppard, Simon Sparks, and Colin Thomas (London: Routledge, 1997), 213.

14. Michel Foucault, *Power/Knowledge*, ed. Colin Gordon (New York: Pantheon, 1980), 81.

15. Herculine Barbin, *Being the Recently Discovered Memoirs of a Nineteenth-Century French Hermaphrodite*, introduced by Michel Foucault, trans. Richard McDougall (New York: Pantheon, 1980), 78.

16. Foucault, Power/Knowledge, 83, 87.

17. Michel Foucault, "Power and Sex," in *Politics, Philosophy, Culture*, ed. Lawrence D. Kritzman, trans. David J. Parent (New York: Routledge, 1988), 124.

18. See Alphonso Lingis, *The Community of Those Who Have Nothing in Common* (Bloomington: Indiana University Press, 1994), 1-10.

19. Alphonso Lingis, "Death Drive," *Journal of Value Inquiry* 29 (1995), 220. Additional discussion on technopoles can be found in Lingis's essay, "In Orbit," *Journal of Social Philosophy* 25, 3 (Winter, 1994).

20. Lingis, *Abuses*, 214.

21. Alphonso Lingis, *Sensation: Intelligibility in Sensibility* (Buffalo: Humanities Books, 1996), 29.

22. Friedrich Nietzsche, *The Gay Science*, trans. Walter Kaufmann (New York: Vintage, 1973), sect. 340.

23. See Alberto Manguel, *A History of Reading* (New York: Viking, 1996).

24. Michel Foucault, *The History of Sexuality, Vol. 2: The Use of Pleasure*, trans. Robert Hurley (New York: Pantheon, 1985), ch. 1 and 2.

25. *Ibid.*, 8.

26. Alphonso Lingis, "The Misunderstanding," *Parallax* (1999), 86.

27. Alphonso Lingis, "Word of Honor," *Paragraph* (2000), 161.

28. Lingis, *Abuses*, viii.

29. Edward Tiryakian, "Hegemonic Schools and the Development of Sociology: Rethinking the History of a Discipline," in *Structures of Knowing*, ed. Richard C. Monk (Lanham, Md.: University Press of America, 1986), 418.

30. Richard C. Monk, *Structures of Knowing*, xxiii.

31. J. B. Schneewind, *The Invention of Autonomy* (Cambridge: Cambridge University Press, 1999).

32. Alponso Lingis, "The Return of Extinct Religions," *New Nietzsche Studies* (Jan. 2002), 27.

Chapter Seven

Foreign Bodies: Interview with Alphonso Lingis (1996)

Mary Zournazi

Foreign Bodies *is a meditation and cultural reflection on the relationships between language, bodies and cultural perception. How do we think about "communities of those who have nothing in common" and the ethics of otherness? How can we understand other histories and life experience from outside the paradigms of western culture? We met in London in April 1996 to talk about his recent writing:* Abuses, The Community of Those Who Have Nothing In Common, *and* Foreign Bodies. *I asked how his writing and experience of different cultures intersect with his philosophical work and thinking on otherness.*

I

Abuses

The first time I went to Khajuraho in India to see the great erotic temples, I had vividly the sense that this was one of the grandest things that my eyes had seen, that could be seen on the planet. I thought it was completely improbable that I would see them: my parents were Lithuanian immigrant farmers and I was the only son; I ended up an intellectual and I never met anybody who had ever gone to Khajuraho. All my colleagues, all the philosophers I had ever known, had never gone to places like India and they certainly don't wander around and confront Khajuraho. When I was there I tried to read everything, but I had no access to Indian languages—so I could only read Indian works in English and guidebooks and so on. And everything I read was just ludicrous. Most Indian writers writing in English reinterpret their own tradition in Hegelian terms. When I left India I had understood very little and I thought this was just one of the grandest things that I had ever seen or could see. I had the idea that when I retire I will return and have more time there, and that before I die I would write something as a kind of acknowledgment of this gift that was given to me.

When I returned to the United States somebody had a cultural conference in Canada and they invited me. I knew most of the people and they said to talk about anything. I thought I would see if I could write something on Khajuraho and to my astonishment I wrote something. It certainly is not any kind of final statement but I was just amazed that I could write something. After that I had this very powerful idea that things that moved me most, not only by their own intrinsic grandeur or mystery but also by the fact that they were addressed personally to me and that they had come into my life, were the things I should write about. Eventually this got put together in *Excesses* but by the time I got to the pieces that got counted in *Abuses*, that was really what I was doing. I wrote about what really moved me most deeply and sometimes it was wonder—like in Antarctica—and sometimes it was deeply troubling and painful, like some of the pieces about torture and the piece about Bangladesh.

I think I write very naively. I don't at all reflect on things and I think that has been true for as long as I can remember. Recently I have become a little more clear about it. It was when I was working with a student who was writing a dissertation on conceptual models. In talking to him I became very resistant to this idea and I thought that the task was to address yourself to some reality and for it to be in your own terms. Several times sacred places were very important to me, like Teotihuacán in Mexico or Borobudo or those that I haven't even written about yet.... When I go to a new temple, I think sort of instinctively—I am always looking toward a "here," what is in this temple. Other studies I had done on temples could not serve as some kind of paradigm or outline to capture this experience. So I think what I would like to happen is that language form itself from what you see or hear, coming from this kind of confrontation.

I don't think I have a policy statement on writing, but I do have some feelings. If I think back on *Abuses*, there were a lot of places in that book where I was very aware of that exploitative presence—for example in the essay about the refugees, the Bangladesh refugee camp in Dhaka. But I didn't take the position of a kind of sovereign outside observer, though on the other hand I also felt a great distance. I think I felt that very, very intensively the first time that I went to India—when I went to Calcutta to stay several months it was beyond what I was in any way prepared for. I was afraid of Calcutta and it had the reputation of a city dreadful at night. I arrived in the evening and as soon as I booked into a hotel I immediately always went out. My hotel was near the center and it was in the middle of the monsoon, sort of raining, and all the streets were lined up with Bangladesh refugees, emaciated, and there were five million—most of them in and around Calcutta. As soon as my white face was visible, I was surrounded by these people, women with emaciated babies at their breast; it was horrifying. I was really shuddering in my hotel that night with the horror.

I somehow had always felt—it was an idea that I found in Nietzsche that suffering does not exceed human capacity. He says that people are afraid of the suffering, of the last agony. He says animals withdraw when they suffer, they don't dread it, they wait for it and don't bother the rest of the herd or the group. And when the pain gets too intense for consciousness to bear it by nature, consciousness fades out. It is the fear of suffering that is worse, it makes cowards of us more than the pain itself. And that is something I verified in a very personal experience—not me personally but my mother's dying. It was an almost unbearable thing to watch, but she bore it with great strength and courage. So she had the strength and that made me believe that one does have the strength. But months later in Calcutta, the last night I was there, I took another midnight walk—I wept, really wept. About a week later I was in Paris seeing friends and talking about India. A friend showed me an account of the refugee situation and again I wept. I had just seen that a week ago but it was like the mind couldn't remember that long, it was a suffering greater than the mind could get any kind of hold on. I thought, I am sleeping in this bed and right on the other side of the world I know there are these people sleeping in the rain on the sidewalk and yet I slept on a bed. And there isn't any kind of justification for that. Some people justify that, saying that I am doing good in my own way by sleeping on a bed. I am saving my strength for some article I might write. I think that is fake justification. I think one is simply guilty.

I always felt that the fact that I was rich and they were poor could never be eliminated from a friendship. When you met someone in the street and you invited them to a restaurant you had to think. You wanted them to get a decent meal but you also wanted them to be brought into a restaurant where you could have a friendship, where that person would not feel embarrassed, out of place. So restaurants I would freely go into would be crossed off the list in my mind while making that invitation. In things like that you are aware that you could never forget that they are impoverished and by comparison I am quite rich. And it was a poison. A lot of people talk about when you go to these poor countries everyone looks at you as a rich guy, that they are going to try and hassle something over. I really have met an awful lot of people and I would certainly say the vast majority of people I encountered did not look at me in this way.

I am all too aware that I am part of a rich culture that is getting richer and richer and more and more dominating, and that you never escape this complicity. The only thing I think is that at least you have to be lucid, you don't want to get hypocritical and justify yourself. I tend to go only to Third World countries, partly because they are the most foreign. But nonetheless when one goes to a country like Haiti a lot of it is going to be miserable, depressing, and a lot of what you see is not at all an interesting, alternative culture; it is just misery.

I think I have always been aware there is an otherness that is irreducible, that there is a suffering in every friendship. But there is another side. I think that nowadays so many cultural critics go all the way, and I don't. There are people who are just analyzing the anthropological discourse, as his own discourse about the people—about his informants and their discourse. The most extreme form you have, well, look at Lévi-Strauss. His own purpose in anthropology is never to give a local person's account of their culture, but instead to give a totally different account in Western scientific terms. It is this language, its analysis and structure, that I have resisted. If I would ever try to say it publicly, people would dismiss it as nineteenth-century romanticism.

I think that there is a way that you can understand people outside of objective structures. I continue to think that you do not just reflect on your own language and perceptions. But so often in my life with people I have met, I have had a friendship—young people, old people, men, women who are radically different in culture. I have been with people who are silent, rural people, peasants in Peru. I think there is an awful lot of deep understanding that goes on without language structures. But there are moments in which I couldn't believe that I understood how someone suffered, saw, or felt. Here again I gather a very explicit example from the first time I went to India. I was walking in the street among the crowds of Calcutta and a young guy smiled and I smiled back. Before long I mentioned I was going up to a restaurant. I was happy to buy somebody a meal. I am sure that is why he made contact, he hoped that I would buy a meal. We ended up being friends. I couldn't believe how he had the kind of understanding he had. He had no education, he was a Bengali refugee, he had grown up in the streets. And I was highly educated from the other side of the world and was also some ten years older than he. In America this wouldn't be possible—I mean first of all someone ten years younger than me would never even want to have any kind of friendly contact, and secondly we would have nothing to talk about. Every day he had such keen sense of what might bore me, what might interest me, what we could do together that would be entertaining to both of us—he sensed these things. At the time I thought, how can he have such tactful understanding of me?

•

Q.: *In some parts of your book* Abuses *there is an address to the reader as "you"—sometimes it is unclear who is the "other," who is writing and whose experiences you are conveying.*

A.: Several people have asked me why I used the term "you." At the time it seemed right and I really in my own mind did not have a reason for it. Of course, on the one hand, "you" is complicit. It ascribes what follows to the reader or the listener. On the other hand, the "me" who had been there I had now a certain distance from. When I write these pieces it is as though I was speaking to myself, asking questions of myself. So I was trying to understand myself at the time; I didn't have a grammatical reason. When I wrote *Lust* I was invited to do a panel session at a conference in France and the topic was "sexual difference." I thought this must be a code word for a current debate, but I hadn't been in France for awhile and at first I didn't know what the specificity of issues around sexual differences were (I was writing this in Peru so I had no access to the French debate on sexual difference; I didn't have any books there). They had invited all the prominent French feminists like Sarah Kofman, Luce Irigaray, and Julia Kristeva.

So my first idea was to write about transvestites. I was dazzled by the great acts they do in Bangkok. It is hard to describe because it is so dazzling. There are these incredible actors in the cabaret. The performer comes out—turns one side to the audience and begins singing an Italian belcanto duet in his tuxedo. Then he flips around with the long hair and a sequinned dress. Then towards the end he faces the audience in an embrace. It is a hoot when they do this—you can't believe what you are seeing!

It is more than copulation because it is the same person. I mean it is really like Aristophanes and these two halves that have come together. I was going to go to Bangkok and ask them to sell me one of these costumes and do the paper in a costume.

This idea of a costume led me to think that the only thing I can talk about on sexual differences and that really moved me deeply was the Bangkok transvestites. When I finished presenting this paper, there was to my complete astonishment, no doubt naivety, an immediate attack by women. I had no sense that this would happen. At one point one of the very vehement objections, and I think that was the only objection I really understood, was a woman who said to me, "you are always saying *you*, but I feel excluded from this *you*—it is a very male *you* that you use in this paper!" And it was then that I thought, "oh people know rhetoric"—when the author uses *you* it is an inclusive *you*, so somehow the things are being attributed to the reader, all these events and so on. And then I thought it is kind of natural that I had an instinct to use *you*, and one of the reasons that it was troubling the audience was that there was complicity throughout. I didn't at all take the position of an observer of this scene, but as a complicitous participant in this scene. I didn't at all say, "those men are dirty old men, pigs all leering and so on." I always included myself and I think this was also instinctual because I completely to this day admire these performers, they are just stunning performers and I am completely wowed by them as people.

II

Memories and Perceptions

Q.: *In your books there are a lot of images accompanying the writing. I am wondering about the photographs and the production of these images in your books, how taking photographs influences your perception and how this affects the way you write about and remember a place.*

A.: I started taking photographs that accompany my books very late. There again it was very naive. For many years I thought there was something completely false in trying to capture the past and it seemed when I would go to a foreign place that what really counted was the way it changed my mind. The whole thing of capturing images was false and was exploitative. You are taking images of other people and very often without them knowing it. At first I just wanted to have buildings and landscapes and then by accident I discovered that children kept jumping and getting into the photograph. They love to be photographed and they thanked me for photographing them even though they would never see it.

I discovered that taking photographs was the best gift I could give. It was more than money. There is something honest about it and it was my technological thing. In Haiti, for example, these people could never afford such a thing. When people have nothing it is the human contact that is the most important. Having the images of their wives, their children, their grandmothers that they can keep years later was wonderful and was most precious to them. So that is how photography became important to me. And when I see these images I am deeply moved because I remember the people or person and their response.

Very often in Third World countries it is very difficult or virtually impossible to photograph women. Peruvian women will actually cover their faces and cross the street if they see the camera pointed in their direction. In India too it is very hard. Sometimes I was taking photographs of street scenes with a zoom lens and not asking the people in advance. You can try to hide the fact that you're photographing them because if they notice they will stop what they are doing. But when I was taking photographs of individuals there was always some kind of permission. I always made some kind of sign and then in every case where I could I tried to return with the photo. Sometimes when I found people were particularly into photographs, I would do a whole study of them and then later on I would give them the images. In this way, I came to see photographs as a way to actually help people. I mean the very act of photographing was an encounter. When I would come back with the photographs, very often they would call in all their friends and insist I come in the house, sit down and have tea and so on.

The other aspect to taking photographs is that I discovered very soon what it did to my own eyes. When you begin to take photographs you begin to see the glitter of light. I remember the last time I was in London and saw the lights—it was so spectacular. This very angular light, winter light, is particularly clear, so that you become sensitive to light, to forms and so on. Photography was a kind of transfiguration of perception that was very precious to me. And I think it was made more dramatic when I started photographing people. I think natural perception tends to take in the person as a whole; when you start photographing it is rare that you would do that. For close-ups you might crop the face or the hands or something like that, and so one begins to see people this way. I also really discovered beauty in physical types and ethnic types that I don't think I would have discovered otherwise. I felt it was a very dramatic development in perception.

•

Q.: *In a different way in relation to images and photographs, the notion of the "face" of the other is important. This imaging process captures a kind of "surface"—a face of others and at the same time a kind of depth to the experiences you shared and captured on film. I am interested in your notion of face and the question of otherness.*

A.: I haven't completely got onto the whole aesthetics of photography, but I think that this is something one should think through, how some photographers really use the face as a purely formal property, like a stone. It seems to me that so much of the formal beauty of the face is inseparable from its action. Maybe just in the very simple sense that as one discovers the beauty of the face one almost reveres it, one wants to protect it, it is precious and fragile.

I think I saw the notion of face in Levinas and went in a somewhat different way than he did. The first thought was when someone faces you they appeal to you and put a demand on you. The act of facing is exposing the surface and the substance—they can put an appeal to you. The simplest possible case is you walk through the door and you are aware of people as forms. Then someone turns and faces you and says "hi." This is already an appeal to interrupt you or your preoccupation, or to direct your attention to him or her and to respond. To not answer a greeting is an offense. As one enters into any kind of prolonged kind of face-to-face relationship in conversation, the one who faces continues to be there as an appeal and a demand. And I think the easiest way to see that is in language. Every statement in the face-to-face conversation that is put forth is addressed to you, who are being faced, and requires some kind of response. But I think it is not just the verbal form and the linguist formulas that contain this evocative and imperative force. It is also the nakedness, the disarmedness of the person before one. One can think of the eyes, the most unprotected part of the body and also the most unstable: the eyes have continual movement. The eyes lack the stability and shield which we associate with self-containment and self-sufficiency—the eyes are always searching. When you look at the eyes, as someone once said, there is a kind of night in the corner of the eyes. The face is unprotected, it is denuded, it is naked. The unprotectedness is on the surface. When you look at the face you don't at all see through it to the bones and so on. It is a surface phenomenon.

I've just had some more thoughts on the nakedness of the whole body that derives from the face. It is the face that reveals itself. Even when one denudes oneself erotically, the view of the body could be erotic because it has a face. The physical reality that marks the wounds and the fatigue is seen on the face. So the face is a kind of surface with whom one stays but it is a kind of sign board—it is where one makes signs to the other. But these signs, because of the physical reality of the flesh, dissolve as soon as they are formed. All of this gives us the sense of a kind of destitution and denuding of the person facing you. I feel this very intensely in other countries. When you walk along the street and you answer someone's greeting, be it a child or a waiter, there is already a feeling you are beginning to expose yourself to judgement, to need, to a desire of the other. And in facing the person there is a kind of nominal denuding and destitution, whereas if you turn away you close yourself back into a kind of self-sufficiency.

The feeling of obligation would be a fundamental ethical fact. If there are any ethics at all it means that I recognize that I am obliged by something outside myself. I started by thinking that this experience, its own basis, is the face of these people. To face other people was the most intense fundamental unquestionable ethical experience. But I have extended this toward other animals in a book I have just finished. It seems to me more and more that it is the material properties of a being that faces us, that make demands on us. What I see on the face of the other is a kind of concentration of light. It seemed to me that when you wake up in the morning and there is a radiant light outside, it is wrong to stay inside. One is called forth by the light. The light is a kind of summons. It summons us in someone's look. I really saw it as the basic ethical experience, not something like an abstracting of a soul but rather the very concrete event of encountering someone who faces me.

Q.: *In this sense, the question of ethics in relation to an other would be very specific to where you are, and I think that provides an interesting rethinking of ethics.*

A.: It is also the experience of the other. Inasmuch as the person who faces me puts demands on me and makes appeals to me, they stand outside as other, outside of this encounter. By just looking at people in the street as they go by or from the window, you get a fundamental experience of similarity. They are like so many different bits of myself. One of these interchangeable forms turns to face me, then something outside, something other stands before me. I think that is the most intense experience in which we discover the other person. I wanted to talk about this architecturally. In authority we don't want to recognize the right or the demands being put on us. The dean has this elevated chair or a kind of throne behind a desk and the student comes in and is maintained at a distance. This kind of physical experience already denies the appeal being made. The student will be treated as another student. The dean will evoke the general rule that applies to all students in order to deny the singular appeal. I think I could talk about the whole architecture of authority and subjugation.

III

Foreign Bodies

Q.: *Your notion of language and sensibility is quite different from a purely linguistic one and informs much of your writing on "foreign" bodies and communities. How would you describe your notion of language and perception?*

A.: I am just starting to think this through in *The Community of Those Who Have Nothing in Common*. In the essay, "The Murmur of the World" it was spelt out in a way that I had never been able to before. I cite authors that helped me as I came to think that there is a sensual, animal quality to language. Jean-Luc Nancy says that the first thing when two people meet and say anything to each other is the tone. When someone comes rushing in, is all excited, frenzied, the first thing you pick up on is the tone. So you say, "What's up?!!" or you might just say, "What's up." That is a refusal of the tone, but the refusal of the tone means that what you caught is the tone. The urgency, the panic in the tone links to the other person's sonorous rhythm, which is a vital rhythm. The connection is made even before language begins to convey messages. One could imagine no end of situations where someone could come to you but with an entirely different tone. Some people would have a kind of hysterical tone and you would realize at once that this is a wrenching, personal suffering they are in. Sometimes from the tone you would sense at once some kind of financial problem that you might help, or something like that, or a practical problem—you know the car broke down. I was so struck with this level of communicating with the tone.

Another thing that struck me a long time ago is that a verbal, let's say a "cinematographic" account of a conversation, shows how much redundancy there is. You know even all the sentences that...well I just said "you know," you know all these little redundancies. The other person is constantly responding with "yeah, yeah" or "understandable" or "yes" or so on, and all this is redundant. If you would write up all of these redundancies in a letter to communicate what I wanted to communicate, it would be a quarter as long again in terms of words used. So there are all those other words that don't really have a message function. There are kinds of verbal functions that continue the sonorous contact.

I just thought of something I had never thought before, both in your question and your own gestures. I think the usual category of body kinaesthetics—at least what I have read people talking about gestures and body kinaesthetics—were really talking about them as part of language, either as mimicking the message that the words were saying, amplifying it, or giving it a certain grammatical place. But there are also other kinds of gestures which involve being in the space, interweaving the same space, a kind of personal presence to the other person. Just as you were speaking I imagined what it would be like for two people to get together and make no gestures. Like people who get up on the podium and during their whole speech they are holding onto the podium without a single gesture. No conversation occurs this way, but suppose a conversation did. What would you think? You would think there was some kind of refusal, there was some kind of wall that was being maintained there. When you and I gesture I don't actually insert my body into the space between your hands—but almost! This is the place of our personal meeting.

Q.: *To follow on from this, it seems to me that your notion of gesture is influenced by Merleau-Ponty and his notion of perception, and I want to ask the tail end of the question before—how do you see the relationship between the body and movement, gesture and perception?*

A.: I think some of the theoretical structures involved in Merleau-Ponty's *Phenomenology of Perception* I have serious objections to that I can spell out. But on the issue that you are pointing to, the relationship between body, body gestures, position, stance, movement, and the perceived, I think Merleau-Ponty is right and I don't think I have much in the way of explicit thoughts that are different from his. But the book *Women Fire Dangerous Things* by George Lakoff is a very important book. He is a Californian linguist. I think that he has actually done what Merleau-Ponty had some outlines of doing in terms of gestural theory. In Merleau-Ponty's theory of language, words and sentences are conceived as gestures. He started to write a book on the origin of truth and he was trying to relate the kind of body language he spoke of in the *Phenomenology of Perception* to abstract thinking, mathematical thinking, and logical thinking. But Lakoff has done this very strikingly. He conceives of concepts as embodied concepts like up and down, and higher and lower. Very often we just think of a concept in a kind of Aristotelian way, as a kind of abstract, inert structure of a thing. But Lakoff has a whole map of different kinds of concepts and they are all very body related. All these kinds of models are related to body postures, body grasps, and movements. I taught that book a few years ago in a graduate seminar and I never wrote anything on it. But that was merely because I was so convinced, so dazzled by his insights, that I haven't gone beyond them in any way. I had nothing of my own to say beyond what he would say.

I think that I move from Merleau-Ponty's idea to certain of Levinas's insights [on body style]. And I am especially thinking of Levinas's very first essay on aesthetics where he has a discussion on rhythm. Rhythm is something that doesn't lend itself to an intentional analysis. It is not that a constitutive mind is synthesizing external data. A rhythm is something that you catch on to, that you are captivated by; in a sense you are no longer free, the mind no longer feels it is spontaneous. It is being rocked along, it is being led. It is captivated and entranced by rhythm and I think that's what happens when one catches on to someone's style. I recognize my mother from two blocks away by the way she walks. What I recognize first is not her complexion, color of her hair or her dress, but that distinctive style of walking. I recognize this at once. The first thing you recognize is the style—the style of movement, the style of sitting, the style of interacting with a person. I think this is not so much knowledge, it is being captivated, like being caught by a rhythm on a dance floor.

•

Q.: *In* Foreign Bodies *you talk about different notions of embodiment in relation to culture and you talk about the "noble" body. For me this raises the question of the "cultivation" of the body, how we produce our bodies in different cultural contexts. I am thinking how one cultivates a body, because different bodies have different forms of cultivation—a female body is differently cultivated to a male body; this poses another question. But in terms of body image, how does the notion of noble body alter "bodily perception"?*

A.: That to me is a very important concept. I first thought about it in terms of Nietzsche. It seems to me that the term "noble," for Nietzsche, is not fundamentally a political, social term. His primary reference is not the feudal aristocracy but animals. Once I picked this up, it seemed to me completely general—in so many ancient cultures there is a sense of noble animals and gregarious animals. There is this whole biological dimension in Nietzsche's thinking. The European aristocracy originally were military men; they were the defenders of the community and achieved a freedom from labor so as to defend the community. But when feudalism set in they no longer had this role and they engaged typically in tournaments with horses, falcons, and so on. Their kinship is with noble animals. And the noble body that they projected culturally, this refinement, is that of a racehorse, tiger or jaguar, and so on. In virtually every culture I have become acquainted with the same things were certainly true—in Japan and among the Incas and Mayas. It seems to me that nobility is a very animal notion. A noble animal that still is left in our Western cultures is the racehorse. The racehorse is a combination of power, instincts, and extreme sensibility. A racehorse is on edge, quick, and has an extremely refined sensitivity and also a physical beauty.

Every culture has something like a body nobility. It occurred to me that every culture covers certain kinds of minds—the Byzantine mind is so distinctly different from the classical Hindu mind or the Roman mind. But there is also distinctive bodily perfection. In India, the yogic bodily postures are very different from the Japanese stance. The whole center of gravity in Japanese physical perfection is different. African dancers, like the Massi that I saw in Kenya, do these great loops, they do this just to amuse themselves on long afternoons (they are herdsmen so they don't actually work, just keep an eye on the herd). Bodybuilders and dancers are both strong, but with totally different kinds of strength. So I think there are many different bodily perfections and they are cultivated in culture, and my suspicion is that every great civilization had a distinctive dominant physical ideal.

Q.: *In a different way, the notion of the nobility of the body I think is a really interesting move away from thinking of the body as somehow outside of the formation of the self. In regards to women's bodies (which is a bit different from what you are saying) there is a bodily perfection created in Western cultures that is often alien to women. But I am thinking the notion of a "noble" body and the cultivation of body, of woman's body in their own image creates another kind of sensibility.*

A.: Perhaps the theme of animal and the notion of animal category may be useful. It means that the body discovers itself, its own powers, and its own instinct, as opposed to the other angle, which would be the ways that a physical ideal is dictated by the culture.

•

Q.: *How does a body become other and alien to the community?*

A.: I had some years ago done a paper on Judge Schreber and his so-called madness. He calls it his nervous illness in *The Memoirs of My Nervous Illness*, where all his visions are attributed to his nervous system. He picks up these visions and rays from God. I was very struck by Lacan and Lévi-Strauss's analysis of him, and there was a very clear article by Susan Sontag giving a completely sociological explanation of his madness. For me the issue was in what way is this discourse of madness excluded as not making sense by the community? With some people, like Nietzsche, there is a discourse whose categories are really diagrams of their affective life. This whole theme of bodies that are excluded from whole communities made me think of Nietzsche and his terms. We should really think of Nietzsche's body, his affective life, his migraines, and his euphorias as diagrams of many of the key concepts, like the eternal return, the will to power, and notions like value. I also began to think of the exclusion of the mystics. As Foucault writes, in the middle ages there wasn't the category of the mentally ill—you were touched by God if you were lucky or you were a demon if you were unlucky. But these people seemed to have distinctive bodies—and that seems to me to continue to be true of shaman or the native Americans and so on, people who have gone through physical crisis. They do have, at least they are perceived by the culture as having, distinctive bodies, and discourse is connected with that. And of course with shamans in their shamanistic culture they have a cultural place, but where they don't have a cultural place they would be seen as not making sense.

I also thought about this in *The Community of Those Who Have Nothing in Common* in connection with those who are tortured. Michel de Certeau was very important to me in thinking those things. Those who are tortured are tortured because of what they say, and they are forced to say something. They are supposed to confess, not that they are wrong but what they were saying didn't make sense. They are reduced to spasmodic, incompetent, brutal bodies in the process of torture. The judges are proving their words are senseless; they are demonstrating they are animals or brute animals. I am very convinced of this. Torture is very connected with language in this way, with a language which is deemed by the community to not make sense to them—demented, absurd, and so on.

I originally thought of that in terms of rape and that there too was a way bodies were excluded in the community through a kind of torture. Violence is not produced by an upsurge of animal impulses in individuals but by recurrence of institutions. The rapist after all has picked up his judgement of the subordination and inferiority of women and so on from the culture. This has been first of all institutionalized in the language of the culture, and secondly the practices of torture are picked up from institutions of torture like the CIA. These are institutions of torture, and as a matter of fact a great many rapists are former special forces commandos from the Vietnam War and so on. I think that maybe not all rapists actually torture, but after all a great deal of rape is torture. To actually torture women the rapist is not releasing individual basic instincts, violent instincts. He is picking up cultural practices which have been institutionalized—institutionalized ways of excluding people. So these are the ways I thought of these various categories of people that are excluded from the community and I thought of them more in bodily terms. It seems to be that the culture is capable of institutionalizing violence and of deadening, disconnecting the body.

IV

Other Communities—Character, Dignity, and the Break in Time

Q.: *What interests me is the question of how people have a bodily "integrity" even in the most oppressive and difficult situations—a kind of "integrity of the self." This type of integrity is implied, I think, when you write about people in "other" communities, but also in connection with death, and particularly your mother's death.*

A.: I think very recently, just this trip, I have gotten a few more thoughts on it. Courage is one dimension of it. I have been thinking more and more about courage. And I haven't got very clear thoughts on it because it has gone in several different directions.... But in the Third World—and it is especially in the Third World where people have great poverty, difficulty, and often personal tragedy—I have felt most the important sense of *character*. Until recently people had character, and you felt that very strongly. In Latin America I was thinking about it in terms of men. Machismo has such a negative connotation, at least it did during a certain period and in recent gender thinking. But I began to think that in Latin America it wasn't completely a matter of domination. The first time I went to Mexico, at the airport there was this Mexican dressed completely in white—with black strings, big white hat, little moustache—looking incredibly glamorous. They have a sense of male beauty in this most spectacular form. Bullfighters are jewelled specimens of male on display, but also they have courage and they have their word of honor. Their word is a commitment and a pledge, that you don't just drop when it becomes advantageous to yourself to do so. When they pledge their word they keep it. So I began to think that when people have nothing to identify themselves with they have character. This is a way poor people have a noble character.

But it also seemed to me that there were physical traits involved—to be brave means you have to maintain yourself as strong. There are certain physical traits that you have to maintain through discipline and a sense of personal, physical dignity. Secondly there are the character traits. The word character has finally dropped out of our psychology and philosophy; nowadays nobody talks about it. When I went to Afghanistan I felt this character so strongly. I remember the first time I went there (which was back in the 1960s when people did go to these places) I came upon two students in Kabul the day I arrived. They were deathly sick with dysentery and so after days of this I suggested we go to an oasis outside of Kabul that was nice and cool and would be restful. As it turned out it was a rather difficult trip. We had to shift from one truck to another for three or four hours before we got there and it was a very dusty road.

When we arrived my friends were in a state of collapse. By luck we saw these trees and we went to sit down to rest from this trip. A man came, an old man dressed in his robes of great dignity; his face was full of dignity. He carried a great pot of cool water, he came and offered us water. My dysentery-afflicted friends were terrified of this water and didn't dare drink it. I drank it freely. And he sat there with us for quite awhile. He had a personal dignity that was in his posture, in his features, in his garb, in his weathered face. There was no communication, I mean no verbal exchange, but there was a kind of silent communication. He stayed with us for awhile and he was just being a friend. That was all. It wasn't watching over us or seeing if there was anything else he could do for us; it was just being with us for awhile. I often think of him when I think of the word "character"—it was so unmistakable that here was a man of character. A kind of inner strength, integrity the word you used—it was so vivid in him. The very idea of going up to foreigners with a conviction that you can be of assistance and that you can really give something good like cold water. There is a sense of character in people who have no other way in which to construct an identity. It seems to me now in our consumer culture we construct our identity with things. We construct our identity with collections, with garb, you know with little things we have in our home, our jazz collection or collection of cars or whatever.

•

My mother was extraordinarily courageous. She died of cancer for months in a hospital and it was the first time I spent a lot of time in a hospital. She lived in a small town near Chicago and when I was with her in the hospital she would say, "go visit that one, she was a neighbor, this one over there we knew her kids." I would meet these women who offhand one wouldn't think anything of, one would think they were just housewives. They didn't even have a job, lived in a small town the whole of their lives. Then I saw with my own eyes again and again the extraordinary bravery of these women. I remember the first woman I visited had leukemia. She told me very calmly as it gets worse she will die. But there was no tears at all, she wanted to talk about me. She wanted to have a relationship, a friendship. I was staggered—I thought this woman is dying of a painful and hopeless illness. I saw this again and again in the weeks that I was there. And I just came out of this thinking we are far more brave than we know, that there is a kind of animal bravery that comes out in the end—certainly in the case of my mother, but not only her. So many other people I saw who were in great suffering and especially hopeless suffering had this animal bravery. Animals are brave and when it is time for them to die they withdraw and stop eating and wait for death to come. They don't cling to the rest of the herd. So I think this bravery is a very animal thing.

More and more in my recent writings I always say, "the other animals." I haven't thought through this concept of "animal" linguistically—the animal side of us which is also the most noble side of and certainly the wellspring of all the kinds of mental, spiritual, cultural nobility that we sometimes achieve. I haven't been able to conceptualize it. But to me the clearest example I could give at the moment is this courage example—when I think "where did these women get this courage?" It seems they certainly did not get it from religion, because what I have read about people dying is that whatever religion you are, or people have no religion, it is not statistically decisive as to whether you die bravely or cowardly. So there are people who die bravely in every religion and in no religion. It seems that they certainly did not get this from their circumstances in society. They lived lives of subordinate housewives in a small town, many of them did not have careers and often they did not have significant jobs, they worked as clerks or something like that. So really this courage was a vital strength that is in our nature. So it was that sense of animal that seemed to me most clear. I would use this as the first case to try and conceptualize this concept of animality.

•

Q.: *To refer back to communities again, there seems to be a "time" that exists outside of the ways that we understand and write about history and cultural experience, a time and otherness excluded in the logical ordering and documenting of other communities and senses of being. In your writing on ethics and other communities are you offering another notion of time and otherness?*

A.: The most important thing I wrote recently was quite a long paper called *Dignity*. I looked at Kant's notion of respecting the other and then at Heidegger and Zizek, then at other figures like Nietzsche. I liked this paper at least for myself because it is the most complete thing I did on a number of important notions about this—about what you respect when you respect someone. In Kant's most narrow view, it is the law as exemplified in the other, the other is a figure of law—woman and certainly animals are excluded. In Zizek's writing, it is the fantasy system of the other that excludes people from the community. I wrote a kind of synthetic study of all these things that gradually builds to my own idea.

But it was only this morning, just before our meeting, that I wrote a little essay on time. For Bataille, there is the time of endurance and there is what he calls catastrophic or explosive time. The other two I worked out this morning very easily and quickly: there is the Aristotelian time, which is the unending succession of time, and there is Heidegger's time, which all seems unified, subjective, and close to death and which is my own life time. Against that, Bataille has the moments of catastrophe—when the course of things or nature or the social world is catastrophically interrupted by revolution, by earthquakes, by tidal waves, by tornadoes, and so on. What is death? The death of a collaborator, which is unthinkable. When I think of someone

I always think of them in a course of projects, and even after someone is dead I can't help thinking about them without thinking what they are doing. I think of my mother speaking to me. And I think of her as a farming woman even though I know she is dead. I think of her in a project; the reality of death is an unthinkable catastrophe. I think I have always felt that. Even when I was an undergraduate working in a hospital, I had a sense that every single death was unthinkable, unacceptable, and catastrophic. It was a very intense feeling.

The second example is nakedness. When you see anyone you see them clothed and groomed, which puts them in a category—all kinds of clothing is a uniform. As soon as someone knocks on your door and you see them clothed and dressed, even though they are a stranger, you have seen the commitments of their past and their future and you can identify a category of responses and behaviors that you are expecting from them and they are expecting from you. But to denude oneself, or for someone to denude himself or herself before you, is to take off these uniforms, these categories. You might end up with a naked body, which is already a uniform. I am thinking of bodybuilders who have body armor according to a model which you might see right away. But then I'm thinking one might see the breasts of a woman which are not muscular, or the belly or the side or the inside of their arms and thigh. Any kind of encounter with this finality of nakedness is by contact. I mean there is a real feeling; you touch it and you feel the spasms of pleasure and feeling. Just to look at it and see it as flesh is a caress—to sense this sensitivity, this sensuality there outside of category. And that is only in the present. That doesn't give you at all the acquaintance of how that flesh will continue to act, or commitment it will be in, or how it has been.

It seems to me that every time you see someone naked and even caress them with your eyes or think of touching them, you always have the sense that it will be a pleasure that they have never felt before, that it will be some kind of surprise to them. The touch will be some kind of surprising pleasure that means the past is cut off and the experience is totally in the present. So that too is a break in time, a catastrophe. It is a time when permanence and endurance break. This understanding of time—time as break and experience in the present—would be a whole new way of understanding and thinking about the other community.

But somehow these words are not the right words. I was struck by watching the tube and seeing the horrifying sights of the civilian massacres in Lebanon. I was wondering, watching the news, what would it be like if I was suddenly trapped in a war. I have never been in a war. What does it mean to suddenly have a foreign country bomb you, civilians, your children, your homes, your roads. It is a total catastrophe for those people. You have seen them on the tube, these people are hysterical with grief, their families, their children, their husbands are killed. That gave me such a sense of catastrophe.

In my life I have always done whatever I have wanted to do. I get this from my father. He was a peasant in Lithuania. He escaped, by hiding in a hay wagon by night, into Prussia in 1910. Somehow he made a way to America without knowing a word of English. He had never been to school, he didn't know how to write. That always gave me the idea that I could do anything. I had this completely privileged position as an academic because I got my first job by mail. And Penn State University later came to me and asked me to apply. To my surprise they gave me tenure. So I had a life that was somehow very determined, and very quickly I realized I could go anywhere in the world on a fluke. This is very privileged on my part and then today I was thinking about this sense of catastrophe. On the tube these people are hysterical with grief and they didn't even enlist in the war. I have this sense that my life has never known a catastrophe.

II

DEPARTURES: SINGULAR AND COMMON REALITIES

I came to the Ganges at Varanasi, like everyone else, to die. Not knowing how old I was nor how young I was yet to be. There I knew you, Gopal Hartilay. You came to me at sunset, frail boy out of so many thousands of Hindus, each silent and alone, descending into the holy river to consign to it the sweat and dirt and fatigue of the day, as, one day, to consign to it the sweat and dirt and fatigue of life. You took me by the hand to the Manikarnika ghat, where among the garlanded cows we watched the fires whisper over the bodies of the dead, and the kites and nightjars circling overhead. One day you will be burned there, and your ashes swept into the strong arms of the river.... How little I understood of it; it was enough for me to watch your black eyes catch the last rays of the sun. When it got completely dark they shone still as you rowed back to the city, where we went to eat a banana leaf of rice under an aswatha tree full of sleeping monkeys.... We stopped at the Durga temple, where you wanted me to contribute something for a blood sacrifice to Kali, who took your mother and father with cholera the year you were born, but who wants you here still. How did I come so far, through so many dense crowds, to find you? What law dictated that you chose to be my friend?

—*"Cargo Cult,"* Excesses

The "Wow, it's you!" with which one responds is an exclamation that breaks the commerce of messages and that responds with a surge of sensuality and with a greeting that is laughter or weeping, blessing or cursing. An exclamation that, by its tone, communicates.... Something passes between one sensuality accomplice to another. Something was understood; the password among accomplices was recognized. Something was said that made you the accomplice of the one that is one of his kind: quetzal bird, savage, aboriginal, guerilla, nomad, Mongol, Aztec, sphinx.

—*"Faces, Idols, Fetishes,"*
The Community of Those Who Have Nothing in Common

Chapter Eight

Limits, Borders, and Shores of Singularity

Jean-Luc Nancy

What is singularity? As what has place at only one instance, one single point—outside time, outside place—it is, in short, an exception. Not a particularity returning to its genre, but a unique, almost exclusive, propriety that escapes all attempts at appropriation, and which, as such, is not even removed from a common element and is not even opposed to itself.

Dasein is singular. The existent whose only place is *je-mein*—in each case mine. It is not necessary to think that this "mine" is marked by the sense of a representation of the "self." The "each case" is the always singular occurrence that determines the instance (or the chance) of a "subject," i.e., what is nothing other than the upsurge of its enunciation (of a "saying 'I'" and not of a "telling oneself, claiming oneself"), of its enunciation and/or of its presentation (in sum, the *ego sum, ego existo* of Descartes).

In this sense, the singular only has a place when it has place. It is bound up with a sudden appearance that implies a correlative and consecutive—in truth, a quasi-simultaneous—disappearance. The singular is hardly different from the case of "saying 'I,'" barely separated from the space-time of a stroke of lightening, that is, from the space-time of a life. A life, an existence: between birth and death, the time of being outside oneself so as to be oneself, oneself excepted from oneself always and only in death.

For this very reason *singuli*, in Latin, is said only in the plural: it is the unity of one for one, as things come "in each case." The "in each case" of exceptional existence implies a double articulation: the different instances of the same "I" *and* those of different "I's" whose multiplicity is a priori present in the difference that one I should make in order to be an *I*, that is to say, present precisely in singularity.

In this manner, the coexistence of singularities as constitutive of existence in all its aspects and in general (and, even more, not only of those we call "mankind," but of all beings) is posed a priori—transcendentally or existentially in a sense that neither Kant, nor Heidegger, despite their having foreseen it, ever entirely established. The existential exception implies the rule of a universal coexception.

This transcendental or existential should also be recognized in what Marx, until now, has been the only one to formally designate: the social production of man, or better, to be more precise, the natural-social production of man and nature. By "social production," one must understand above all not a dimension adjoining or supplementing something that from the start and in itself would comprise "man" or "nature." On the contrary, one must understand, well ahead of representations of the operations of production (work or exchange), the singular plural constitution of existence: the fact that existence comes to light in the space-time of its existing, *through*, *in*, and *as* plural singularity. This does not occur in a distinct manner, with "man" on one side and "nature" on the other, but through what is an already existential sharing, one that carries with it the instance of a work and an exchange themselves a priori.

•

The thought of singularity has become necessary for us in the same measure as the collapse of representation, according to which unity had been thought, in the final instance, as unitary rather than as unicity, as synthesizing rather than as distributive, as monovalent and monotelic rather than as polyvalent and polytelic—or, more so, as beyond value and *telos*. The word "collapse" is no accident. It is, in a new sense, the very reason for our history, its reopening and its revival, if I may be permitted to say so in this manner.

The "social-natural production of man and nature," or even what I shall highlight in a moment through the more nuanced expression of a *creation technique of the singular plural world*, is what thinking demands of us at the start of the twenty-first century.

•

The singular implies its own limit. It does more than imply its limit: the singular poses its limit with itself, it poses itself as its limit, and it poses the limit as *its own*. To be *jemeinig*, to be "mine" or "his or hers," not "in each case" in the sense of at all times and always, but on the contrary according to the discontinuity and discretion of *time*, of the space-time or having-place that is always outside-time-outside-place. It is not unending, but according to cessation, interruption, and interval. An interval separates the singular so that it can be singular, if one can say so in terms so apparently final.

Because, without doubt, this does not concern a finality, it is not appropriate to say that the singular would be an end of nature (or of history or God). Rather, in the transcendental-existential regime that I outline, the singular is the condition of possibility (or of necessity—or even, beyond this opposition, a free provenance, liberation itself, i.e., from nothing, from being in general without end).

Though we are not concerned with finality, it is, on the other hand, finitude which constitutes, in these conditions, the very essence of singularity. Finitude yields to understanding not as a limitation or lack in reference to infinity, but on the contrary as the proper mode of access to being or sense. In singular finitude the sharing of being and sense is given place—of the sense of being, or the being of sense—a sharing that neither overcomes nor effaces the limits or ends of the singular. This sharing, on the contrary, distributes them and does so, in each case, according to their exception. An eminently affirmative finitude of what is *unending in a nonprivative sense*.

•

It is therefore necessary to examine this very particular nature or constitution that the limit or end of the singular possesses. Without this examination, we will not be able to know what there is of the plural singularity, i.e., with it, of being-in-common which we make or found (that we share) and whose comprehension remains still torn between integration, or fusion, with the interior of a commonality and a narrowing and absolutizing in an encompassing individuality. Ordinary representation remains caught between these two poles, for which, according to its strongest architecture, there is more than one reason in the very structure of Occidental thought. Perhaps, in effect, what has been called the Occident has been nothing other, since its birth, than the dissolution of a certain *given* state of being-together. More exactly, what in myth and in rite is given to the group. This signifies, therefore, that to think singularity is necessarily to think outside of myth—there is neither myth nor rite for the singular—and also to the extremity of metaphysics in Nietzsche's sense, to this extremity to which Marx, once again, signaled the point of inflection when positing the "social nature of man" as an object for ontology, i.e., its nonnaturality, and through this the nonnaturality of the world in general and its singular plural constitution.[1]

•

Of what sort then is the limit that limits and singularizes the singular?

I propose to approach this question through the combination of three notions: limit, border, and bank. It seems to me that the play or the braiding of these three notions perhaps opens up an initial view upon singular finitude, on this finitude that forms both the singular's discrete plurality and its infinite sense or truth.

From the very start, finitude gives itself to thought as limit. The limit is the end, the extremity beyond which there is nothing more—nothing more, at least, of the thing or the being of which one reaches the limit. The limit is the end insofar as it places end, that it sanctions an achievement which is also a cessation and an interruption if nothing comes to justify in right the arising of this end. The end of a story bases itself in right through the very organization of the story, just as the limits of a painting are ordained by the conception of the image, and not by the imposition of an arbitrary order. But the end of existence—its double end of birth and death, simultaneously symmetric and asymmetric, only begins and is completed by interruption, therefore by incompletion. No reputedly "natural" or "technological" processes can provide for a completion that is not an interruption, beginning and ending (and therefore neither beginning nor ending) in the universe *ex nihilo* and in leading humanity with it *in nihilum*....(one understanding that everything here turns on the question of "nihilism"!).

The completion, the truly *final* end, can occur only in the measure that one end—*telos*—corresponds with one end-limit. But if the singular is atelic, its limit cannot complete it. The limit circumscribes it, rigorously, but it circumscribes it in an incompletion that is essential to it. Essential, its incompletion is also its completion. A completion without end, *sine die*.

In this sense, one will never reach the limit—or, better, one is always already exposed and one does not cease to touch, i.e., to approach it, to brush against it, and to thereby remain distant. Birth and death strictly limiting my existence and defining as infinitesimal the access this existence has to its primary reason and final end. This definition by and in the infinitesimal constitutes the finite singularity.

Always and never affected, the limit is in sum both inherent to and exterior to the singular: it is ex-posed. It is immediately and conjointly the strict contour of an "inside" *and* the design or outline of an "outside." In itself, the limit is nothing. The Latin *limes* designates the way that traverses the length of a domain. One side of the domain appearing to the *dominium*, the other appearing to an other, or to the public *dominium*, or even to a *no-man's-land* that escapes all *imperium*. The way itself is the limit. Or, rather, it is again and again the unknowable median line of the way or the breadth of its width. The limit is thus an interval, separated and yet without thickness, that spaces out the plurality of singulars. The limit is their mutual exteriority and the circulation between them.

As a consequence, the limit is also what singulars have in common. In other words, they share in the inexistence of a line or the undecidability of a distance. Existents sharing the negativity of a common path, upon which each singularity imprints something of itself while at the same time withdrawing from it. The path leads toward no common destination, neither as a point of departure nor totality: it plays only upon the overture between them, the circulation between all, the contact and distance between finitudes. The limit is the "nothing-in-common" through which communication takes place: if one wishes, the sharing of birth and death, and therefore that of a *nothing* or a "negativity without use"—to use an expression of Bataille's that could equally be transcribed as: "sense without signification." But this sharing of an outside deprived of substance and signification nonetheless contains its own possibility of co-existence and the necessity of co-existence in the very definition of existence in general.

•

In this manner, the circulation of the limit passes and crosses between two borders. It separates and reunites border to border what it de-limits, i.e., beings. The limit is nothing, but it has or it separates two distinct borders, much in the same way as a geometrical line, while possessing no thickness, still has no fewer than two sides. The property of a limit, in-itself without properties, that forms an extraterritoriality in reference to all property, consists in its doubling, what can also be called its excess: a distinction between the borders, an evasion of the "nothing" on its two borders.

The border is an extremity where a structure comes to a stop. In the origins of the French word—both Norse and Saxon—it is from the very beginning the "hull" of a boat, and in general an extremity, much like a cut off board or plank. The border has partly the nature of a limit: an incision, a division, that in itself is nothing, that makes or works the nothing of a separation. Yet, on the other hand, the border has the consistency of what has been cut off, according to the law of division, and therefore of a trace conforming to the limit and actually giving, not only an outline, but also a relief that constitutes the contour of a singularity.

Through the border the limit makes contact or makes contact with itself. At the limit, singulars are border to border. In this way, they touch, i.e., they separate themselves from nothing—more exactly, from nothing that they have in common. The borders are the ones for the others in a double rapport of attraction and repulsion. Through the border, one approaches the other border, that is, surrenders to a collision. Precisely by colliding with the other side, until spread only in the nothing of its limit, one can also go beyond. This depends upon the energy, the impetuosity with which one dashes forward.

The border is the part or dimension that exposes or has exposed the singular. It exposes at the limit, in the end it is the limit itself, not in the sense of a line with no thickness, but insofar as the side is, first of all, the appearance and aspect of a delimited being. On the border, the limit is something or someone. It becomes the nothing configured, an existent or an other, or even this or that space-time of a single existent. The configuration of a nothing is the fashioning of an end. If one can say: nothing insofar as *something* (not "something rather than nothing," but much more, and more problematically, "something form nothing," "a thing of nothing"—something or some*one*). In this way, nothing departs from nothing exposed, presented or represented, addressed or alongside, confronted or affronted (perhaps, in this manner, touching upon the connection between *nothing* and thing [*res*]).

In exposing and being exposed, the configuration of a border retains what it contains. It is the border of a content, the end of a defined, and the horizon that it in this manner presents. Contrary to the limit, the border has a thickness and this amasses until it approximates the thing and its other borders. It is otherwise impossible to determine if a being has several borders or only one, the same as to discern if, how, and where a border is external or internal, being moreover always one or the other in some fashion. The unique limit pluralizes itself there by singularizing itself. The border or borders resemble the consistency of a substance and hold it firm in itself. This is also why borders, by uniting, permit resemblance: the identification of a figure, always singular but each time the figure *of* the same substance or subject, traced of the same limit that finitude hollows out in the middle of the same substance, rendering it in this way inaccessible and restoring it to the endless circulation between singularities. Through these borders, every subject overflows itself and is only, each time, in this excess. ("Subject," here, should be understood as referring to every being, material substance or being-for-itself.)

•

On the border, the limit thus loses and recovers itself in the same movement. This movement is the gesture of the singular. It is its ownmost impulse, its thrust, the force of its singularization, what has place each time that it has place (and this "each time" is equally, in some sense, both permanent and intermittent, continuous and discrete; this movement is frequent—it is the frequency through which the singular vibrates, its own wavelength—and yet infrequent—the rarity and brevity of its singular manifestation, of its own radiance).

This force is not an attribute of the singular. Rather, the singular constitutes it. *Singulus* is formed, in its first element *sin-*, from the root *sem*, which designates the one (as in *simplex*, and already there, the one as things come, not the one—*unus* of unicity) and, in its second element, from another root, traceable to the gothic *ainakis*, whose sense is of eagerness, enthusiasm, and impetuosity.

With or without *etymon*, the singular singularizes itself in the impulse that it produces, or, better, by which it overcomes itself. It is itself the force, the *impetus* or the *conatus* that knows or allows to be known through one "time" (an occasion, an occurrence, a chance, an encounter, a good or bad hour, a *kairos*, i.e., nothing inasmuch as favor, radiance, the contingency of being and of sense).

Through its radiance, the singular tears itself away from the continuous—i.e., in the first place, from unity in the sense of unicity and indifferentiation. It uproots the one (*sem-*) of *a time* with the one of no time. It brings out *time* itself, the circumstance, the occasion, i.e., the *case* or occurrence of a unitotality that knows no case (and which does not exist), or of a universality that would not make the world, that is to say, a differential overture of sense. Otherwise said, the singular assumes the limit, it gathers there and borders the excess and its force. The limit is nothing given in advance. It redraws itself at each birth, at each death, and at each singular appropriation of *Jemeinigkeit*. The border is the completion, the body, i.e., being outside of self, the matter and the force of an existence, its fragile upsurge and hard effacement within the nothing that it has bordered for an instant. But this nothing is nothing other than the indefinite totality of forces which it traverses. From it, returning to it, the nothing is snatched from existents, from the concrete radiance of sense.

•

These forces, or this unique, discontinuous force, open the limit and detach the borders. The border as separation, wrenching, forms a *bank*. *Ripa* comes from a root meaning rift. It also comes close to the Greek *ereipein* (to fall, to collapse) and *eripné* (slope, side). A *bank* is separated or hollowed out, furrowed, by the water which falls past it and from which it gets in return its name *river*. The bank is an elevation through excavation and through fall or decline. Inclined, sloped, sometimes torn, the bank resembles something of a ruin (in Greek, *ereipia*, and one can suppose, in common with *ereikô*, the root *rei*— to tear up, break, or smash). The stream flows into the river and this into the sea: banks become shores. No longer are there only two opposed borders, but an interminable sinuosity of sides from out of which the land emerges. Or, better, the emergence of all lands is exposed to the liquid, mobile elements, both another place and no place, separating the places, huge width, absolute breadth, remote.

The shore appears as what is nearest, the *here* where I hold myself in surety and from where I can see the difficulties and perils of those who are abandoned, on the brink of subjugation, to the sea and winds (it is the *suave mari magno* of Lucretius, who, not by chance, holds a gnomic place in our culture).

However, the shore can also appear as what is most distant, as what lies beneath the horizon, from where another world approaches, both dreaded in its strangeness and hoped for as an assurance of yet another border from the perilous elements, as the possible term of a *traversing*—which is the fundamental meaning of experience—that is to say, as the chance of *arriving* upon some other shore, close to another proximity.

The shore is the place from where one departs and upon which one lands: a place that is neither exactly limit, nor border (neither the negativity of the trace, nor the positivity of force), but passage, the broken up, frayed side of a rock crumbling into the sand, mixing with the froth and soil, sliding into the water where the strait gives way.

This can also be the passage of speech, the sonorous sense that reaches out to the other: Mallermé, for example, speaks of lips as the "rose shores."

In mythology, *Actéon* is the hero of the shore. He tells himself *akté*. As we know, he is changed into a stag by Artemis, who surprises him in a bath, and is then devoured by his own dogs. Jean-Pierre Vernant understands this myth as the experience of the passage from adolescence to adulthood. Delacroix painted this scene by placing the protagonists on the two banks of a narrow, turbulent river.

To think the singular plural should be to think the rift of a bank, the experience of setting off for the distant and uncertain, with the peril of the crossing and with the possibility of being pulled off course in addition to that of arriving. The other shore has been, in the best of myths, what one would find on the other side of death. Where there is no longer a myth to represent another world than this one, and when this world, on the contrary, disposes itself in a reticulated geometry of singular worlds, the ones entirely exposed for the others, the other bank is always the shore of the other singular, and the other bank of death is still this world, otherwise broken up, otherwise accosted. Existence holds itself in this cartography of being border-to-border and dispersed in an ocean that is every time another and the same world at once, only configured around a different shore.

All existents are rivers, i.e., river-dwellers of the same waters and for that rivals, those who together claim the favors of a single source. This rivalry places the singulars at the borders of war and the competition for excellence, on the edges of desire, appropriation, extortion and exchange, on the edge of a cold rupture of some feverous contagion, on that of a general equivalence or even absolute value, one incommensurable and unconvertible. To think this general rivalry without either suppressing or stirring it up, it is necessary to invent a thought of the banks, of their borders and their limits: a thought of extremes, of an existence extreme in its finitude.

The world of shores with no banks other than the mutual exposition of all shores would appear to us as the most shattered world, the one most exposed to its own conflagration. This is a world where at every moment the bank risks disappearing as a place of passage and arrival, as a place to go beyond the one in another, of an element in its contrary or of life in death. A world where the bank and the ruin compete.

At the place of the shore, the border hardens and the limit solidifies. This concerns frontier and closure, boundary and rampart, ring or wound. Finitude exacerbates itself in a bad infinity or even in non-sense. No redemption is here possible. There is neither tragic truth nor the movement of history. On the Occidental shore, it seems that one can only embark upon the limitless ocean of nihilism.

But this is our shore, it still falls to us to face, to hold and to think this murky and abyssal element. We have always wanted to depart and traverse, always searched for a way to drift off and pull away from our peninsulas. We recognize ourselves in the cape and the promontory, in the bluff, the point where the bank drops off. It comes back to us to recover this adventure, to reappropriate the risks of extremes. The world of singularities still remains to be opened up and mapped, the banks to be retraced: to interpret *and* to transform this new world.

This can begin if we remain watchful upon the shore, attentive to the night and to the unlimited obscurity of the ocean where the sun of the Occident sets. Not, perhaps, so as to await some always uncertain dawn, but so as to adjust our gaze and our hearing to an unforeseen truth, to the night itself and the proximity of the far-off in it. The ones for the others refer us to Rilke's verse:

> Make of me the warden of your spaces,
> Make of me the lookout on her boulder
> Give to me the eyes I would embrace
> The solitude of your seas;
> Let me follow the coursing of rivers,
> With them to distance myself from the crying banks
> And sink into the nocturnal tumult.[2]

English translation by Michael Sanders, Department of Philosophy, State University of New York at Stony Brook, Stony Brook, NY 11794

Notes

1. Karl Marx, 1844 Manuscripts.

2. *Le Livre de la Pauvrete et la Mort*, in *Oeuvres Poetique et Theatrical*, trans. J. Crespy (Paris: Gallimard, 1987). [*The Book of Hours* (1905), English translation by Peter Vere Warden.]

Chapter Nine

Dream of a Blind Sculptress

Gerald Majer

The dream goes like this.
  I'm in a city, perhaps London, Chicago, New York. There's a woman, a pretty woman. She doesn't resemble anyone I know. She's an artist, a sculptress, and she's blind. She has a gallery, in this same place I've moved. It's as though she's followed me here out of love.
  In the morning we're in bed together. The idea is we don't have to worry about the kids—they don't get up until 2:45 or so.
  The idea of her body, the sensation, is that she can't see you, all is touch, but she also *hears*, of course.
  She knows many things—a line like that.
  Then there's another woman, maybe an old girlfriend, she wants to see me, too.
  The last image is the sculptures—the figures are prone, and are like bodies sizzling out of the stone, the marble, bubbling over.
  My first take on this dream connects it to having trouble sleeping. I live in a fairly noisy neighborhood, directly across the street from a tavern that closes at two in the morning. Often enough people call out, shouting back and forth on the way to their cars or on their way home; sometimes there's a loud argument, trouble. After two years I'm more or less accustomed to the sounds, but once in awhile, especially if I'm restless—allergy problems, too many thoughts turning through my mind—the noises break into my sleep. I'm annoyed when that happens because the immediate thought is to go downstairs and make sure all is well, no one's up to anything, the doors are locked, and the windows secured. Once I'm done with pondering, dismissing, and finally making the inspection, I'm wide awake. I look out at a street that's already empty, the noisemakers gone home, the lights off on the tavern sign with a figure of a green pool-player on it preparing to make a shot. It seems I'm the only one in the neighborhood still about, night-watching over a sudden quiet of sidewalks and doors and windows, not a soul in sight. Thoughts start rolling, an hour passes before I drift off again, and all the while I'm

angry about being awakened, worried about not getting enough rest, anxious too about being worried, not being able to relax.

I suspect, then, that the dream was an attempt at protecting my sleep. The disturbing sounds were managed in a way that incorporated them into sleep instead of letting them disturb it (though ultimately I was awakened; was it by the noise, or by the dream itself?). The dream served a very basic wish—for me to keep sleeping, to get my rest, to avoid annoyance and anger and anxiety. It did this first by offering a fantasy satisfaction of other wishes that the wish to sleep could lean on. The first wish: to be in a major city, to be where things were happening, someplace important, interesting, of a higher status than other places (to my mind, that is). Not Baltimore, where I am, but one of the big ones, Chicago or New York. Second wish: patently egotistical and so continuing in the same strain—to be pursued by a woman, to be that important, that desirable, that powerful. And the kind of woman she is—the artist, the sculptress—is yet more gratifying: a successful person, highly successful, with a gallery of her own in a place like New York. (This desire is echoed by the other woman's pursuing me as well.) Along the same lines, the erotic component is pretty obvious: the blind sculptress suggests a kind of ultimate lover and thus is a character certain to keep me inside the dream with a promise of some unimaginable bliss, her realm one of pure *touch*.

Granted the protective function of these images—they're saying something like Well look, you're so great, nothing can bother you, including those noises at the edge of sleep, that business outside that's just about to wake you up—I get a sense that the blind sculptress may be more complicated. First, it might be that the character in the dream embodies what I want—to be lacking in one of the senses; to be insensible not to sight per se but to what is going on outside, the noise that perhaps I'm hearing in my sleep and that's right on the verge of waking me. The blind sculptress in this case would be an image of how I want to shape my own condition in sleep so that I'll remain deaf to those potentially disturbing noises.

And of course there's more to say, really no end of things. The blind sculptress suggests a comforting maternal image of total acceptance: her favoritism—like blind faith, I suppose—might be a judgement that sees me objectively, fairly, like blind Justice (herself a sculpture if not a sculptress) who views things neutrally. The figure of Justice leads me to think of another, also connecting a woman, stone or statues, and matters of sight and blindness. The Medusa: I remember yet, as though memory itself was astonished into a particular vividness, the first image of her I saw in a childhood storybook, an illustrated treatment of the Greek heroes and myths. On the colored page—they were weak tints, product of some inexpensive process and washed unevenly over the pen-and-ink drawings—her raving face was a chalky white. It was as though she as well as the men who were her victims had the character of stone. The blind sculptress pursuing me, the marbles agitated into a frozen burning perhaps like the serpent curls of her wild hair—was the dream some face of the Medusa still following me?

Yet the feeling of the dream was not one of terror; it was no nightmare but rather, as I noted to myself in the morning, a very satisfactory dream. There was an exhilaration in it, a delight, even though in retrospect those sizzling statues seem a possibly sinister image. As a child the story of Perseus always had delighted me. Standard fare—the impossible task assigned to the young hero, the power of his various magical devices, an ingenious victory over the castrating dangerous feminine in the guise of the Medusa. Considering more closely the elements of the story I can trace a few resonances with my dream. The helmet of invisibility, for example—one of Perseus' three gifts from the nymphs—is the helmet of Hades, lord of the Underworld, the dead. The helmet is said to give Perseus the face of a shade, a ghost. In my desire to sleep undisturbed, was it such a helmet—rather like a pillow over my head—that I wanted to put on? Thus the blind sculptress and the marble figures would connect from another direction to my wish for sleep: like Perseus I would not be seen, would in fact be like one of the dead, myself a part of the night rather than a creature of day waking into the middle of it.

I can explain the other two gifts of the nymphs—the sandals of instant flight, the hunter's pouch for carrying the slain Medusa's head—in a similar way. Instant flight, the power to move anywhere and everywhere one desires, speaks of my ambitious desires to be in some other city and to be judged favorably, as well as my sleeper's desire simply to escape the noises in the street that are disturbing me. I have the power to be somewhere else, without transition, immediately. And perhaps in the hunter's pouch the head I'm carrying is not Medusa's but my own—a head removed from the seat of its life, the body, and hence in one regard insensible, sleeping like a rock, perhaps too like the rock that Medusa's head turns men into when they gaze upon her face.

Having gone this far in considering the dream of the blind sculptress I realize that while my interpretations have as their general trend a demystifying of my desires and my pretensions, at the same time the very analysis of the dream in such detail becomes a sort of self-inflation, as though the exposure of so many and such insistently elaborated meanings testifies, just as the dream seemed to do, to my own importance. And by now many readers will have elaborated some counterinterpretation that strips away yet further my pretensions. But what if the dream isn't about me after all? It could be that my procedure so far has been blinded by the presupposition that the dream served only to protect my sleep, to excite and assuage my desires and fears. Perhaps the dream in one respect had nothing to do with me. Perhaps the dream was in some sense about itself.

How could a dream be about itself? It sounds like nonsense, since someone is the dreamer and thus the dream must have some connection to the condition of the one who is dreaming. But perhaps this someone would not be me, but only "someone," an aspect of the dream's own grammar, like a subject of a predicate. Someone is dreaming—this might mean, a dream happens, and its happening involves "someone" in the position of the dreamer. A dream might just be an emotive and imagistic machinery that runs on its own, a language that speaks itself without necessarily being centered on the desires and fears of the subject, on the I or me.

In the story of Perseus and Medusa, one of the dangers of the Gorgon is the extreme difficulty of approaching her, of ever surprising her. This is so because

Medusa, even when sleeping, always had one eye open—an eternal insomnia. This detail points to a disturbing possibility—that in approaching the dream of the blind sculptress there is a danger of paralysis, perhaps a blind narcissism in which interpretation would go on endlessly with its reference the security and the pleasure of the ego-self and thus no chance then of ever coming to anything beyond what the eye would see of the I. The dream would be sculpting a form of blindness paradoxically comprised by my eye, my I, in its self-surveillance.

About itself—but how? My thought stops here, and I'm tempted to return to more comfortable concepts. Couldn't the blind sculptress have been, for example, a shadow-image of elements of myself I deny—perhaps the realm of touch and intuiting as contrasted to vision and analytical rationality? Then the sizzling statues would represent a potential awakening of a neglected aspect of myself, the hard marble precipitating into a new activity of life, some buried or repressed energy breaking out of its freeze.

And yet: in the story of Perseus, Medusa is mastered through the bronze shield which is used as a mirror. Not looking upon her face directly, Perseus is able to behead the Gorgon, to gain the power of her terror for himself. So the Medusa, and perhaps the blind sculptress, suggest that one can never really see what lies beyond the I of the dream. One can only see its image, its copy in the mirror, itself an equivocal thing, would-be sign of one's mastery but nonetheless an image still infected with a barely contained power of astonishment.

In that mirror—which I imagine would cling to the touch, fogged with a heat or clouded with a mortal cold—the blind sculptress is perhaps dreaming. Not of me, but only dreaming.

Royan, 1928: Roger Caillois

What exactly are the trees that bend there in the wind, what is the precise texture of the dissolving sound of the waves on the beach?

The leaves are like coins thrown across the light, on every one a writing of its single existence, tracking of veins and spading or toothing of its edge, a skin smooth or grating or surprisingly dense, thick with green juices, a thing trembling and rolling and bending in its body's exposure to the sun and wind and the mild salt air of Royan. A soliciting of the eyes and of the other senses, too—the smell of sand and trees and sea moving out beyond like a drifting ship along with the halting march of the schoolboy's walk here at the seaside, the tread of his boots on the wooden planks sounding against the murmuring tongues of the leaves, a sort of music that verges on a desire to leap into the air or to fall down in terror and which infiltrates the swing of his arms drawing the wind closer to him even as he feels he sails across and through it. The press of the air on the delicate skin of his face is beginning to form a mask: he doesn't only see the world but the world sees itself through him; he is the blind mirror of the wind and the leaves and the sea. With a second surge of the wind, another shivering rattling of the trees, he is becoming its writing, its word, poem that strings across the air, turns back, verses, again, again, through imagings and soundings, an unspoked wheeling axled by the caesuras of the wind, the leaves, the freshening trail of some recompounded scent of wood and water, sloshing and draining of the sea toward him, away from him, the staggered collapse of the waves, their pacings, a calling to his feet to walk farther, to relinquish the orderly path of the boardwalk and like some boy from the village run heedlessly to the beach as if there is not a moment to spare.

For an instant he imagines doing it—his boots removed, his bare feet pounding the sand, his heart pounding too. Without a shred of dignity, his smooth naked feet doubling and mocking his delicate hands, usurping their rule, an apparition of his body revolved in some helpless cartwheeling before the maddening stalling, the bland foaming avarice of the sea.

Yet he keeps walking. In back of everything he does today, he hears a thin wailing, a tone inside his own ear or floating somewhere on the fine summer air almost oppressively lucid in the Mediterranean sun.

On the whitewashed wall of his room, a sort of crucifixion. The body of the death's-head moth. Unlike the leggy, organic-plastic form of the mantis, that pure machining, the moth had a formidable weight about it—a flocked thickness, a density as of a severed finger. In the excitement of the capture—walking past the neglected orchard, he had caught a subtle motion along one of its avenues, inside the damp sweet air a folding and unfolding like a book in the wind—he had nearly damaged the superb specimen of *Acherontia atropos*. His collector's avidity had given way to near-paralysis, his fingers going numb as he positioned the silken net, the eyed wings distracting and confusing his usually effortless method so he finally swooped down clumsily, blindly.

Yet when in his room he had carefully peeled away the net, the moth had been miraculously intact—perfect, the fine dusting of its wings; perfect, the enclosing irises that rayed through chromatics of sun and blood and that flashed for an instant a bluish tinge across the blind stare of the ocelli, their flat and absolute black.

He had fallen back on his bed, the same bed where he tried to dream while waking, to experience the precise moment of the slide from everyday consciousness into a world of the night. In that world, one hovered over life and death like the moth in the orchard, the air and the trees and the scent of the leaves melting together with one's own body, some kind of writing or tattooing inscribing landscapes and trails and then swiftly erasing them, each instant a suspended fluttering, drag and pulsation and opening again of a tracking, colors helplessly vibrating, somewhere a resonant flute-tone heavy as a syrup.

Some confused trail had led there—to his room quiet with its light, the sounds of the villagers outdoors, the sea airs touching through the shutters. A brief spasm, a frenzy in which a sexual current had galvanized the clinical pleasures of handling the specimen, managing the silver tongs and the killing-jar supersaturated with cyanide. Gazing into that jar and the fateful white floor under its glass—the glass as hard as ice, the poison as pure as Alpine snow—he had witnessed many times the final convulsions of living beauty, the awful instant when the ghost was given up, the wings settling down into the first magnificence of death. Today, however, he felt not only the usual distracted stirring but also a fast rising in his blood, a thrust of which he was warden and prisoner, a thrust that carried itself through in the stab of the mounting-pin through the live body of the moth and its brutal affixing to the frame over the window.

When he managed the capture, the moth, unbelievably, had released a tiny sound of dismay, a minuscule but almost-human scream—sound of an etching or cutting into glass protected with a heavy cloth, or of a voice on some remote unreachable mountain-peak broadcasting its disaster. In his room, later, the thick body in his hand electric with its expiring life, the pin between his soft fingers, he heard the sound again. A piercing subsonic kind of cry, issuing from an uncertain location—the moth's body or his own dry mouth whistling out his breath.

As the evening comes on, he continues his strolling on the boardwalk and the wall alongside the sea. He cannot eat, cannot go to his room and rest. He can only walk, an extended pacing like that of a deluded man who imagines himself a general or admiral, pondering some vague conquest and watching for some equally vague threat looming on the horizon. He feels everything as if it is collecting itself in back of him. He recalls the unsettling notion (from a teacher or shopkeeper, a pompous uncle) of *having eyes in the back of one's head*, feels as though his forward progress as it slips insensibly into a circular procession—the stalls, the beach, the seawall, the temptation every moment to turn around just here, here, but then going on anyway to the end—might soon become something altogether delirious, insensibly transformed into a mad walking in reverse.

Eyes in the back of his head—it would first be a stumbling, his arms stretched out like wings searching for purchase, balance, and then a lugubrious perambulation among the forward-pressing bodies of the thickening summer evening crowd here along the quay. The gaze of those backward other eyes would not be of the light and the day but rather of the dark and night; they would be eyes that would not see but be seen; eyes that would not blink but instead be swimming among the sea of faces like some feverbacillus, germ of a swooning. One must be overcome by the crush of drowsy and eager bodies in the summer air; one must be overcome by a discomposing odor, a deathscent, of warm human skin; one must be overcome by the bare possibility of showing that other face and by the bare possibility of the one who would see it.

Come with me, she says, the girl, the woman, there near the green-painted benches, hot silver of the evening star and the stopped turmoil of the sea behind her. *Come with me*, she says again. *You'll have a good time. I promise.* Her voice, like her eyes, is languid and sleepy as though it is through her body that she gazes on his anxious gesture, droops inexorably as a flower at his silence, his refusal of her. He flees into the crowd, the soft milling of the night. There are bonfires now along the strand, red fireworks wasting their light in guttering sparks over a distant pier. When he finally reaches the trolley-station he finds the mob there at its thickest, the air heavy as a dream, her face perhaps somewhere still seeking him, her body drifting toward him through the brief spaces that open in the crowd, close up again, convulsive valving of some fragmented heart, blind tearing of an impossible eye he dreams upon as he breathes the cooler air of empty streets where he walks beneath the ranks of the lamps, follows the rays of their boxed flames.

But one must be overcome. Later, he will go with another, older woman. Learn her rages and knowledges, her seductive talk of dreams, clouds of unknowing, books of hermetica, dark religions of the stars. She told him she had killed a man, a lover, with a magic mirror. He imagines that mirror as the breastplate of a machine-creature, a woman-body fetishized and transformed by some sustained hypertrophy of the optic nerve: she is all eye. She would exist in an immaculate vision, or a supreme blindness. In this *femme fatale* would be embodied the ultimate secret of his own existence, perhaps of all existence—past all reasons, the tangling of love and death, the necessity of convulsion, an overcoming by the night.

Mimetism and the Imperative

One must be overcome: in some way, this seeming invention of his own mind would transfix Roger Caillois; it would irrevocably mold his writing and his life. Five years after what he viewed as that fateful summer of 1928—he was now twenty years old—he would consider his own dreams and the behavior of the mantis and the moth. Fascinated by mimicry, *mimetisme*, he would write a book (published posthumously) in which he used his own experiences to argue that, beyond biological functionality, mimetism exhibited a strange drive toward pure resemblance—not toward resembling anything in particular, but just toward resembling.[1] Ultimately, all creatures exist not only as discrete entities following their individual trajectories of survival but are marked by what is other than themselves. Solicited by the forces and faces of the worlds through which they pass, they put on masks—not to deceive other creatures but as a form of play, as a movement of spacing by which they differ from themselves, crossing the boundaries of fixed identities. In Caillois's words, "they invent the spaces of which they are the convulsive possession."

Thirty years later, with a broader scientific and sociological approach, he would follow the same idea in another book, *The Mask of Medusa*.[2] Phenomena such as the eyes on the moth's wings are not only useful adaptations which serve to intimidate or defend but are marks of an othering, are evidence of a permeable and uncertain boundary between living things and their worlds. They just resemble: they do not dominate or exploit a space but in the play of mimetism open up spaces, not just in terms of survival and mastery but in terms of a "convulsive possession"; this latter phrase attempts to register the difficult notion of a simultaneous taking-hold and being-taken-hold-of, along with its indefinite oscillation—what in another vocabulary might be called an experience of finitude, a being-toward the world.[3]

In his ethnographic and theoretical work, Michael Taussig has followed this path marked by Caillois.[4] Taussig suggests that we consider culture and representation not in terms of how images can imitate and thus give us a functional mastery over nature but rather in terms of how images relate us to the world's otherness. In the image, Taussig sees a kind of gift exchanged between the world and ourselves: nature is not only ordered and dominated by our inventory of representations; images are born through our yielding or joyfully responding to the world. This is an "active yielding" and a "bodily copying of the other," like what Caillois saw in animal mimicry and in himself. Against our privileging of vision, our insistence upon images as a way of knowing and controlling the world, Taussig proposes we understand images as a way of reconnecting to the world—not in some sentimental fusion but in an encounter with its otherness. Mimetism would be a movement of touching, and of allowing ourselves to be touched by, alterity.

Caillois saw in the figures of the praying mantis and the death's-head moth and the femme fatale a call of his destiny—of "the force of things," of a "lyrical necessity" beyond what would appear in a merely personal-psychological description. Taussig notes too this force of things, the ways the world touches us, the ways we live in the betweens of ourselves and the world, every imitation at the same time a making-contact, every mimesis also a contagion.

The dream of the blind sculptress—rather than an image of personal anxieties and desires, was it instead a call, a directive of the world itself, of my own path or wandering through the world? Was it indeed a call to do what I have been embarked upon in these pages—to try to understand something other than the familiar truths of image and interpretation and to *touch* upon or be touched by something other?

Alphonso Lingis speaks of such directives coming to us in dreams and creative visions, a realm that he distinguishes from the world of doing, the practical sphere of everyday instrumentality.[5] In Lingis's words, the dream brings us to an imperative of the night, "an alien depth and an enigmatic significance." While it may seem that dreams simply repeat and rehearse fragments of everyday experiences and concerns, they possess a different sort of modality. Rather than being made from images of the world's objects molded by the desires and anxieties of the personality, dreams expose a mimetism characteristic of all our experience of the world: "things themselves engender, along with their graspable counters, images of their presence in multiple locations and in impracticable spaces"; "a thing *is*...by engendering images of itself, reflections, shadows, masks, caricatures of itself."

In this view, it appears that our everyday world of work and utility is not primary; instead it is the world of vision and dream that is so: "is not to exist as a sector of the geographical space laid out in perspective simultaneously to exist as a landscape of revery?" In the mimetisms and contagions, the touching-betweens, of the world and ourselves, we invent the spaces of which we are the convulsive possession. Indeed, Lingis argues that "it is because [things] engender carnal, caricatural images of their characteristics...that they also engender a practicable field. Reality is this parturition."

An unsettling idea—the day as perhaps only a partition of the night, waking as perhaps no more than another form of what we call dream-life. And the dream of the blind sculptress—what mask or omen was speaking to me, what in the world was touching me with its demand, its imperative? Perhaps it was the night itself—a mortal night of insomnia, the one eye always open, the world dreaming through or with me in the terror and delight of an active passivity, a profound and disquieting exposure. The blind sculptress: seen rather than seeing, touching rather than grasping, things coming to shape not in the light of a practicable vision but in a contact, a contagion, a clinging of the world to invisible hands themselves made of world.

While such a call of the night may seem to be unpleasant or disturbing, suggestive of anxiety and distress and neurosis, of our fears of life and of death, Lingis asks whether our distress may instead be caused by our insistence upon forcing such experiences into the framework of personal-psychological explanations, our habit of referring all phenomena to the I and its projects and instrumentalizations of the world. Experiences of dreaming and creativity are misconstrued and trivialized by such a habit of explanation. Solicited by the echoes and masks and resonances of the world, by enigmatic directives which materialize in the dream or the creative process, the dreamer and the artist touch and are touched, less creators than created. In the realm of what Lingis calls unpracticable fields—where things double and mimic and dance, where things contagiously touch and are touched—one encounters a call of what is other, of an ordinance that commands.

What is this ordinance which seems to deny what we hold most dear, our autonomy and our freedom, our privilege of making a world? It is a call of the night, the night as opposed to the daylight world of grasping and managing all things to our benefit—that too-familiar world whose law would be our own will, where every thing and every image would be brought to its graspable meaning and its orderly truth. In the realm of the dream we fall prey to uncanny words and images, songs and musics, cryptic soundings which do not serve our practicable purposes, do not function as markers or signals. Communication is no longer the conveyance of a message but a condition in which we are washed over by a motioning of the world—we are caressed, we are shaped and unshaped, sculpted by an indefinite and inscrutable gesture like that of a roiling sea, its heavings and breakings and backwashes a baffling, singular field where we move as we are moved, where we feel that which touches and smooths and roughens and unworks the grain of our existence, the sense of our world. An encompassing night carries us away from the projects and purposes of the day.

In describing the realm of night, Lingis calls us to a reorientation of our world, a facing toward what he names the phantom equator—one which draws us into journeys of wandering, draws us to unpracticable and unaccountable destinies and assignations. Coming to us from this other realm, our dreams are not personal dramas cobbled together from images of everyday experience, nor are they projections and myths of some psychic therapeutics. The dream is born from a "a realm of exteriority that exists with the exteriority of an imperative": the dream, then, may be intersected by the lines of this phantom equator, this tracing of alterity which runs through all of our existence, calling us to the imperatives of an otherness that touches and traverses and exceeds us. The shifting and metamorphosing lines and forces of Lingis's phantom equator would perhaps return us to Freud's image of what is ultimately unknowable in the dream: the floating matrix of the dream-navel beyond which interpretation cannot penetrate, that indeterminate place where the dream-thoughts weave and unweave themselves.[6] The dream's fateful other eye, blind and never-sleeping: that movement of a spacing by virtue of which every word I have written here does not only mean but also records a trembling, an undoing, a being-overcome.

The blind sculptress—is it tears that blind her, tears that would obscure the distinct forms of an intelligible and practicable world, tears in which the shapes of objects and intentions would blur and bind and contagiously melt together, would be born then with the force of a command, a summons—a call to a different world, not the world of project and mastery but of a not-doing, an encounter that changes for us the very definition of world?

In the mirror of these words, she is dreaming. Not of me, but only dreaming.

Someone dreams: dreams the world, the space of which one is the possession in a movement-with, a convulsion of night.

Envoi

On that night of September 22, 1998: my wife sleeping alongside me. Before we drifted off, a play of our hands, our flesh, our bodies, our laughter. Between us a fragile motion, a rippling-through of our forces, a mixing of our breaths and airs, our limbs and skins in a confusion and then a frenzy of passions, ourselves possessed, dispossessed. At first our eyes were open, avid and enjoying; after awhile they closed, slowly, heavily: a black swooning.

Blind to the world, in the night. A night-world where it seems it is we who are seen, are exposed, the sculpting of our hands and our flesh a blind visioning of what might be the lineaments and the mortal weight of what is our birth, what is our death, what is our love.

The world of the dream; the dream of the world.

Notes

1. Roger Caillois, *The Necessity of the Mind*. Trans. Michael Syrotinski (Venice: Lapis Press, 1990).

2. Roger Caillois, *The Mask of Medusa*. Trans. George Ordish (New York: Clarkson Potter, 1964).

3. As in Jean-Luc Nancy; for example, 29-33, *The Sense of the World*. Trans. Jeffrey S. Librett (Minneapolis and London: University of Minneapolis Press, 1997).

4. Michael Taussig, *Mimesis and Alterity* (New York and London: Routledge, 1993).

5. Alphonso Lingis, "Phantom Equator," *The Imperative* (Bloomington and Indianapolis: Indiana University Press, 1998).

6. Sigmund Freud, *The Interpretation of Dreams*. Trans. James Strachey (New York: Allen and Unwin, 1965), ch. 8.

> AUTHOR'S NOTE: *Although this chapter was not written specifically on the work of Alphonso Lingis, nonetheless it is written in the spirit of Lingis's quite unique and moving vision of the world. No one else takes the kinds of intellectual and personal risks as Lingis, while at the same time remaining absolutely sensitive to the personal and conceptual sensitivities of a situation. Risk-taking, or perhaps a better concept is courage and valor, usually involves a kind of bravado, the swaggering moves of a hero, a role-model rendered insensitive to his particularity through his allegiance to a principle or cause. But in Lingis's case, this is the risk of absolute openness, the risk of complete vulnerability, both one's own and in one's understanding of one's own position in the revelation of the other's vulnerability. What Lingis proposes is a kind of raw philosophy, a philosophy that is both thoroughly immersed in its delight of conceptuality while never losing touch with its thorough immersion in the materiality or social, interpersonal, and erotic life, a philosophy adequate to the wildness of being, as rich, complex, and ambiguous as the open unfolding of events and encounters themselves, a philosophy adequate to the naked being of the human. Thus it is for Lingis, and with Lingis, that this paper was written and is presented here.*

Chapter Ten

Naked[1]

Elizabeth Grosz

> [The other's eyes] turn to me a liquid pool waiting for unforeseeable disturbances. They are more naked than the flesh without pelt or hide, without clothing.... They are more naked than things can be, than walls bared of their adornments and revolvers stripped of their camouflage; they bare a substance susceptible and vulnerable. Their nudity exposes them to whatever message I may want to impose, whatever offense I can contrive.
> —Alphonso Lingis, "Imperative Surfaces," Foreign Bodies

1. Mammalian Orchids

Human bodies, indeed bodies of all kinds, are the product of an extraordinary intrication of a nature that must be regarded as considerably more complex, convoluted, emergent, nonlinear, nondeterministic than we had once believed; and a history that cannot be contained in culture alone. This history includes, but is not restricted to, the social, economic, geographical, and representational practices which surround and sustain bodies. But such a history, the history of culture, cannot be conceived as wholly outside of or autonomous from nature, for it is nature, a reconceived and open nature, an evolutionary nature, that both produces all environments, as well the bodies sustained in and by those environments. In a certain sense, it is nature that requires and accomplishes culture, but nature must be conceived as richly open in possibilities rather than rigidly determined in its outcomes, in other words, nature driven not by the forces and closures of the past, but fundamentally directed to the future, a nonteleological or evolutionary nature. A history of culture is in a certain sense the ever-expanding history of nature.

Nietzsche called for a history of culture that would not simply include or focus on scientific, cultural, economic, or military achievements but would explore the self-cultivation of minds and bodies, the human production of itself as a species. In this sense, his work is not entirely alien to that of Darwin and the biological tradition that follows him, though Nietzsche remains ever suspicious of "the school of Darwinism," that is, of Darwin's contemporaries and followers. Every culture and social group, Nietzsche maintained, can be understood not only in terms of its social and cultural products but also in terms of the particularities of its corporeal arrangements and body ideals, its management, representation, and production of bodies, and thus of nature.[2]

Nietzsche claimed that the first artists worked with the noblest of resources, the clay, canvas, and oil of flesh and blood. In a certain sense, they were the founders of culture. The first art is one developed from out of the core of one's own body and its products. This impulse to make something other of oneself, to make one's body other than what it is—the primordial moment of the artistic impulse—is the very explosion of culture itself and the input that such a reconceived nature gives to the human, and the human-yet-to-come. One can see in the products of culture, its technological, political, and scientific achievements the exteriorization of this primitive artist's impulse, the directing outward of this primordial body art. A history of culture *could* be written as the history of the way man makes his body other, and does so indirectly, through the meandering feedback that action and production impose on and as the nature of bodies.

In spite of Nietzsche's self-evident hostility to Darwinism, we find striking confirmation of the bodily origins of art in the work of the more palatable Darwinians. We could see, for example, in the writings of the French paleoanthropologist, André Leroi-Gourhan a detailed elaboration of *homo sapiens*'s increasing externalization of bodily organs in the form of language, art, and technology.[3] What characterizes the human, from the earliest emergence of the human to its present varieties, is the increasing capacity to store the functions of organs, muscles, and neurological processes in external or "technical" devices, prostheses—paintings, tools, machines, religious objects, domestic arrangements, books, computers, and so on. We could, with some liberties, reconstruct Leroi-Gourhan's complex genealogy of human physiology and culture, his account of the technological history of humanity, by dividing it into four broad stages which roughly coincide with the biological evolution of the species. This history reveals the intertwining of, and undecidability between biological-evolutionary and cultural techniques in the transformation of bodies. Bodies and technologies function in a self-feeding relation where transformations in the one produce transformations in the other, which in turn feedback on both. The history of nature and civilization coincide insofar as they are both a function of the bodily impulses which produce and are transformed by technological impulses:

i. This history "begins" with the most primitive use of tools, tools that in the first instance are parts, and then are extensions, of the body itself, and above all, of its privileged organs and functions: cutting, chopping, and grinding—tools modeled, at the outset, on teeth and their capacity for cutting, and on hands, and their capacity for pounding and their various rhythmic operations. The baboon, the chimpanzee, and the ape forage and manipulate using their teeth, and the first baboon and *Australopithecine* implements, forged by chipping stones, branches, or bones between the front legs, exteriorize this function of chewing and grinding. As the four-legged gait gives way to upright posture, the privilege of the teeth and nose give way to the primacy of the eyes and the hands. The mouth no longer explores, encounters, and manipulates nature directly; rather, the legs propel the creature into the world, and its hands serve to mediate between the world it samples and its mouth. It now reacts to a world that is manually organized, and thus considerably more open to movement. The hand/face pairing will eventually in human development prepare the way for a parallel emergence of tools and language.[4] Leroi-Gourhan suggests that the evolutionary path that lead to the emergence of the human originated, not with the development of a larger brain, but rather with the advent of upright posture, that is, with organic transformations in the structure of the foot, which in turn lead to transformations of gait, spinal realignments, the shortening of the face, and the positioning of face and hands as the primary modes of territorial exploration. As he claims "human evolution did not begin with the brain, but with the feet…" (*Gesture and Speech*, 229) Tools exteriorizing and supplementing the atrophying senses (nose, snout, mouth, teeth) emerge, tools that are part of the process of this gradual atrophy of bodily organs and organic functions and their accumulating replacement through prostheses.

ii. Technological history harnesses externally driven motor power, the power of water, winds, and animals, to power the tools thus devised. These devices—the plough, the windmill, the sail—enable a wider locus of control than that available to either the individual's or the group's labor power. The power of vision is even further privileged, insofar as the externally driven forces require regular and careful supervision. In addition, this transfer of energy and force from musculature to external energy sources helps participate in the supercession of muscular power, its reservation for tasks of nobility, piety, and bravery rather than mere survival. Moreover, as Freud hypothesized, with the privileging of the visual and the repression of the sense of smell, sexuality becomes unseasonal, no longer confined to an estrus cycle, no longer inflamed by the enticements proffered by smell but excited by the now-upright creature's visually exposed genitalia.

iii. Replacing the utilization of these rather unpredictable or erratic natural resources comes the invention of machines, nonhuman and nonorganic devices, which are able to be regulated and used with increasing reliability and control. The key image of the controllable machine is the mechanical clock, which is not only a self-regulating mechanism, but also one into which other sorts of mechanical connections could be made, and other, more complex machines devised, a replacement, not only for muscular power but also for efforts of bodily coordination. Another example is the steam engine, while it replaces the brute force of animals and nature it nevertheless requires the neurological input, which is to say, the skills of judgement necessary for the ongoing functioning of such machines. Mechanism has the advantage over external motor power insofar as it requires ever-diminishing surveillance, through perhaps a more minute vision of the mechanism and its functioning. Moreover, although it requires some muscular input on the part of the human, above all, it requires their discernment, their capacity to begin, end, and direct the operations of these mechanical devices. This is accompanied by the increasing atrophy of musculature, and an ever-escalating emphasis on capacities for conceptualization.

iv. The externalization of the brain itself in the form of electronic machines designed to record, code, and analyze data of various kinds, the augmentation and replacement of conceptual skills through information or data storage, processing, and retrieval. This is an evolution into a pure spectatorial state and its correlative display. Lingis, following Leroi-Gourhan, describes it as an orchid existence, the becoming of what we might understand as a mammalian orchid, a combination orchid-muscle.[5] We must recall that orchids are genetical monstrosities, plants with atrophied trunks and limbs, pure, spectacular sexual organs enticing bees for their frenzied cross-species union. As a species, we may extrapolate from his speculations on the origins of human art, language, and technology, that we are in the process of becoming huge eyes, feeding into a massive brain, in the hope of engorged genital pleasures, Nietzsche's giant organs on tiny bodies, the drastically shrunken homunculus whose body shrinks as its brain expands, for whom the hand no longer links with the genitals, but give way to the primacy of the eyes. A huge brain linked to big eyes and dexterous hands, with a spindly body attached.

If there is some plausibility in Leroi-Gourhan's techno morphological genealogy, it implies that history, or at least human history, is both an inward and an outward movement: outward, insofar as the species produces from out of its interior, from its body and its condensed and compressed, projected rhythms to create cultural forms, its various arts (including dance, painting, pottery, poetry, and "architecture"); and inward, insofar as external resources (natural forces, mechanical forces, electronic forces) are gradually incorporated into and become capable of replacing human organs and tissue.

There are here two salient characteristics of the evolutionary tendency toward the obsolescence of musculature and the atrophy of sensory organs: the first is that the human body has tended, through the period of its history on earth, to subordinate and render secondary all the other sense organs than those of vision, to which it grants an extraordinary priority. The movement from mouth and nose, to hand, and eventually to the eyes (the parallel and consequent of the transitive from quadrupedal to bipedal gait) is an increasing movement toward the spectacular, an ever-increasing orientation to the visual, and thus to the artistic, and the representational. The second is that there is at the same time a movement toward display, toward the rendering of the body as exhibition. In other words, correlative with the development of the organs for seeing is the heightened development of organs to be seen. The transformation from quadrupedal to bipedal locomotion, the movement from a crouched to an upright posture, Freud argued, made the visual organs pivotal in both the mastery of nature and in the transformation of sexuality from a cyclical to a unseasonable form.[6] The privileging of the visual goes together with the repositioning of genital organs for frontal viewing. The protohuman creature becomes simultaneously a viewing and a viewed object, its organs for viewing being closely identified and articulated with its organs to be viewed.

It is thus hardly surprising that art, and especially the visual arts, have become a primary medium for the socially sanctioned and culturally binding relations of sexual spectacle and sexual viewing. Art, the art of self-making, transformed bit by bit to the highly abstract and formulaic art of our earliest human records, growing through realistic or representational art (an early acquisition in human prehistory) to an art of depiction, to functional art, and to experimental art, is crucial in the entwining processes of transforming of both body and nature, a pivotal hinge midway between sexual and erotic practices, and the practices of self-making that constitute culture. Art lies at the heart of culture as much as sexuality and sex lie at the heart of art.

2. Naked Vulnerability

I am interested in this chapter in exploring the interface between sexuality, bodies, and art that Lingis, and the tradition on which he relies—that of a Nietzschean genealogy of corporeality and affect, of a Merleau-Pontian phenomenology of the lived, a Levinasian ethics of absolute alterity—focus on thinking about the body as both the object and the medium of art. I want to reconsider some of the terms that have become central to the ways in which art, and visual representation more generally, have been theorized, and to problematize some prevailing intellectual models by which they are understood. In particular, I want to rethink notions like the gaze, voyeurism, exhibitionism, in other words, the relations between representation and eroticism that have dominated both visual theory and feminist theory in the last two decades and more, not so much to provide a new theory of art and spectatorship, but to attempt to provide some refinement and subtlety to these overwrought terms and concepts, to bring some freshness to this significant nexus of bodies, looking at bodies through and as art, and to bring some of the particularity that Lingis brings to his explorations of limits, whether of life, of activity, of otherness, or of representation to questions of visual representation.

An initial hypothesis: we don't know what bodies are capable of. Whether in the realm of the biomedical (genetics, embryology, molecular biology), or in the sphere of sports and bodily exertion (bodybuilding, exercise, competitive sports), or in the order of the production and labor power, though we have a broad understanding of bodily capacities, we have very little understanding of the limits and boundaries, the threshold between what is bodily possible and not possible. This is not simply true because of the limitations in our current forms of knowledge, the lack of refinement in our instruments of knowledge, but more profoundly, because the body has and is a history, and under the procedures of testing, the body itself extends its limits, transforms its capacities, entering into a continuous process of becoming, becoming something other than itself. This capacity for becoming other, or simply becoming, is not something that culture imposes on an otherwise inert nature, but is part of the nature of nature itself. Becoming is what suffuses bodies from both outside (through the imposition of increasingly difficult tasks) and from within (through the unfolding of a nature that never was fixed, through the self-overcoming that is inherent in the very being and ontology of bodies).

A body is produced from other bodies, and its cohesion and continuing existence and integrity as a body is contingent upon its ability to glean energy from other bodies, the bodies it ingests and from which it gains energy to not only continue its existence but to proliferate itself in its products, including its offspring. This was the physicist, Erwin Schroedinger's response to the biological dilemma that physics posed to all studies of life. If all physical systems tend toward disorganization and disorder, maximum entropy or thermodynamic equilibrium, then how does the living organism avoid decay? His answer was as simple as it was profound: "The obvious answer is: By eating, drinking, breathing and (in the case of plants) assimilating."[7] We prevent ourselves from plunging into atomic simplicity, physical or systemic annihilation, through the assimilation, in effect, the annihilation, of other organic existences. These give us the energy to maintain cohesion and growth. Bodies thus live in debt to the life that they destroy, the organic supplementation they require. They must give back something of themselves, of their own bodily cohesion for anything more than mere existence to be possible. I have already suggested, extrapolating from Leroi-Gourhan, that culture can be understood as an extension, as a protraction and projection, of the interior of the body itself. This is what the body gives back to the life on which it feeds and which it must destroy, as Bataille recognized, a sacrificial excess that produces not only the most noble and elevated cultural achievements, but, even more richly, the surprising and ever-productive possibility for the subversion of these achievements and their transformation into different, often equally prodigious, accomplishments. This is what life is—the ever-transforming, ever-recontextualizing of what has been done so that it can be done differently.

A body reproduces itself not only biologically but through the rigors of its practice. It is at this point that art figures itself as a bodily practice. While much of art merely re-presents the body, depicts or pictures it, at its most provocative, art also contains the possibility of refiguring, transforming, functioning at the very limit of the body's capacities, especially if, as Nietzsche outlines, the origin of art is the very exploration and use of the body. Good art, as much as good science, presents us with the possibilities of bodies that are barely conceivable, that challenge and problematize the very stability and givenness of bodies, both organic and nonorganic, that force us to rethink our presumptions and our understanding of what bodies are.

We can follow Alphonso Lingis, with whose words I began this chapter, in arguing that it is in part the ridiculousness of the human form, its simultaneous vulnerability and infinite productivity, that is the very motive and force for the history of art and the history of technology:

> Is not the conviction that our anatomy, ridiculous by nature, has to serve as

the material for art coextensive with all civilization? The civilization our species has launched and pursued to relay its evolution appears in nature as the exteriorization not only of the powers but also of the splendours in our organs. (*Foreign Bodies,* 38)

Can art be seen as a way of forcing this anatomical ridiculousness into productivity? Of both enforcing this status of the ridiculous while pleasurably and productively exploiting it? Perhaps this may be one of the more profound differences between erotic and aesthetic attachment: that erotic attachment induces a voluntary reciprocity in vulnerability, it produces the overcoming, the normalization or naturalization of ridiculousness, a reveling in its splendors and intensities; while aesthetic practices serve to denaturalize and heighten it (while in their own ways renormalizing and renaturalizing it, at least in terms of artistic conventions).

Maybe another way of asking this question is: what is it about bodies, and particularly about viewing bodily organs, what is it about *naked* bodies, that propels us to produce and to view art, and most especially, to produce and view the body as *nude*. What is the difference between naked and nude—an old theoretical question, but one whose range as a question is not yet exhausted and whose provocations we must still, on occasion, address. If, as Leonardo da Vinci claimed, human genitalia and nakedness are "of an irremediable unsightliness," if, as Lingis suggests, humans have no bodily equivalent to the lure of the peacock, the inwardly coiling horns of mountain sheep, and the lasciviously scarlet buttocks of the baboon, if there is nothing inherent in the bodily rather unspectacular or bare human to make it orchidlike, then is art—including the art of fabrics, the art of cosmetics, the art of car design, the art of prosthetics—indeed art as prosthetics—that serves as our sexual lure, the visual snag that rents our vision.[8]

A second hypothesis: we are not "allowed" or encouraged in our culture, nor indeed in other known cultures, to either exhibit ourselves or to observe the bodies of others, *except* in highly restricted and codified contexts. While nakedness seems a sometime necessity and a convenience in all cultures, almost all cultures cultivate some kind of clothing or covering, some sense of shame or modesty, some stretch or limitation on the reach of nakedness. We are discouraged from nakedness ourselves except on condition that (1) we are children; (2) we are lovers or in some intimate sexual context; or (3) we are mediated in a relationship to nudity through representations—in art, in pornography, in advertising, in medicine, in religion, in cinematic and fictional contexts, and so on. These three broad contexts seem the privileged spaces of bodily intimacy, not where nakedness takes place, but rather where nakedness is automatically coupled with the desire, possibly even the imperative, to look and with the pleasure of looking. It is in intimate and/or nurturing relations that we are encouraged not just to look but also to show, not just to look, but also to induce a touching.

Nakedness is a lure to intimacy and proximity because it invites the other's care and solicitude.[9] Nakedness is a state of vulnerability, not simply because one is open to the elements, at the mercy of the environment, unprotected, but also because one is prone, more prone than usual, to the affect and the impact of the other. There is so little to mediate, only the most intimate surfaces of the skin. And mutual nakedness modulates this vulnerability by making it reciprocal, by making each vulnerable to the look, the touch, and the intimate judgement of the other.[10] A singular nakedness, the nakedness of one alone, is the most naked and prone, the most vulnerable, for the model, but also, in a sense, for the observer.[11] This is why the boundary of the frame, the mediation of the image, the protection afforded by the artistic representation of the naked body—the emergence of the nude from the naked—makes that nakedness even more alluring in its representational form than it may be in the flesh. Nakedness is not the most alluring state: it is the veiling of nakedness, its suggestion or intimation, its promise or possibility that entices. This has long been recognized, by both artists and pornographers, and the lure of eroticism, the props, veils, adornments, the half-dressed, the near-naked—that is, the naked in promise alone—is the body adorned by representation:

> Without the gearing-into the tool—or without bravery at grips with death—the unathletic male nudity is ridiculous. The female anatomy verges on the ridiculous too, as our advertising, our high art, and our pornography know; it has to be relayed with stage props—be they reduced to the minimum, as in Nô theater, to high-heeled shoes, a garter, atmosphere spread with vaseline on the camera lens, or, as Marilyn Monroe said, perfume. (Lingis, *Foreign Bodies*, 34)

Lacan has already made it clear that the human infant is even more fascinated with the image or depiction of an object than it is with the object itself.[12] The image holds the promise of a richness and a controllability that is unavailable in life. This is the allure of the cinema, of fiction, and art: the mediation of an object or objects so powerful as to entice one to identify with them, to desire to watch them, to be entertained and amused by them. The allure of the image, the evocation and simultaneously, the containment of, nakedness that the image affords is the perfect context and setting for the depiction of bodies, bodies in their rich openness, and in their sexual provocation. The nude brings together the eros of intimate encounters, the lure of the image, and the passion of contact, but without a real encounter or anything but visual contact; it enables us to indulge in this encounter but also to subordinate it to a "higher" purpose, a cultural rather than an erotic goal:

> It can happen that erotic excitement is fastened on a whole human body. Apart from the pattern of lips, breasts, hands and genital zone accentuated for sexual contact, beauty organizes the entire body into another pattern, linking up its contours, colors, and movements into a snare for the eye. (Lingis, *Dangerous Emotions*, 143)

We augment our skin to entice and signal our openness: we do not do this through displaying our plumage, the magnificence of our horns or tusks, or the beauty and luster of our markings, stripes, or spots, or through flashing our genital organs.[13] We do not do this through our organs directly, at least not usually, but rather through the supplementation that allows us to signify our organs without designating them, through sheer underwear, through provocative low-cut or tight clothing, pendants worn at breast level, weapons and tools carried on the hip, through insinuation rather than explication. In short, through what Leroi-Gourhan has claimed is our very human proclivity to externalize our organs, to produce prosthetic representations to replace or supplement them.

The naked becomes nude only through a fundamental equivocation, by suffusing of the image of nakedness with a context, a purpose, and a possible signification, which in a sense form a covering for that nakedness, in other words, through immersing the naked body with beauty, grace, form, solidity, a frame which contains it (even the frame of the art gallery or museum itself in the case of a work not literally framed: the frame, in other words, that designates some thing or activity as a work of art. The frame, in this sense, thus functions just as pervasively in nonpainterly and nontraditional modes of art—in performance, in dance, in video, in installations—as it does in the traditions of academic painting). This containment of nakedness in the nude enhances the naked form through the idealization performed by representation on the one hand, and, on the other, it induces an authorization for a spectator to watch, to look, without the overwhelming obligation for intimacy that the naked or the erotic body, poses. The spectator is insulated from the usual obligations of naked intimacy, and can thus watch the spectacle in pleasure or in discomfort, with a distance of the voluntary. This is because representation intercedes between nakedness and the spectator to enable the spectator to dwell on, to savor and enjoy—without erotic obligation.

3. Nudity Veils

Kenneth Clark has argued for a certain Platonic elevation of art over pornography: art represents the nude, the female nude in particular, as an object, not for the senses, but for the mind or reason.[14] It is elevated, "sublimated" from its bodily origins and set up for noble purposes. This nobility is secured through a kind of distancing that removes the depicted objects from their more sensory and base implications, and instead presents the naked body for intellectual and aesthetic contemplation. In other words, at a certain level, Clark is, in spite of himself, recognizing the power of the image to veil nakedness, to produce nakedness as nudity. The naked body has a force that can give rise to bodily impulses in a spectator. Art is what protects the spectator from the more mundane and venal of these impulses, art is a veil of modesty here, not for the model or object of the nude but for the spectator.

Instead of seeing how to veil this nakedness most aesthetically, to refine it into a moderate, consumable nudity, the most provocative art since the time of Courbet has not strived to present the most beautiful and aesthetically appealing images. Quite the contrary: modern art has sought to problematize beauty, the assumed norms of the aesthetically appealing, and instead to bring back something of the visceral force of bodies through their representation, whether through the direct presentation of bodily momentum in the work of Jackson Pollock, or whether through the intensified viscerality of depiction in the work of Francis Bacon. Art has become exploratory of how to view bodies differently, how to see them from angles and perspectives unthought of, to bring out latencies within them that may not be obvious in everyday life, and to make them speak with a directness that has been blunted through what is now the most stylized and ritualistic forms of sexual depiction, pornography. It is not that art and pornography differ in what they depict, or even necessarily in how they depict nakedness, nor am I suggesting that a hard and fast line can be drawn between art and pornography: simply that pornography can only function as such insofar as it is ritualized, fundamentally repetitive, a series of infinite variations of a very small number of themes, governed by a preordained goal. Pornography refuses innovation in a way that, ideally at least, art does not. Pornography relies upon its formula, its theme, its script, to induce its desired effects through a more or less guaranteed pathway. Its eros resides in its insistence on infinite repetition. This makes it no "better" or "worse" than art: simply less resourceful.

What pornography and art do share in common is this: whatever their quality, originality, framing, or viewing context, whatever their audience and cost, they consist of representational practices that both render what is historically private, that is, a relation between a very limited and select number of individuals, into a publicly and anonymously accessible form; and that veil naked bodies through a representational structure that makes their image, their diegetical content, as desirable or appealing as their materiality. Both pornography and art produce nudity as a form out of nakedness as a content. Both materialize bodies (theirs is not a project of dematerialization—from the real to representation—as much as a process of rematerialization, the transformation from one mode of materiality, flesh, to another, paint, canvas, photographic paper, choreographed movements etc.) whose materiality is contained, bordered with and as representation. And in doing so, both license an audience to develop a particular set of relations of seeing which are commonly not available in everyday life, at least not at will: one is authorized to look—not to gaze, but to look—in any way one chooses. One need not be captivated, but could also be bored, indifferent, disgusted. One is not implicated in the other's vulnerability, not simply because, as traditional feminist theories of the gaze suggest, the other cannot look back, but because one, as spectator, has free reign with the kind of look one can utilize. In intimate bodily relations, one is already committed in some sense to a relation of positivity, a relation of nonindifference, nondisgust, a relation of desire. One is, in Levinasian terms, called, called upon by the open giving up of a certain vulnerability that the other offers to us as naked. It is this that we are protected against in observing the work of art. We are not called to protect, or to bare ourselves to, this other that we observe. Our observation is given free range. We are liberated from the impulse towards reciprocity.

If Clark is naive in relation to the distinction between pornography or salacious representation and pure or high art—what shocks the sensibilities of one period becomes the high art of another; one century's pornography becomes the classical tradition of another's—there also seems to be a misunderstanding of the nature of perception itself and the role of looking. Looking is, of course, no more refined, no more cerebral, no more intellectual than any of the senses. And, more subtly, this kind of argument—which draws a clear-cut dividing line between pornography and art—reduces the kinds of looking to only two: an ennobled looking which illuminates the soul and a salacious, perverse looking which feeds only the body, and particularly the other organs.

Psychoanalytic discourse too, reduces the various modalities of looking to only two: the look of the voyeur (reduced, in feminist discourse, to "the gaze"), and the desire to be looked at of the exhibitionist, active and passive variants of scopophilia. What is needed instead is a *typology* of looking, a mode of thinking of spectatorship that, instead of relying on the vast apparatus of projection, identification, fetishism, and unconscious processes—what psychoanalysis has offered to film theory and theorists of the visual arts have borrowed as their primary model of spectatorship. Voyeurism is not the only modality of looking: seeing has many particular forms, well beyond the purview of the gaze, which is, in psychoanalytic terms, necessarily aligned with sadism, the desire for mastery and the masculine privileging of the phallus. Long recognized by feminists as an expression of male domination of psychical structuring in patriarchal cultures, more recently many feminists have also recognized that the apparatus generated through the structuring of the gaze leaves the female subject, or for that matter, the male subject, with no position other than a masterful phallic one. Instead of pushing this description further, regarding it as a fundamental political truth of the ways patriarchy has structured seeing, a limitation on the kinds of seeing available to women, I would suggest instead that seeing needs to be retrieved by feminists, and that vision needs to be freed from the constrictions imposed on it by the apparatus of the gaze.

In addition to the gaze, for example, there is, the seductive fleeting glance, the glance that overviews without detailing; there is laborious observation, a slow, penetration inspection that seeks details without establishing a global whole, there is a sweeping survey, there is the wink and the blink, speeded up perceptions that foreclose part of the visual field to focus on elements within it, the squint which reduces the vertical to the horizontal, and many other modalities. The history of art cannot be regarded as the history of the male rendering of the female as passive object and the reduction of the female spectator to masculine voyeur. If these are the terms in which the history of art are viewed, we have nothing but the eternal subjection of women, and no understanding of many, many modes of resistance to patriarchal circumscription. The point is that not only do men but also women look in many different ways, and it is this plurality of possible ways of seeing—depending on one's interests, investments, commitments, and beliefs—that dictates how objects are seen, and even which ones are seen.

In place of this understanding, we must instead understand that bodies are not simply the loci of power but also of resistance, and particularly, resistance because of their excess. Bodies exceed whatever limits politics and representation, management, or desire impose on them: the bodies of women, even the depicted bodies of women, are no more passive, no more exhibitionistic, no more the objects of consumption, than male bodies, animal bodies, or natural bodies. And the ways in which women, as well as men, look, the ways in which they engage with images and representations of bodies is not singular or monolithic either. One can inspect, survey, peer, glance, peek, scour, one can focus on or look through.[15] Art itself has in fact always elicited looks other than the gaze. This of course is not unknown by artists, whose work is commonly an attempt to engage with, and perhaps produce, other ways of looking that may move beyond the mundane and the habitual, and hopefully beyond the apparatus of the gaze. (This indeed is one of the founding assumptions of installation art, of conceptual art, and most art of the twentieth century: the art of surprise, the art of re-looking, the art of the double-take.)

4. Looking Good

Given the limits of conventional art historical analysis and of feminist versions of psychoanalytic theory, which both reduce the look to the gaze, reduce the body to the nude, and presume a fixed set of politically given significations, it is important not just to celebrate the body as the universal object and medium of both culture in general and art in particular—as has been the fashion over the last few years—but also to use its rich and uncontained complexity to problematize and rethink this conceptual edifice that surrounds art production (an edifice or frame, of course, as Derrida recognized, always suffuses the interior, parergonally[16]). To use conceptions and theories about the body to rethink the role of the body both in its representation and its reception.

While the nude is of course not the only domain in which such a reconceptualizing or re-presentation of the body is possible, it is a place where these issues can be tackled most directly, for the human body, in its relation to other human bodies, animal bodies, props, and scenery, has been its primary focus. In the wake of the simultaneous becoming-redundant of the body, the vestigial structures of muscles, sense organs, hair, tissue of the human body; and the ever-pressing focus on the body as the locus of enjoyment, pleasure, gratification, and display, it seems that art, especially erotic art, art that deals with bodies, whether with their depiction or their refiguration, has become one of the most intense loci for the body's transformation. On the cusp of redundancy, through its own inherent capacities for excess, for production over and above survival or need, yet because of that excess, no longer bound only to need or survival, bodies must make the trajectory of that redundancy into the very condition of art itself. To make oneself into a work of art is in a sense the only response to an immanent and ridiculous redundancy of the specific forms of the body: and to make oneself into a work of art, as Nietzsche, and following him, Foucault, suggest, is not simply to aestheticize life, to dandify it, nor is it to make oneself into an object or spectacle for the artistic investigations of others. It is to live one's life and one's body in excess of what is required, in excess of discipline, and even in excess of aesthetics.[17]

To live one's life as a work of art is, among other things, to once again return to one's body as the site and source, the origin, of pleasure and productivity; to utilize it differently, to move and act in ways other than those to which one is habitually confined. This is not only to act different, but also to be acted on differently, i.e., to sense differently, not only developing each of the senses beyond its usual biological reach but to inquire into the limits and transformability of biology itself. It is also to synaesthetically cross-map the senses onto each other, to experiment with how to sense differently, how to use senses in terms of the range and scope of the other senses, to explore how each sense functions or is capable of functioning quite differently from its assumed and normalized role. To develop these alternatives is inherently invested in artistic activity. It is to render the body differently in representation, for representation is, as I have argued, almost a second skin, a diaphanous sheathing for bodies that transforms what the body is and does. It is to looking good in both senses: to look at something well (outside the domain or order of the gaze), and to be looked at as well.

Notes

1. Terry Smith, ed., *Impossible Presence: Surface Screen in the Photogenic Era* (Sydney: Power Institute Publications, 2001).

2. Friedrich Nietzsche, *The Genealogy of Morals/Ecce Homo*, trans. Walter Kauffman (New York: Vintage Books, 1969).

3. André Leroi-Gourhan, *Le geste et la parole: Technique et langage*, Paris: A. Michel; trans. as *Gesture and Speech*, trans. Anna Bostock Berger (Cambridge: The MIT Press, 1993).

4. "...we saw the bi-polar technicity of many vertebrate cultures in anthropoids in the forming of two functional pairs (hand/tools, face/language), making the motor function of the hand and of the face the decisive factor in the process of modeling thought into instruments of material action, on the one hand, and into sound symbols, on the other. (187)

5. See "Orchids and Muscles" in *Foreign Bodies*:
"With our sight disconnected from any decision or motor functions, its content determined by the image-industry programming, our bulbous and succulent organisms, hoisted into the space of visibility on the massive trunks of cybernetic forests, are biologically evolving into mammalian orchids." (32)

6. Sigmund Freud, *Civilization and Its Discontents*, trans. James Strachey, Standard Edition of the Complete Works of Freud, Vol. 21 (London: The Hogarth Press, 1929).

7. Erwin Schroedinger, *What is Life?* (Cambridge: Cambridge University Press, 1944), 74.

8. "In some species of birds, females mate preferentially with long-tailed males. The shimmering iridescence and extension of the peacock's feathers exemplify traits that may have been selected not because they offer any survival advantage to the peacock, but because they please, sexually excite or otherwise charm the peahen." Lynne Margulis and Dorion Sagan, *Mystery Dance* (New York: Summit Books, 1991), 100.

9. This naked vulnerability is an extension of the vulnerability of the face-to-face relation that Levinas poses as the foundation of all ethics. The other faces me, and his face, which is not a sign of vulnerability is living, breathing vulnerability, a call to and upon the subject. See Emmanuel Levinas, *Otherwise than Being or Beyond Essence* (The Hague: Martinus Nijhoff), 45-50, 85-94.

10. As Lingis makes clear, the intimacy of erotic love is connected both to a fear of vulnerability the other imposes on or extracts from me, but also to a kind of animal passion that directs us to an intimate encounter in spite of risks to our sense of security or well-being, a kind of noble wildness:
"How rarely do humans find the courage to say those fearful words 'I love you'—fearful because we are never so vulnerable, never so open to being so easily and so deeply hurt, as when we give ourselves over in love to someone! But from early infancy we have come to understand that instinct—in our kitten that so unreservedly gave itself over to its affections for us, in our cockatoo that in all her excitement upon seeing us wants nothing but to give us all her tenderness and high spirits. *Dangerous Emotions* (Berkeley: University of California Press, 2000), 63.

11. For a pointed example, see Helmut Newton's famous and often reproduced photo-

graph of 1981, "Self-Portrait with June and Models."

12. Jacques Lacan, "The Mirror-Stage as Formative of the Function of the I," *Ecrits: A Selection*, trans. Alan Sheridan (London: Tavistock, 1977).

13. Lynne Margulis and Dorion Sagan (1991) illustrate the strange proclivities of the squirrel monkey, almost a compulsive reflex of self-exhibition:

"These monkeys show off their erections not only to indicate sexual desire, but to greet and to threaten. In one species of squirrel monkeys, males invariably raise their erection to their own reflection when seen in a mirror. Apparently in doing this, squirrel monkeys are trying to frighten away what they see as rivals." (133)

14. Kenneth Clark, *The Nude: A Study of Ideal Art* (London: John Murray, 1956).

15. Here I am indebted to the insights of Edward Casey, "The Time of the Glance," in *Becomings: Explorations of Time, Memory and Futures*, ed. E. Grosz (Ithaca: Cornell University Press, 1999).

16. Jacques Derrida, *The Truth in Painting*, trans. Geoffrey Bennington and Ian McLeod (Chicago: University of Chicago Press, 1987).

17. Michel Foucault, *The History of Sexuality: Volume 1: An Introduction*, trans. Robert Hurley (London: Allen Lane, 1978).

Chapter Eleven

There Is Always Another Island

David Karnos

In Michel Tournier's *Friday or the Other Island*, a novel retelling of the Robinson Crusoe myth, there is a passage that always turns my mind to Alphonso Lingis. Crusoe has been diligently working at reforming his newfound aboriginal island mate, but perplexing frustrations meet his every effort at civilizing the man. One day Friday flips over a giant turtle in the sand and quickly sets about "slow-roasting" it over low coals till the singed and seared creature crawls out from its bloodied moorings and lurches toward the water. A horrified Robinson watches as Friday, without pity or malice goes about the business of making a warriors shield. That night Robinson writes in his journal,

> It is a part of our English nature to show more mercy to animals than we do to men, an attitude of mind which is perhaps open to discussion. The fact remains that nothing has set me apart from Friday as that unspeakable torture of an animal. Yet his is not a simple case and it raises many questions.[1]

Many questions indeed! For,

> Not long after this Friday became interested in a fledgling vulture which he rescued after its mother had turned it out of the nest for reasons of her own...

> Friday at first thrust scraps of fresh meat into its mouth and these were gulped down with an eagerness which suggested that they would be swallowed no less readily if they had been pebbles. But a day or two later the little creature fell sick....In a word, it showed symptoms of acute and possible fatal indigestion.

> Accordingly Friday put some goat's entrails to cook in the sun, where they lay in a cloud of flies, giving off a stench that turned Robinson's stomach but seemed to revive the vulture's appetite. And when a quantity of small white

grubs appeared on the nauseous, half-liquid mess Friday performed an operation which Robinson was never to forget. Scraping at some of it with a shell he put it in his mouth, grubs and all, and sat methodically chewing while he gazed absently about him. Then, bending over his foster-child's beak, which was held out to him like a blind man's begging bowl, he let the unspeakable white pap dribble into it, while the little creature quivered with delight.

"Living worms too fresh," he explained to Robinson. "Little bird ill, so chew-chew. Always chew for little birds."[2]

Such literary passages impress. They can haunt or taunt one's memory of what once was shocking to them. Like an epiphany, such passages can serve to illuminate certain sudden and momentous events in one's journey that particularly reveal what is with utter truth and candor. And in this passage from Tournier you are called. And you recall.

The conclusion of a week's trip with your daughter visiting a dozen colleges from Amherst to Swarthmore. You had flown to Boston from Montana: she, from San Francisco. A rental car, coupled with a maniacal itinerary interrupt Fall semester. Visiting old friends and colleagues while she interviews with admission officers. Grading papers at night in the local motel while she overnights in the freshman dorms. Your mind curdles, like many parents, at the thought of that nest of iniquity; especially, remembering your own first debacles....You've been dreaming about this cherished moment for some time now, and proudly jabber away about the advantages of a great liberal arts education, such as your own.... Then, before the final orchestrated visits you took a *piccolo pausa*, and a little diversion of self-indulgence.

You take her to meet one of your teachers.

You drive a few hundred miles off the Eastern seaboard highway, take some back roads, and come to downtown State College, Pennsylvania. Arriving at a little wood-sheathed home tucked discreetly between towering concrete student apartments you park, illegally, in the midst of threatening signs of tow-locks and unconscionable fines that would cost a week's salary for a professor in Montana, and work your way through the thick tangle of brush and vine sheltering the cackle of incongruous sounds recognized vaguely as grouse and peahens, and knock on the door.

His grin appears. You cross the threshold. Inside, your eye darts everywhere hastily panning the continuous shelves of books, record albums, travel journals comingling with exotic fish tanks, odd furniture, eclectic poster art, and your eye and heart together smile comfortably. After twenty years it is as it always was when you were last here as a gawky and gaping graduate student ready to party at his professor's home: comfortably bizarre. Then, you sense your daughter's stillness. Though her stance is frozen her eyes are wide and wild. You forgot to tell her about the birds.

As we stood making introductions midst the cockatoos, macaws, toucans, and a host of jungle avian surprises, iridescent hummingbirds darting hither and thither around the corners and crannies of the household and, for but a brief midflight hover during which you "thought" you saw a critter, snatch unseen morsels from the *Orthropodae* family of flying insects just three inches from your nose, reverse direction and disappear. This moment lasted who knows how long, for flinching was useless, and we were mesmerized anyway, caught in this intensely busy intersection of crisscrossing flashes of whirring and blurring color. We turn to Lingis. He has noticed my daughter's incredulity, and his welcoming grin instantly changes to mirror her own moment of wonder. "You know," his voice trails off in a murmur, "they must eat their own weight in insects daily..."

•

Was it first torturing the turtle then nurturing the vulture that turned Robinson's stomach inside out and his mind upside down? Or, was it seeing both side by side in a single glance, that, as Robinson writes in his journal immediately thereafter, forever changed his perception of reality from that day onward? Was it that horror and beauty could coexist side by side so readily in a noncivilized world, or that they were in fact epiphanic apperceptions of a reality simply devoid of judgements? Preferring the latter interpretation I am convinced that out there in the middle, the geographic center of Pennsylvania, there is a man who lives on that "other" island.

I

Friday or the Other Island has been revisited in the work and writings of Lingis for over thirty years. It has been discussed in class lectures, and referenced in letters sent to friends from abroad. It appears in his essays, and almost all his books. It is a text that both informs Lingis philosophically, and perhaps is performed by him in the course of his own daily engagement with the stuff that makes him tick.

Where did this "Other" island begin?

In February of 1709, Captain Woodes Rogers, commander of the HMS *Duke*, while on an expedition against the French and Spanish, put in at the island of Juan Fernandez off the coast of Chile to replenish his supplies. His pinnace returned loaded with crayfish and "a man clothed in goat's skins, who looked wilder than the first owners of them."[3] After four years and four months of dwelling alone on the island, Alexander Selcraig, a Scotsman, returned to England. Six years later he was interviewed by a journalist who reported:

> When I first saw him I thought if I had not been let into his character and story I could have discerned that he had been much separated from company from his aspect and gesture; there was a strong but cheerful seriousness in his look, and a certain disregard to the ordinary things about him, as if he had been sunk in thought. When the ship which brought him off the island came in, he received them with the greatest indifference with relation to the prospect of going off with them, but with great satisfaction in an opportunity to refresh and help them. The man frequently bewailed his return to the world, which could not, he said, with all its enjoyments, restore him to the tranquility of his solitude.[4]

Six years later yet, in 1719, Daniel Defoe would publish a novel version of this event entitled *The Life and Strange Surprising Adventures of Robinson Crusoe, of York, Mariner; who lived eight and twenty years all alone, on an uninhabited Island on the coast of America, near the mouth of the great river of Oroonoque; having been cast on shore by a shipwreck, wherein all the men perished but himself. With an Account how he was at least strangely delivered by the Pirates. Written by Himself.*

So began the story that would evolve and devolve countless spin-offs for another quarter millennium. Along the way the story acquired enough mythic proportions to make it suitable for the classroom. In 1762, Jean-Jacques Rousseau published *Emile: General Principles of Education* which argued that the only good education is one that keeps children away from books until they are twelve years old. And then Rousseau had his Emile read **only** *Robinson Crusoe* because that at least taught the possibility of solving the problems of living without any aid beyond one's resources. For to Rousseau, "the surest way to rise above prejudices and to make one's judgements according to the true relationships of things is to put yourself in the place of an isolated man, and to judge everything as that man would, in reference to what is useful to him."[5] Needless to say, Rousseau was not heeded. Today, children do not read *Robinson Crusoe*, and philosophers are not likely to be born from being stranded on deserted islands.

With the publication of his first novel, *Friday, or the Other Island* which won the *Grand Prix du Roman* in 1967, Michel Tournier revisited the adventure, perhaps rescuing Rousseau from the embarrassment of having promoted a racist sexist imperialist text. Four years later he revised that book into a children's edition, *Friday and Robinson, Life on Speranza Island*, which soon became required reading in French schools.[6] By then Lingis was already teaching *Friday* in America, and writing strange letters from other islands.

So what did he find in this text that struck such an epiphanous chord? It has lots of solitude coupled with lots of sex, woven together with a binding charm—the allure of Otherness. But this Otherness is more than phenomenological alterity, or existential strangeness, or metaphysical ultimacy. It's even beyond the familiar Lingian discussions on conditionals and imperatives.

In the Preface to *Foreign Bodies* (1994), Lingis writes,

> *We found in Michel Tournier's novel* Friday *a destiny we have found understood in no philosophical literature.* In Tournier's narrative, Robinson sets sail from the objectives of his English world, sets sail too from paternal and reproductive sexuality. On the island of Speranza...he finds himself led from the mire of immediate gratification, beyond the surface island subjected to cultivation and law, beyond the tellurian island in which he finds rebirth—still further, led now by Friday, to an elemental domain, that of the free winds, earth, skies, sun, that of vegetative and solar sexuality...The exemplary destiny of Tournier's Robinson makes us understand that our bodies are not just, as existential philosophy and also as our technological society taught us to think, contrivances destined for things, that is objects-objectives, destined for implements or wealth. They are substances destined to stand with the earth and to ground, to capture the way of the light and illuminate, to breathe the wind and chant.[7] *(emphasis mine)*

The penultimate chapter of *Foreign Bodies*, "Elemental Bodies," is devoted to an exegesis of this destinate nature. Many themes run like leitmotifs, undercurrents, and updrafts texturizing the discussion—Solitude, the Look, the Other, Sex, Language, Time. They rise and fall wavelike, crescendos building toward inevitable climaxes and sublime conclusions. But it is what Tournier and Lingis call tellurian and uranian, that is, transformed notions of the earthly and the celestial, which interests me the most.

•

First, what is this destiny not understood in any philosophical literature? What did Tournier conceive in *Friday* that is so unique? Assuredly, retelling Daniel Defoe's Robinson Crusoe as seen through the eyes of Freud, Jung, Claude Lévi-Strauss, the films of Buñuel, as the first English edition's flyleaf suggests, is different. But what twists and turns Tournier provides in the fate of a man mythologized for two hundred years as the epitome of Anglo adventure survivor are indeed very different. To begin with, whereas Robinson dominated in the tale of Defoe, it is Tournier's Friday that masters the situation, turns the tables and offers an alternative to conquest-minded racist sexist political philosophy.

Dispensing with the tedious self-flattering first lines of *Robinson Crusoe* with which Defoe began ("I was born in the year 1632, in the city of York, of a good family..."), Tournier throws us out to sea in a storm "*With the precision of a lead line the lantern hanging from the cabin roof measured by the extent of its swing the roll of the brig Virginia in a sea that was growing steadily worse.*" Not only is the action immediate rather than autobiographical, cartographic, and lineal; it is graphic, microcosmic, and convoluted. Convoluted because doubling the action of the storm going on outside is a tense swinging of fortunes on a tabletop inside the captain's room. The captain is reading Robinson's future through twelve tarot cards. While the lantern sways the tenth card is read.

> *In the City of the Sun, set between Time and Eternity, between Life and Death, the inhabitants are clothed with childlike innocence, having attained to solar sexuality, which is not merely androgynous but* circular. *A snake biting its tail is the symbol of that self-enclosed eroticism, in which there is no leak or flaw. It is the zenith of human perfectability, infinitely difficult to achieve, more difficult still to sustain. It seems that you are destined to rise even to these heights, or so the Egyptian tarot cards say.*[8]

In the cast of these twelve cards, soon to unfold into twelve chapters of a book, Robinson receives glimpses of a future that promises much more than a simple return to the ordinary world of Daniel Defoe and an English yardstick destiny. Immediately after the twelfth card is read the ship wrecks; and the next twenty-eight years, two months, and twenty days begin.

In his essay Lingis triangulates this destiny through three phases of Robinson's metamorphosis from tradition-bound civilized man to brave new world order uranian man. These coordinates are the condition of the self in solitude, the case of the Other's sexuality, and the place of the subtitle that binds them together in the alembic vessel, "the Other Island." Lingis shows us how Robinson, whose modern sensitivities lead him to willfully overcome his racial prejudices, lets himself become initiated into the rites of Speranza's springtime couplings with the luxuriant and exotic foliage about him. He lets go of Defoe's crippling colonial constraints and their inward commanding drive to master and administer things according to their utility as prescribed in the Book of Books. He lets go the drive to label, count, classify, identify, and attach to things a civilized value. Instead, he undertakes the laborious process of letting himself become akin to things by letting them flow, flux, congeal, and take their own form. Realizing the fruitlessness of reproducing his mundane world for a cast of phantoms who never come to rescue him with their looks of approval and smiles of familiarity, Robinson adapts. Rather than domesticate, he follows Friday's example and begins to masticate.

Then it happens.

One day Robinson's carefully engineered cave-world goes up in smoke, caused by Friday's capriciously taking tokes off a pipe earlier rescued by Robinson from the flotsam of the shipwreck. When Robinson breaches the cave entrance, Friday, in panic for partaking of the sacred tobacco, tosses the lit pipe further down the "tube" into the womb of Speranza where Robinson has stored his ultimate defense arsenal. The result of this Big Bang explosion will be a born-anew Robinson, one no longer in need of prophylactics or taboos. Shaken and dazed from the mighty explosion which casts him flat upon his back facing skyward he suddenly sees with dread the impending doom of a crashing giant cedar tree, itself shaken from its ancient bed by the explosion in Speranza's womb. As the tree's crown falls toward him, a hand appears as if off the vault of the Sistine Chapel and he grasps Friday with all his heart. Henceforth, Robinson shucks the grip of mundanity and welcomes in all his nakedness the tellurian magical, libidinal, and elemental forces of the Other island. "A new Robinson was sloughing off his old skin.... He would never let go the hand that had reached down to save him on the night the tree fell."[9] Lingis's remarks on this episode are pregnant.

> It was not because Friday recognized in Robinson a duplicate in himself that his hand reached out to save him the night the tree fell. He had fled to the magnolia trees because he had come to see on Robinson only the appalling face of the demented. Robinson saw in him the one who destroyed all the intelligibility he had put on the island and whose touch now uprooted the trees to replant their roots in the sky. It was at the extreme point of recognizing the alien in one another that their hands clasped never to let go again.[10]

When he read Tournier did Lingis, too, shed his Self—that self-first molten in the crucible of Husserl, then tattooed on the flesh of Merleau-Ponty? Was it upon the lap of Freud, the altar of Levinas, or the anvil of Nietzsche where he laid his head so often that he made his last sacrifice to the Western canon? Who cares? Lingis found *Friday*. And for him it became destinate.

II

"Beware of purity. It is the acid of the soul."
(Van Deyssel's last words to Robinson, spoken while scooping out a pipeful of tobacco the moment the ship crashed)[11]

Lingis travels a lot. Usually, to home, to classes, and to conferences. Otherwise, he wanders. He writes,

> In most traveling...one drags oneself along, and goes everywhere to accu-

mulate still more photographs, experiences, memories, reports, revenue, return. The further one goes one finds oneself only the more in oneself, the more wearied with the weight of oneself. The true nomadism is rather that which drives one, when one goes far, not to find, on each shore on which one arrives, someone with whom one shares a language, a belief, or practical concerns, but to find someone with whom one shares nothing, the stranger, and, reduced to the solitude in which one has been mired by contracting an existence one's own, one is delivered by the carnal arms of a stranger. If one starts with this access to the other, outside all contracts, one will hear the thoughts and see the perspectives and glimpse the visions of another land, without the inevitable deviation and misunderstanding and parody, the unending Western recording. One would know *depaysment*, one would find oneself *elsewhere*.[12]

Usually, what drives one to travel involves the desire to escape and to explore. To leave the baggage of one's ordinary, civil, conventional existence, and strike out for another place where one is not recognized. Lingis rejects this circuit of self-gratification. If the desire is truly to find oneself elsewhere, one needs to link with particular Others in order to identify the emplacement of one anywhere. After all, how could urban, suburban, country, or rural people really fathom an Other place? It's not just a lateral transition to wider spaces, less people, and a diminishing of familiar and comfortable infrastructures (billboards and power lines, cell phones and toilets, SUVs and bottled water). It's more than quiet, big vistas, and longitudinal space. It is depth. Being elsewhere is like a thermal inversion in winter: places devour spaces as chinooks "eat snow."

Earlier, the clepsydra Robinson had devised to mark his calendrical existence stopped and suddenly he "seemed to discern *another island* behind the one where he had labored so long in solitude."[13] In his last journal entries many years later he recalled:

> There were also those moments of prophetic vision which, with instinctive perception, I termed "my moments of innocence." I seemed to glimpse another island hidden beneath the buildings and tilled fields which I had created on Speranza. Now I have been transported to that other Speranz. I live perpetually in a moment of innocence. Speranza is no longer a virgin land which I must make fruitful, nor Friday a savage whom I must teach to behave. Both call for my attention, a watchful and marveling vigilance, for it seems to me—nay, I know it—that at every moment I am seeing them for the first time, and that nothing will dull their magical freshness.[14]

Knowing he liked to spend Christmas in Bangkok I tried tracking Lingis once. It was my fiftieth birthday and I decided to treat myself to something bizarre. Asia and Al. Early in January, I found him holed up in a colonial French hotel. In my excitement I eagerly rattled off the possibilities: the Calypso, and a few other night spots of transvalued fame. Cockfights and snake charming, kickboxing and crocodile farms. His ever-buoyant grin waned.

I offered alternatives. The royal barges, the emerald Buddha, the gold Buddha....His grin turned to wax. To hide my disappointment I changed the topic. I told him of my morning's visit to the U.S. Embassy and a family friend who worked there in the Cambodian sector. Just the day before, Pol Pot had been reported and photographed as he lay dying. His eyes widened. *Could it be true?* Two days later Lingis left for Angkor Watt.

Somehow I had thought that if I came to Thailand I could see what he had seen. Or, I could see what he had said and written about what he'd seen. Caught up in my own eagerness I had forgotten Nietzsche's admonition; "This is my way, where's yours?" With a wide-open grin bigger than the upcurved smiles of the giant Buddhas guarding Angkor Watt, Lingis bid me farewell, knowing I would have adventures of my own no doubt.[15] He left for Cambodia and a place where, surrounded by pockmarked craters of exploded and yet-to-be-exploded land mines, an island of timeless otherness rises. There, he could find solitude, for a moment, before the inevitable waves of tourist terror struck. He could renew himself before the eyes of others colored the freshness of the Khmer Kingdom's greatest moment of innocence. Perhaps, he remembers his writing of four years earlier in *The Community of Those Who Have Nothing in Common*.

> In solitude, Robinson Crusoe learns the frightening nakedness of his eyes. He realizes that the eyes of others had extended beyond the narrow radius of things he sees, fields of things already seen or being seen by us; alien eyes extend the map of the visible. His solitude means that these other lights are gone and black night narrows the visible to what he himself actually sees.[16]

In *Friday* solitude is first experienced as the lack of others' eyes. In order to survive, Robinson builds a boat he names *Escape* so he may leave the island he has named *Speranza*. But his boat is built despairingly too far from shore and inevitably it rots high and dry. Hope sours and he soon mires in a never-ending circuit of self-pity—a second form or phase of solitude. It takes a magical, momentous, and thoroughly spontaneous event to sublimate the two former phases—the appearance of a Stranger at the end of a very hard week. The Other that Lingis so often writes of is really not so strange or categorically other (alienlike). These visions are but variations of our expectations. The stranger he denotes is a welcoming, a fresh breeze that brings an elemental change of behavior. What normally results in one's reactionary motions (e.g., repulsion, aversion, shock, alarm, fear, terror, etc.)—redundant tendencies to protect and *secure the world as it is known*—vanishes, evaporates, like a shadow that one is no longer able to ignore.

It's also an excuse to get carnal.

On one of his annual trips to Carnival, yet another island, Lingis writes his friends:

> Read in Tournier:
>
> J'ai un amil qui est le plus parfait don Juan. Ses conquêtes ne se comptent pas —ce qui est un façon de parlar, car il en tient scrupuleusment registre, comme faisat Dom Juan au demeurant. Je l'ai longtemps observe et j'ai fini par lui dire: "Comment fais-tu? Tu ne's ne beau, ni brillant causeur, ni riche, et ta reputation est détestable. Pourtant aucune femme ne te résiste?"
>
> —C'est simple, m'a-t-il répondu. Je ne suis pas sportif. Je ne cherche pas la difficulté. Au contraire, je la fuis comme la peste. Tout mon art consiste à

repérer la femme qui ne me resistera pas. Et à ne m'en prendre qu'elle. De là mon constant bonheur.

My own practice had been for years simply yea-saying to anyone anywhere who indicated she/he? Wanted to make love with me. Tonight I reflected that this practice had broken down in Copacabana; if every evening I go out for an evening stroll I did that I would never get two blocks down the street, and would never get any exercise. So, I had been appraising, choosing. But that method is bad: one merely ends up with a bedpartner that fit one's preconceived image. So remembering the *amour fou* methods of the surrealists, I decided to reintroduce chance. I cleared my mind and thought of a number. The number that happened to come up was 11. I strolled down Avenida Atlantic, and counted the eyes turned my way, tongues wetting lips, until I reached eleven, and we went off together, and indeed there were surprises.[17]

Lingis still stands away from normal methods of everyday couplings and mundane linkings. He prefers intercourse with the tellurian. "In such lovemaking, outside the network of rules that organizes the city spread behind us, they will lead us, as Friday led Robinson Crusoe to an elemental world made of sands, sea, and sun in Michel Tournier's *Friday*."[18] This is dangerous politics, if not, then certainly unconventional in a wild sort of sense. But "sowing mandrakes" in a lovely garden patch called the "pink coomb" as Robinson comes to indulge in during moments of mating urges only satisfies the vegetative and Freudian compulsions. It also gets you to jail or an asylum if observed by the ubiquitous eyes of Society.

In the mundane framework we express ourselves sexually in terms of a civil habitat. But on that "other" island expressions and all their dictates, imperatives, and taboos are transmuted, dissolved in the vessel of otherness. Robinson responds to the gift of Friday's hand out-of-nowhere. Previously, he became stymied, stifled, and goatskin-harnessed by his worldviews in the very place he had sought Hope. Hope for a new world is rotten-thighed, unless one changes and adapts. Then Friday came and joined the dance. Friday shifts attention away from the mundane traditional value paradigms of myopic Robinson to his own vegetative and tellurian responsiveness. It's axiological; it's elemental. It's not a matter of choosing how to act in accordance with an acquired or inherited set of principles, maxims, values, and systems—these things merely make living on earth controlled, commonsensical, and civilized. Rather, it's letting the earth's constituents themselves draw forth a response, an action automatically linking object and objective if you wish. The earth simply extends itself; fluidly, foamingly, loamly, slimely, stormily, volcanically, caressingly sublime. Such is the tellurian response. Lingis calls it the elemental imperative.

III

"What is a friend? A single soul dwelling in two bodies."
—Aristotle, *Diogenes Laertius*, Bk. V, Sec. 20

To follow Lingis on earthly adventures may be dangerous. Following his writings about those endeavors may be daunting, but they are always delightful. Especially if you surround yourself with a nice world globe, an atlas, an encyclopedia, and a dictionary. But only a dictionary friendly to Lingis; that is, like any globe or atlas, one that pertains to the facts and the times of what one describes. Merriam Webster's Collegiate Dictionary, tenth edition, flyleafed as "'The Voice of Authority,'" continuing its 150-year tradition of excellence....America's best-selling dictionary" won't get you into Lingis. It's too civilized. You won't find Tellus or tellurian. You will find something on telluric and tellurium, but they will be misleading. You'll need to find something old, even out of tune or place with modernity, and probably crusty and barnacled with bookshelf sediments. In one such set of dictionaries I found:

> **tellurian** (te-lu'ri-an), a. and n. [< L. tellus (tellur-), the earth, + -i-an.]
>
> I. a. Pertaining, relating to, or characteristic of the earth or an inhabitant of the earth.
>
> They absolutely hear the tellurian *lungs* wheezing, panting, crying "Bellows to mend" periodically, as the earth approaches her aphelion.
> De Quincey, *System of the Heavens* (*Davies*)
>
> II. n. 1. an inhabitant of the earth: so called with references to supposed inhabitants of other planets.
>
> If any distant worlds (which may be the case) are so far ahead of us Tellurians in optical resources as to see distinctly through their telescopes all that we do on earth, what is the grandest sight to which we ever treat them?
> De Quincey, *Joan of Arc* (*Davies*)
>
> **telluric** (te-lu'rik), a. [= F. *tellurique* = Sp. telurico. < L. *tellus* (*tellur-*), the earth.]
>
> I. Pertaining to or proceeding from the earth: as, a disease of *telluric* origin; *telluric* deities.
>
> How the Coleridge moonshine comported itself amid these hot *telluric* flames...must be left to conjecture.
> *Carlyle*, Sterling, i. 10. (*Davies*)[19]

Tellurian lungs. Telluric flames. Deities. This is not a conception of earth as Ptolemaic or Copernican, revolving, circumvolving. It's not really a Gaia either, for its neither gendered nor mythic. Here is designated an earth that is uroboric, earthy, cthonic. It is not about the position of a body, the role of an authority, the status of an ego. It is as it might appear to a stranger, its ownmost Other, the sky. Earth and sky solarized become tellurian and uranian.

Lingis writes "We live our lives on the surface of the planet, among things we can detach and manipulate; we live under the sky. The sky is without surface, without shape, without inner structure, ungraspable. We see in the sky the sovereign realm of chance."[20] Perhaps the most relevant image to consider in *Friday* is the day Andoar, a big shaggy goat, comes to fly and sing. The theme of rebirth requires another doubling back to the tarot cards cast in the Prologue, as well as a little unpacking of the legend of Robinson Crusoe. It's the "other" island we are seeking that Lingis keeps pushing us toward in his writings, namely that "otherness" beneath, above, and all around our own shell of everydayness.

In the original account of Captain Woodes Rogers, Alexander Selcraig had arrived on board the rescue ship "looking all the worse for it like a 'goat-man.'" After all, he had been living with the goats for four years. Steele's interview with him in 1719 records:

> When his clothes were quite worn out he dried and tacked together the skins of goats, with which he clothed himself.... It happened once to him that running on a summit of a hill he made a stretch to seize a goat, with which under him he fell down a precipice and lay senseless for the space of three days, the length of which he measured by the moon's growth since his last observation.[21]

Tournier takes this strange account and converts it into something descriptive of the uranian. One day Robinson observes Friday playing with his goats, the same goats he has very carefully herded for twenty years, the same ones that have sustained, nourished, and clothed him. His economy. Upon some tellurian impulse Friday seizes a chance to become ramlike (as the tarot cards had suggested). High up on the shelf of a cliff, and for the fun of it, he wrestles with the head goat Andoar. The scene is charmingly crafted. The two elemental beings collide, crash, and storm about awhile until Friday fatigues, and losing the battle and fearing the worst he clutches old Andoar in a reverse Odyssean like hold and together they thrash about the cliff's edge more violently than ever. Then, Friday covers Andoar's eyes with his hands. Suddenly, Andoar and Friday go over the cliff.

Watching the event from afar through his telescope, a terrified Robinson rushes to the cliff bottom's rubble to discover Friday sitting atop the dead Andoar. It is not compassion that moves Friday's next response. It is instant love. He sets himself to making sacrifice. In the ensuing days Friday conducts his own native alchemical tasks skinning, gutting, cleaning, boiling, chewing, and stringing Andoar's vitals. What he does to Andoar resembles what Robinson did to the goats that provided his clothes. The doing is transformatory. Only, Friday's production is not a self-centered economy; it is sacrificial. "He died and saved me with his skin," he tells Robinson, "The great goat is dead, but I shall make him fly and sing."[22] And so he makes a kite, one that sings. An aeolian goat-harp (it really is an incredible imaging to read). One night sometime later, "huddled together in the shelter of an overhanging boulder, Robinson and Friday lost all sense of themselves in the splendor of this mystery wherein the naked elements combined—earth, tree, and wind joined in celebrating the nocturnal apotheosis of Andoar."[23] To this Lingis lisps "In dissolute ecstacy the body that had become ligneous, ferrous, coral, now curdles, dissolves, liquifies, vaporizes, becomes radioactive, solar, nocturnal."[24]

The philosophical destiny of the body for Lingis is to become a hollow for wind and song. It is a destiny approached only after the fundamental characters of earth and sky, the earthly and the celestial, the vegetative and the solar, have been apperceived as the tellurian and the uranian. For Lingis, "Robinson's sensuality, invaded by the uranian elements, his body laid out, like the body of the island under the skies, in total submission, now resounds with such an instantaneous symphony. The aeolian harp replaces the clepsydra to mark the form of time in which the imperative is heard."[25]

"He goes to the sky, on the wind." So says a line in the poem from the ancient pharaoh Akhnaten's "Hymn to Aten." So goes the double, the ba of the pharaoh, living god, Horus to the sky: to become its Other.

•

In Defoe's tale, Robinson and Friday return to the world of England there to continue propagating the absurdity of Victorian conquest. In Tournier, Robinson chooses to stay on the island only to learn that Friday has to sail away into new ventures and other worlds. Robinson does not cry, does not go mad. He smiles. No longer bound by reactionary emotions and ego-centered thoughts, Robinson watches. Soon he discovers someone has come ashore, having absconded in the night from the departing schooner. Robinson receives another day of life, as the Egyptian tarot cards had foresaid, and in the generous exchange of things given freely under the sun, he names his new mate Sunday.

Sometimes I wonder what the philosophical destiny of Lingis might be. He is a kind of Friday, quite at ease chewing others' sensibilities, or stringing them along for a very good ride. But more so, is he not like a Stranger before whom you stand enchanted?

And I recall later, that mid-Fall afternoon in State College, as my daughter found a book, a place to sit, and adjusted to the hummingbird symphony in E-zap minor, I accompanied Lingis to the front porch aviary. He introduced me to the macaws, toucans, and cockatoos by their names, and told stories about each. Using my finger he demonstrated the deceiving appearance of the toucan's mighty looking but hollow bill, explaining that it had not the power to even break the skin. He spoke of the cockatoo's little beak, power capable of snapping macadamia nuts: no demonstration necessary, thank you. He sat upon the floor, back to the wall, knees drawn up as a perch for his favorite. Taking a single green grape to his lips. He made an offering. Jouncing along, the cockatoo inched down his legs, across the valley of his abdomen and up the crest of his chest where it lingered for a moment and looking Lingis dead in the eye plucked the grape.

...*il y a toujours une autre île.*

Of course, to come to this conclusion, one could read Defoe's *Robinson Crusoe*. One should read Tournier's *Friday*...

One *must* read Lingis.

Notes

1. Michel Tournier, *Friday, or the Other Island*, trans. Norman Denny (London: William Collins, Sons, and Co. Inc., 1969). All references are to the New York, Pantheon paperback edition of 1985 entitled *Friday* in accordance with the text to which Lingis refers. There are differences in these two printings, 161.

2. *Ibid.*, 162-163.

3. "Steeles' Account of Selkirk," in Daniel Defoe, *The Life and Strange Adventures of Robinson Crusoe*, 3 volumes (New York: George D. Sproul, 1903), 339-40. Originally published in *The Englishman*, Dec. 1-3, 1713.

4. "Captain Woodes Rogers's Account of the Rescue of Alexander Selkirk," in *Ibid.*, 330-331. Cf. Woodes D. Rogers, *A Cruising Voyage Around the World* (New York: Dover, 1970), and P. B. Grove, *"The Robinsonade," The Imaginary Voyage in Prose Fiction: a History of its Criticism and a Guide for its Study, with an Annotated Check-list of 215 Imaginary Voyages from 1700-1800* (New York: Columbia University Press, 1941). Note: in *The Critique of Dialectical Reason*, Sartre criticizes some thinkers for "robinsonades": thinking which justifies and reproduces existing conditions.

5. Cited in Lester G. Crocker, *Jean-Jacques Rousseau: The Prophetic Voice 1758-1778*, Vol. 2 (New York and London: Macmillan Publishing Co., 1973), 140.

6. Since 1980 all fictional texts of Tournier's work are marketed for children. Tournier believes (somewhat like Rousseau) that the transmission of knowledge requires a storytelling tradition that relies on myths involving initiations. Simone Viernes notes that all of Tournier's novels involve initiatory quests through three stages: separation from society, encounters with death, and rebirth into a cosmic, or what Lingis calls uranian harmony. For further reading on Michel Tournier, see: *Michel Tournier*, W. Cloonan (1985); *Michel Tournier*, S. Koster (1985); *Michel Tournier*, ed. P. E. Knabe (1987); *Michel Tournier, Philosophy and Fiction*, C. Davis (1988); *Michel Tournier's Metaphysical Fiction*, S. Petit (1991); *Michel Tournier's Children*, C. Anderson (1998). For an account of the tarot card symbolism in *Friday*, see L. Sbiroli, *Michel Tournier: La Seduction du jeu* (1987).

7. Alphonso Lingis, *Foreign Bodies* (New York: Routledge, 1994), xii.

8. Michel Tournier, *Friday*, 12.

9. *Ibid.*, 180-181.

10. Alphonso Lingis, "Elemental Bodies," in *Foreign Bodies*, 204.

11. *Ibid.*, 13.

12. Alphonso Lingis, "Being Elsewhere" in *Falling in Love with Wisdom*, ed. David Karnos and Robert Shoemaker (New York: Oxford University Press, 1993), 260-61.

13. Michel Tournier, *Friday*, 90.

14. *Ibid.*, 205.

15. See photographs in Alphonso Lingis, *The Imperative* (Bloomington: Indiana University Press, 1998), 12; and Alphonso Lingis, *Dangerous Emotions* (Berkeley: The University of California, 2000), 40.

16. Alphonso Lingis, *The Community of Those Who Have Nothing in Common* (Bloomington: Indiana University Press, 1994), 129-130.

17. "I have a friend who is the most perfect Don Juan. His conquests do not count, which is just a manner of speaking, because he keeps scrupulously a register, as Don Juan

did moreover. I have observed him for a long time and finally said to him: How do you do it? You are not handsome, nor a brilliant conversationalist, nor rich, and your reputation is detestable. Nevertheless, no woman resists you.

"'It's simple,' he answered. 'I am not a sportsman. I do not seek the difficult. In fact, I flee it like the plague. All my art consists in seeking out and identifying the woman who will not resist me. And dealing only with her. Therefore...lies the source of my constant happiness.'" [Letter from Lingis, March 23, 1993; my translation.]

18. Alphonso Lingis, "Beauty and Lust," in *Dangerous Emotions*, 154.

19. *The Century Dictionary and Cyclopedia*, vol. 6, 1891 (New York: The Century Co.), 6220.

20. Alphonso Lingis, "Gifts," in *Dangerous Emotions*, 114.

21. "Steeles' Account of Selkirk," in Daniel Defoe, *The Life and Times of Robinson Crusoe...*, Vol. 3, 339.

22. Michel Tournier, *Friday*, 190.

23. *Ibid.*, 198.

24. Alphonso Lingis, *Dangerous Emotions*, 148.

25. Alphonso Lingis, *Foreign Bodies*, 209.

Chapter Twelve

Mapping the Earth Otherwise

Edward Casey

For Al Lingis: *whose inimitable writings map the earth otherwise in eloquent words.*

What distinguishes the map from the tracing is that it is entirely oriented toward an experimentation in contact with the real.... It fosters connections between fields, the removal of blockages on bodies without organs, the maximum opening of bodies without organs onto a plane of consistency.... The map has to do with performance, whereas the tracing always involves an "alleged competence."
—Deleuze & Guattari, A Thousand Plateaus

Spatial concepts can only effectively predict these results by becoming active themselves, by operating on physical objects, and not simply evoking memory images of them.
—Jean Piaget & Barbel Inhelder, The Child's Conception of Space

I

If maps and paintings are considered as ways of representing the world in images drawn or painted on flat paper or canvas, they seem very different, without common ground. It is tempting to think that a painting is a colorful rendering of the world as we perceive it, capturing it in a tableau which, however dynamic it may be, fixes the painter's vision in a lasting format. Hence we "hang" paintings on walls, as if they were just so much dead weight; and we put them, thus immobilized, into living rooms and museums as if they were so many embalmed objects to be preserved just as they are—or rather *were*: were at the moment of being finished in the artist's eye. Maps, too, we regard as mere objects, completed once and for all, then deposited in printed atlases or, again, hung on walls for decorative purposes. On this view, maps are quite literally stillborn: once published, they are taken as definitive representations of the known world; they stand as authoritative renditions of this world —until corrected by other maps (or later editions of the same map) that claim even greater representational authority. Construed thus, a map is a statement about the way the world is. It is a literally objective claim in linear form about a supposedly settled state of affairs.

Regarded as objects to be hung on walls or included in books and seen as alternative modes of representing the world, maps and paintings have strong affinities with each other. But it is precisely in the domain of objective representation that they also part ways. For maps trump paintings when it comes to accuracy of representation; their formidable armamentarium of metrically exact techniques for measuring and reproducing the lay of the land keeps them legions ahead of paintings when it comes to the depiction of space.

This was not always so: before the eighteenth century in the West, what were called "landskips" and other topographic paintings (including those painted by J. M. W. Turner in his early career) were as much prized as maps for their delineation of particular landscape features. The advent of modern mapping techniques, along with the rise of Romantic sensibilities in painting (to which Turner's later paintings contributed so significantly), changed all this. From that point onward, e.g., the middle of the nineteenth century, paintings and maps went their separate ways as two diverse ways of representing the earth and its many landforms. The scientific status of the one came to be seen as increasingly antithetical to the inspired state of the other.

Curiously, it was when painters turned away from earlier aims of representing the natural world in some recognizable and reliable way that they cleared the way for a renewed convergence with mapmakers. In part, this was due to their willingness to acknowledge that maps—and, more recently and on a different register, photographs—were bound to win out in any contest for representational verisimilitude. In another part, it was due to an increasing interest in eclecticism in art, breaking down traditional boundaries of what is and is not art and importing into art what did not traditionally belong there, including poetry and political comment and philosophy (Dada, Surrealism, conceptual art), as well as photographs and maps themselves. In the rising experimental spirit of a specifically "modern" art, the doors were flung open to former rivals or enemies of painting and new forms of collaboration arose: e.g., the extensive use of photography by artists as diverse as Man Ray, Robert Rauschenberg, and Andy Warhol.

The collusion between painting and mapwork has been comparatively recent— a creature of the past several decades. It has characterized earth artists in particular: most notably, Robert Smithson and Michelle Stuart, Eve Ingalls and Jasper Johns. Each of these artists makes express use of maps in their work. Others may not employ maps per se—i.e., recognizable cartographic inscriptions—but they nonetheless employ mapping techniques such as aerial views, grids (including parallels and meridians), projections, and the like. They are mapping even if they do not make explicit use of maps as such. As Margot McLean remarks in reference to her work, "I don't like to talk of maps but of mapping."[1]

Mapping may be regarded as an activity of certain artists who refuse to stay within the established bounds of painting. Evidence of this activity is to be found in many different forms. Sometimes, it occurs in the specific form of remembering places and bringing their presence to bear in the artwork. This obtains for McLean herself: her memories of her childhood home in Virginia were sustained by the materials she brought back to her New York studio from that homeplace. These *souvenirs*, displayed in transparent plastic bags on the walls of the studio, constituted a first level of mapping—a concrete synedochal relation to her past in the workplace of her present. A second level was achieved when the same materials were integrated into paintings of the early 1990s such as "Virginia" (1993), which brings soil and leaves from her homeplace into its very constitution. These materials allude to a past and a place without indicating them in any strict sense. This is memorial mapping in which a painting does not represent something but commemorates it.

In an equal but opposite move, Michelle Stuart maps in an imaginary mode. Her "Mariners Chart" (part of the larger installation, "Sacred Precincts" [1984]) projects possible South Sea islands and dotted lines of voyage between them. There is a commemorative edge to this chart insofar as it alludes to the part of the Pacific where the ill-fated *Essex* was destroyed by the whale that became the inspiration for Melville's *Moby Dick*. But unlike "Virginia," this work does not look back primarily; it looks out onto an entire imaginative world that rejoins the literary world where virtually anything is possible. It maps by *charting*, i.e., by projecting an open future of possible happenings in which earthbound actualities no longer constrict the imagination: in contrast with *plotting*, which is tied to the actualities of land or sea. Much the same sensibility (though conveyed by a very different way of working) is found in De Kooning's paintings of the beach and ocean on the southern shore of Long Island, e.g., "Montauk Highway" (1958) or "Door to the River" (1960). Here, too, the realm of the possible beckons: the vividly colored water invites movements as free as those laid out in "Mariners Chart."

All such movements, whether oriented to the past or the future, or linked to the actual or the possible, can be considered "psychokinetic." By this I mean motions of the mind taken in the expansive sense of psychical outreach. This outreach, which occurs at the level of feeling rather than of intellect, is not only into temporal modalities such as past or future. It is also into spatial situations that involve direction and distance, near space and far space, the earth underfoot and the horizon out there. Into each of these parameters of place the psyche feels its way and gains orientation. Feeling at the level of psyche—not to be confused with emotion—is able to ingress into the particularity of place in the midst of open stretches of space.[2] It has a genius for sensing what is special to a place and for moving itself, on the wings of memory or desire, into that place. Psychokinetic motion, then, is any such movement that occurs by the outreach of psychically based feeling. This is a movement that, true to its name of origin (*kinēsis*), does not merely move through space but changes what it moves through—changes it from within, alters its very character.

Artworks are testimonials to such change. They map out what happens to paint and other materials as they are invested with the psychokinetic motions of the artist.

To talk of mapping is thus to talk of motion, and to begin with the feelingwise ingression of the artist's psyche into his or her chosen materials. But the full activity of mapping in paintings and other artworks requires the commensurate motions of the artist's body. Paul Valéry said that the artist "lends his body" to the painting he creates.[3] Here lending is not just loaning for a certain period of time, say, that of the creation of the work; it is more like a permanent loan in which the body's active contribution remains evident as long as the work itself lasts. This contribution is that of animating matter. The active participial locution, "mapp*ing*," signifies such animating motion, a somatokinetic power that prevails in paint or stone, soil or glass, earth or water.

It is not accidental that earth artists have literally moved out of their studios and into the landscape. Robert Smithson led the exodus with his excursions into abandoned quarries and industrial wastelands in New Jersey—another world in comparison with the sophisticated spaces of New York City. He went in search of a "site," a real place where the body could interact directly with matter, whether natural (e.g., rock) or man-made (e.g., slag).[4] On that site, he left an earth work that changed the very landscape itself. Michelle Stuart has gone in search of exotic places far from her studio—in the Galapagos Islands, in New Zealand, in Alaska, in Sweden, and many other places. Other artists may have traveled less far, but they sought the *other place* that would inform their work back in the known place of the studio: De Kooning moved to Springs from New York City, Ingalls lives in the wilderness of Idaho in summers, McLean goes to the Orinoco region.

What matters, however, is not the literal trip, the displacement of the artist's body in geographic space: that way lies the transportational essence of *phora*, the other Greek word for "motion." As Al Lingis knows better than anyone, travel is important not as merely "going from one point to another"[5] or for the sake of the exotic—or even as a way to collect materials, important as this collection may be—but for the opportunities it offers to *immerse oneself more thoroughly in matter*: matter different from that which one is used to back home. What matters is to move in the midst of foreign matter—to become attuned to it and to enter into intimate embrace with it. This embrace need not be as ecstatic as that of Robert Smithson's in his discovery of the site for the Spiral Jetty in Utah. What is needed for the bodily immersion that is at play in active mapping is something more modest, yet of decisive importance: to feel oneself, bodily as well as psychically, at one with the materiality of one's immediate landscape: to bring one's own body into synchronous relation with the world's body, to be the world in which you walk.[6] This can happen at the edge of the Great Salt Lake or in the Cook Inlet in Alaska or in Thailand (where Lingis goes frequently), but it can also take place just outside your own apartment where, like Sandy Gellis, you collect the daily results of rain in jars whose contents are then employed in paintings. Indeed, it can occur anywhere—even where you are just now sitting while noticing the matter around you as if it were something new. As long as the experience is intense and intimate enough, the impulse to map earthwise can be awakened: you receive an invitation to trace out the new experience of matter in an artistic medium of your own choosing.

The body at stake in mapping is thus not the vehicle of metaphoric motion or literal transference but the lived body immersed in the material realm. This does not mean that the body is passively merged with matter, much less its mere witness. Instead, it is its animator, converting it from found matter ("dross") to material for art ("subtilized matter"). This is the body that is the subject of what we could call "concrete mapping" or better yet, "absorptive mapping." The bestraddling of earth by women in certain of De Kooning's paintings of the early 1960s, for example, shows us an intensive engagement with the earth: the women are virtually indistinguishable from the earth they cover, becoming part of the depth of its surface. No proud walking here—no striding over the earth with Promethean prowess. Not even a bare upright posture. Instead, a leveling with the earth is presented, coming to terms with its materiality at its level, getting down on all fours and getting dirty. This impression of the body into the earth has its counterpart in Ingalls's recent body sculptures, made from soft but fast-drying material into which she presses parts of her body, e.g., "Of Gravity and Breath" (1996). Just as these body parts are absorbed into the plasticene substance, so De Kooning's writhing bodies are absorbed into the earth over which they crawl so inelegantly. In his painting "Two Figures in a Landscape" (1967), we witness such concrete, absorptive bodily motions in all their awkwardness. As such, they contrast with the deft and highly skilled movements of the cartographer's hand, which traces out pregiven shapes with unerring precision. The tightly configured hand-eye coordination of the professional mapper gives way to the loose and bumptious motions of the corpulent body, its inept flesh arrayed against the equally unmannered flesh of the earth. And yet mapping is going on in and by such motions. Even if not recognized by cartographic officialdom, this is a mapping which every/body—everyone in their obdurate and sagging flesh—knows to be happening whenever we move on land. Every time we make our way across the merest plot of earth our bodies map out the movement, tell us which way to go, and report to us the "coefficient of adversity" we encounter.[7]

Since cartographers take no interest in this unofficial course of action—and since most human beings take it for granted—it remains for artists to underscore its importance. Contemporary earth artists are especially sensitive to its potentialities for mapping. For them, mapping is anything that pushes out the limits of their chosen medium while retaining an allusion to the earth, even if not importing soil as such into the painting or installation. For them, mapping "permits a kind of excavation (downward) and extension (outward) to expose, reveal, and construct latent possibilities within a greater *milieu*."[8] This greater *milieu* is the earth, and such artists see their own activities as speleological soundings into its depths by means of their own bodies—depths that are to be found on the earth's surface.[9] A number of earth artists literally dig into the earth (e.g., Smithson, Heizer, Stuart), while others trace out paths on the earth (e.g., Richard Long).[10] Any mapping they do in this bodily digging into the earth or walking on it is meant to manifest its depths, not to demonstrate cartographic rectitude on the paper surface of a map: "One does not *impose*, but rather *exposes* the site."[11]

Considering the work of such earth artists makes us realize that mapping, fully extended, is at once psychical and somatic—and in both regards, kinetic. Just as it changes the surface of the artwork (e.g., as when Stuart pounds and perforates the surface of rag paper, making it into something itself earthlike), so it changes its bulk and shape, its heft. Earth works in particular are hefty amassments of soil or rock, grass or trees, that reconfigure already existing things on earth. Sometimes the reconfiguring is very slight—as in Long's walking paths, which consist in trampled grass or flowers across an open field. Sometimes it is massive, as in Smithson's Spiral Jetty (1969-1970)—where earth has been moved and removed to create a new shape at the edge of the Great Salt Lake. As the two-dimensional surface of paper and canvas are left behind in such a massive work, we move closer to sculpture as well as architecture.[12] But the aim is not to alter the surface of the earth in any permanent, monumental way. Just as "the rationality of a grid on a map sinks into what it is supposed to define,"[13] so an earth work is meant to subside with time—to be taken away (as in Christo's cloth fence in California), to sink back into the earth, or even to fall under water (as in the case of the Spiral Jetty). What matters is that matter has been reanimated and redirected in such a way that "maps of material, as opposed to maps of paper,"[14] have been set forth on earth, whatever their degree of permanency and without regard to questions of accurate representation.

For lack of a better term, I call these quasi-sculptural productions "earth-maps." Shared by the artists who create them are these traits: (i) respect for the earth and its surface formations; (ii) ability and willingness to immerse oneself kinetically in the earth, whether by way of psychical insinuation or bodily insertion (optimally by both); (iii) a commitment to creating material maps, whether from canvas, paper, earth, or water; and (iv) a passion for performance, not in the sense of "performance art" (in which the artist's body and/or others' bodies are theatricalized), but in the sense of an active engagement with the materials at hand and the earth under foot.

II

I take "performance" here in Deleuze and Guattari's sense of an activity that exceeds any mere tracing of a prior or underlying reality, yet that has a life and structuration of its own. As James Corner reformulates the claim of *A Thousand Plateaus* cited as the epigraph to this Epilogue:

> Mapping is neither secondary nor representational but doubly operative: digging, finding, and exposing on the one hand, and relating, connecting, and structuring on the other....In this sense, mapping is returned to its origins as a process of exploration, discovery, and enablement....Like a nomadic grazer, the exploratory mapper detours around the obvious so as to engage what remains hidden.[15]

Tracing is tied to an existing object—to its edge and shape, to what is superficial, the *superficies*, the outer surface that does not contain depths of its own. The line that does the tracing is bound to the internal and external edges of the surface in this delimited sense. Plato claimed that form or shape (*eidos*) is "the limit of a solid."[16] Tracing is eidetic replay. It is the basis of much standard cartographic mapping, which hews to what is already known—and known for sure—about the configuration of a given group of sites.

Performance, in contrast, is finding the form *through* (*per-*) experimental action. Instead of seeking to copy an existing shape, it discovers new shapes by its own activity. This activity is that of the whole body—not just the hand which is the exclusive implement of tracing. Even in its ordinary acceptation, "performance" implies getting the lived and moving body fully into the act: making it *operative* and not just *operational*. When Michelle Stuart rubs soil into rag paper, she will sometimes put the paper over an object such as a stone or even a piece of metal. These latter exert their influence, they make their presence felt; yet they are not simply traced by Stuart's rubbing. She does not seek to reproduce their outline as if this were a detachable property which her merely operational hand could lift off the object and transfer to the surface of the paper: as in the fantasy of perfect replication which underlies so much of scientific cartography as well as hyperrealism in art. Instead, her entire body is engaged in the arduous procedure of rubbing, which consists in pummeling and pounding with her hands and arms, bestriding and straddling the paper, and in many other micromovements of her lived body. This body elicits new forms from its total engagement with the matters at hand—paper and soil. These latter are as indeterminate as is matter for Aristotle: i.e., the potentiality (*dynamis*) for form. Matter solicits activities that draw forms out. Such per*form*ances embody the very sense intended by Deleuze and Guattari: "an experimentation in contact with the real."

Mapping is performative in another, closely related sense. It is *productive*. A map regarded as a tracing is reproductive of existing objects and structures, land masses or sea straits; experiment has no part in its sober creation. This is doubtless why Borges lampoons such tedious sobriety by his fable of the imaginary map that had a scale of 1:1 and thus covered an entire empire point by point: as sheerly redundant, it is otiose to begin with.[17] A productive map, on the other hand, does not suffer from any such spirit of gravity; it is more economic and selective; most importantly, it elicits new forms from the region it maps.[18]

If a reproductive map is the tracing of *what is*, and is bound to its shape and surface—a matter of formal eidetics—a productive map brings out *what is not yet*, thanks to its experimental and performative spirit. But production is not altogether novel in detachment from the known; as the word itself says, it "draws out" from what is known new directions, "new grounds," finally new worlds. Hence it is a matter of a material eidetics that "re*form*ulates" what already exists materially. In contrast with abstraction—which literally "pushes away"—production leads out. In the case of earth-mapping, it teases new forms from the landscape, thus from within the immanence of earth. The productive process here at stake is neither that of the free-floating imaginary of pure possibility nor that of advanced technology. This is a deliberately primitive productivity that finds the unexpected within the expected, new forms in old matter, new ways to map the same terrain: a Spiral Jetty in an ancient Salt Lake.

Mapping that is more than mere tracing is productive in three majors ways. (i) It manages to *re-present* its subject matter in innovative and unanticipated ways instead of merely representing it as it is and has been. This latter is the task of tracing, a reproductive activity. The former is realized by such steps as literally re-presenting earthen material in the art work, giving it a new and second life there: rocks from open quarries in specially made boxes, water from the Hudson River in jars, leaves from various places in paintings that incorporate them bodily. (ii) Mapping *re-implaces* parts of the landscape in strikingly new ways. A house lot in Virginia, a remote farm in New

Zealand, are re-located in the work of McLean and Stuart. The work of art offers a new place for perceived or remembered landscapes—a new scene in which they can be re-presented. Just as it does not merely "represent" them, it does not just reposition them either. It creates a new aesthetic and eidetic world in which a former world of experience can find new significance.[19] (iii) By the same token and in the same productive process, paintings or earth works can effectively *re-embody* their artists and viewers. Given their way of exacting full engagement, they provide new senses of being embodied—new virtual as well as actual modes of embodiment. As these are in effect potentialities of the lived body, we have to do once more with the dynamics of matter, the forms it holds within itself that are liberated in the productions of art. These contrast with the habitualities of routinized bodily conduct that concern overt behavior, thus the body's external surfaces and measured motions.

We can sum up the contrast between productive and reproductive mapping in this schematic way:

Production	*Reproduction*
Operative	Operational
Re-presentation	Representation
Re-implacement	Repositioning
Re-embodiment	Repetition

III

All of this calls for an extended meditation on the mixing of art and maps—on the promise of this commixture as well as the actual achievements of those who manage to map as they create art. Their achievements exhibits not only the dissolution of any dogmatic binarism between making art and mapping—as if the two were antithetical or incompatible enterprises—but also the mutual enhancement of one by the other. Gadamer claims that all significant art brings with it an "augmentation of being" (*Seinszuwachs*), and if so this is especially true for artworks that bring mapping into their domain. Such enhancement has happened before—in Northern Sung scroll paintings that are also maps, in nineteenth-century Japanese mapping that is equally an art form, in Vermeer's remarkable employment of maps in his paintings (most notably, "The Art of Painting").[20] But in the last thirty years in America there has been a virtual explosion of experimentation in the creation of earth works and paintings that also map. But just how has there been two-way enrichment between such very different forms of endeavor?

If painting is not to be utterly self-absorbed—as it almost became in the middle 1960s in the case of abstract expressionism—it needs to have a certain quasi indexicality. Not indexicality in any strict sense, as seen in topographical realism in Canaletto's paintings of Venice or Turner's early renditions of the Swiss Alps or Church's detailed paintings of Ecuador. This way lies the isomorphic snares of representation, repositioning, and repetition: visual reproduction in short. But quasi indexicality is something else again, for if it sometimes gestures toward representation and reproduction, this is usually with considerable irony. When Smithson presents rocks from Franklin, New

Jersey, in trapezoidal wood bins that correspond to sections of an aerial photo-map of the site from which the rocks were taken, this is not in the interest of establishing exact location and its representation—not even if the size of each rock bin is proportional to the size of one of the areas shown in the photograph.

This work, entitled "Non-Site, Franklin, New Jersey" (1968), does not serve the interest of geographic truth. Despite the actuality of the rocks, their place-of-origin, and the accurate cartographic representation, something else is happening in the re-presentation that occurred in the "nonsite" of the gallery. The work in the gallery is not a straightforward index of a preexisting site; no such one-way indexical relation obtains between the artificiality of the nonsite and the naturality of the original site. Instead, there is (in Smithson's own word) a "dialectic" between the two in which both are caught up. The nonsite is indeed a "map" of the site, but it is a strange map indeed, since it does not resemble the site; it only resituates it in boxes in a gallery in an act of double containment that literally closes off nonsite from site. Mapping here thrives as much on difference as on similarity. Neither indexicality nor iconicity in any rigorous sense is present. Yet mapping is going on, and the viewer is intrigued and moved by the irreverent and indeterminate commixture of art and map.[21] In particular, what would otherwise be a mere box of rocks gains from its quasi-indexical reference to the site—thanks very much to the presence of the actual map—while the mapping activity gains from the unconventionality and ingenuity of the installation. Artwork and mapping both gain from their ironic interchange.

What does mapping gain more generally from its productive association with earth works and paintings? In earlier times, one would have said: pictoriality and coloration and figuration. (I refer to eighteenth-century English and French maps which were enlivened by water color, not to mention sixteenth- and seventeenth-century maps that displayed "topographic views" of cities and other notable *endroits* along their edges.) But today? I would suggest such different gains as the texture of the medium and the expressiveness of the image. Jasper Johns's painting-maps of America are cases in point. These embellish wholly conventional road maps of the United States with freely applied thick paint whose very surface tempts the viewer to touch it; and the blurring and slashing of state boundaries give to this extraordinary image an intensity and energy utterly lacking in the Rand-McNally original. The result is not just an expressive painting; but a map that has been significantly transformed in the process: what was once a mere map in an ordinary road atlas has become an instance of *mapping* in the strong performative sense.

In the end, the quasi indexicality which mapping lends to paintings or earth works and the aesthetic aura (e.g., the expressivity) which artworks add to maps conjoin and collaborate closely in the most convincing cases. These include the use of photographs of sites by certain contemporary artists: as we see in Stuart's "Passages: Mesa Verde" (1977-1979), where the photographic images of the prehistoric cliff dwelling lend geographic specificity to the utterly indeterminate rubbing between them as well as the unlabeled rock books below. On the other hand, the rubbed paper and the books extend the subject matter of the photographs beyond their manifest pictorial identity—into the work as a whole. This is not an installation of photos plus indeterminate objects but a genuine *Gesamtkunstwerk* with several jointly animating parts. Even when there is no obvious maplike presence at all—not even photographs—we witness the same interanimation of painting and mapping. This is surely the case with De Kooning's landscape paintings, in which barely recognizable human figures lead the way into the absorption in the land which is the common aim of all those who create earth-maps.

IV

Certain basic questions remain. Who is the subject of such intermingled earth work/painting/mapping? What is being worked or painted or mapped? How does this happen? Where is it happening? Here I can only sketch out possible responses to these four quandaries.

The question of *who* is the question of the subject who does mapping as an artwork or vice versa. This is not just the professional artist who has a distinct identity, i.e., address, training, reputation, life history, etc. It is the person who, often despite an established identity, wishes to invest him or herself in the earth through the work—to do an earth work in a sense broad enough to encompass painting as well as "earth works" in the narrower meaning familiar to admirers of Smithson, Heizer, Oppenheim, Holt, De Maria, and others. *To find oneself in the earth*: that is the insistent aim of an earth-oriented artist. This means in turn: *finding the earth as oneself*, i.e., finding that one's own deeper identity and interests are continuous with those of the planet as a whole. At stake here is not so much the imperatives of "environmentalism" but the profound link between the artist's self, the ultimate who who one is, and a sense of the earth as an organic entity with distinctive strengths and vulnerabilities that must be heeded. When Smithson planted mirrors in the ground in the Yucatan, he removed them immediately afterwards, restoring the ground to the condition in which he first found it. Gellis is determined not to tamper with the course of events on earth—hence her waterworks that stem from the sheer reception of rain or the bottling of limited samplings of the Hudson River. The Idaho landscape is left intact by Ingalls as she walks through it in search of scenes to paint. Animals are natural denizens of the earth, and are the subject of special concern on the part of McLean and Stuart, who find space for them in their work directly or indirectly. In all such forms of earth awareness, these artists expand their personal subjectivity to include the material identity of the earth. The ultimate subject of their work is not limited to discrete objects on earth, much less their own isolated personalities, but the circumambient self who is continuous with the earth on which it lives. The subjectivity of the viewer who is moved by this work undergoes a comparable expansion into a larger sense of self. However momentary this extension of self may be, it embodies the potential for lasting change—for a permanent psychophysical *kinēsis*.

What is being mapped or painted? Nothing other than the very same earth just discussed. But this "what" is no more reducible to a determinate substance than is the subject who creates or views the work. If anything, it is closer to Aristotle's notion of "prime matter": a matter that underlies any specification into the discrete identity of substance. This is a level of matter that borders on chaos, yet is always part of the cosmos; it is matter as "chaosmis" in Joyce's term. Stuart's later work brings us to this very point: e.g., her "Paradisi: A Garden Mural" (1986), in which encaustic, pigment, plants, and flowers are intermixed and create a vibrant, pulsating whole.

A work such as this exists on the very border between the ordered (being composed from a vast rectangle made up of smaller squares) and the disordered (as suggested by the wildly changing patterns, as seen both close-up and farther away). Indeed, one and the same basic figure, the grid, provides both predictability and chance.[22] This means that the ultimate subject matter at stake is indeterminate with respect to this very choice—and to other definite dyads that tempt us to reduce the complexity of earth art to a binary description: painting vs. mapping, form vs. matter, self vs. earth, close-up vs. far-away, etc. We must recognize the misleadingness of such bifurcated descriptions and the need to undo their stranglehold on our conceptual imaginations.

And *how* are earth works and paintings that map constructed? In no single way—or even in any definite set of ways. Earth-mapping occurs with extreme variety. It ranges from traditional painting techniques (e.g., as employed by Ingalls and Richard Diebenkorn in their otherwise very different landscapes) to modifications thereof (e.g., the use of natural debris by McLean and Stuart). But it also includes the direct modification of the earth independently of anything painted on canvas, reshaping it as a three-dimensional earth work in the stricter sense (most notably by Smithson). Given such differences of material production, it is perhaps surprising that these artists have so much in common. But they are deeply affiliated by virtue of their shared commitment to put art back into touch with the earth, and to present a lively record of this contact in various modes of mapping.

Where, then, do such mappings occur? It occurs *in relation to the earth's surface*—a surface that has its own chthonic depths stirring under the outer pellicule of earth, its topsoil or rock-bound exterior or the upper surface of seas and rivers. For each artist, the surface of the artwork—whether canvas or paper, a group of rocks or a jar of water—relates to the surface of the earth by means of a spontaneous mimetism that is the equivalent of the material eidetics singled out above. This mimetism is not to be reduced to the isomorphic projections of representational artworks, that is to say, to the reproductive tracings of already extant structures of the earth. Operative here is a kinetic connection between work and world in which both are changed by their interaction. The place world is the larger scene of this interaction, the ultimate where of the mapping that artworks (paintings as well as earth works) effect in the hands, and with the bodies, of the artists to which I have alluded. In the space of that capacious world, new directions emerge, new worlds are produced, new works are created, a new vision of the earth comes into being. The familiar earth is mapped out and brought into view as if for the first time.

V

Any thorough discussion of earth-mapping must consider such mapping in the light of four basic kinds of mapping: mapping of, mapping for, mapping with/in, and mapping out.

(i) *mapping of.* This is the sense of mapping that attempts to delineate the precise lay of the land in terms of shape and distance. It is "cartographic" in the rigorous sense of being a tracing of territory, its exact extent and full features. Almost always it furnishes a view *in plan*, i.e., a view from above that purports to give the fullest and most objective representation of the land or sea below. Thus it implies both *taking distance*—in order to be as neutral as possible in making an objective assessment—and *determining distance*, that is, measuring the spatial interval between points. These points are preestablished and possess simple location; they are either landmarks or human habitations such as cities or towns. Hence their practical value as the basis for moving between known actualities in a given landscape. No wonder that travelers consult atlases and road maps for such information; it is the most assured basis for deciding the best route to follow and how long it will take. Its reliable and steady character allows us to plot our way—where "plot" again implies planning a trip from one definite place to another.

It is revealing that while we speak easily of a "map of X," we do not say that we are engaged in a "mapping of X" unless we mean the cartographer's practice of creating a particular map. The objective genitive "of" fits best with a discrete object, a fully constituted map, rather than with an activity or performance of mapping—which is just what is at stake in earth works and paintings that map. Since these latter are at best quasi indexical, they do not count as objects that direct us to definite locations. Or if they do, it is often an ironic gesture, as in Smithson's use of the photo-map of Franklin, New Jersey. Even if not intended ironically, the use of a map or photograph in earth-maps remains extraordinary; it is not locatory or orientational; nor does it offer geographical information for its own sake. At the most, it may serve as a simple acknowledgment of the source of materials or as designating the place of inspiration (as in Stuart's "Passages: Mesa Verde"), where both of these latter criteria obtain). Even so, in none of the instances in which a recognizable map (or a photograph intended as a map) is employed does it direct us to leave the artwork or suggest that we should go somewhere else. It is *part of the artwork* and not a reason for abandoning it.

(ii) *mapping for*. This last remark obtains all the more strongly for maps that are designed to tell you where to go in a delimited local setting, e.g., "You Are Here" maps that simplify (and even distort) the representation of the landscape in order to indicate more clearly the best single route from X to Y. In the case of an ordinary road map, all significant features are presented, including all viable routes; it is up to the map reader to decide which is most expeditious to follow. In the case of the kind of map that is posted in the center of a city or on a college campus, only a few possible routes are displayed and these only to the most obvious destinations (e.g., the campus library, the nearby post office, the town hall). Such maps, then, are wholly utilitarian; unlike the standard cartographical map, they do not display information for its own sake but such that it is meant to be acted on in a very practical way in a limited local context. Once a cartographical map has been completed and printed in an atlas, its destiny is complete, whether it is subsequently used or not; the aim of an orientational map is exhausted in its actual employment; its being is wholly pragmatic; its meaning is its use. Such maps are always *for others*—for those others who, including myself, wish to find their way.

Such maps are at the farthest remove from the work of earth artists we have considered. Any mapping they do (and despite its remarkable variety) is not for the sake of telling viewers how to find a particular location. To specify a source of materials or a locus of creation (e.g., "Cook's Inlet, Alaska," "The Great Salt Lake, Utah") is not to suggest that the viewer should ever go to this source or locus. Far from it! The work is itself the destination of the viewer's visual voyage; it is an "intransitive object"[23]—if it is an object at all—that is designed to attract and keep the viewer's attention throughout his or her engagement with it. It is not a matter of going from Here (the place of the work) to There (some other place, a definite destination in relation to Here). Instead, the viewer's look is meant to stop just Here, at the work itself. This is true even if the work is in fact located in an open landscape, as in the case of many earth works. In that event, we go There in order to experience the work in its sheer Hereness, its unyielding otherness, its implacable confrontation with ourselves. I go to the Niagara River Gorge to see just how Stuart's ribbon of linked rag papers fits into that landscape, how it falls down over the escarpment that is partly natural and partly sculpted (I refer to Stuart's outdoor installation entitled "Niagara River Gorge Path Relocated" [1975]). Once there, I have found the only Here that matters; I need not go elsewhere but can remain with the work itself. The earth work has become a work for me the beholder; it is not a work for others unless these others are willing to enter into the magical circle of its Hereness.

(iii) *mapping with/in.* This third kind of mapping comes closer to capturing what is happening in earth works and paintings that bear primarily on the earth. For these artworks map by way of adumbration rather than indication. Even the quasi-indexical character of some of these works operates by indirection; it does not really point us to a source or origin; or if it does so, it is only as a gesture that falls away as soon as it is made; it does not persist as a pointer—as is required by a genuine indicative sign, which possesses a consistent reality (*Bestand* in Husserl's term) that motivates a steady belief in the existence of something else. It is instead a matter of adumbrating—literally, shadowing forth—the earth.

When mapping that is with/in occurs, we encounter a situation very like what I have been calling "immersion in matter." The in of mapping with/in concerns the way in which such mapping refuses to remain above in a detached position—e.g., the privileged bird's-eye view of the cartographer—but moves down into the material it maps. The map is immanent in what is mapped; it sinks into the matter it projects so that it can understand it better from within: thus to let it show forth. This means to understand matter on its own terms instead of those brought by prior considerations such as accurate depiction or practical usefulness. Instead of imposing the map on the landscape, it is a matter of exposing the landscape itself: *exhibiting* it.

Such is the direction of what I have called "absorptive mapping." In this effort, what matters most is the way the body of the mapper—and by invitation and identification, that of the viewer—is drawn into the map work, finding his or her bodily bearings there. This is the corporeal analogue of Stuart's rubbings: just as the soil is absorbed by the muslim-back rag paper into whose surface she presses this matter, so the experience of the earth artist is to become absorbed in the work. So much so that the separate identity of that artist dissolves into the work—into the earth which it is or re-presents. As Smithson described his experience at the moment of conceiving the Spiral Jetty:

All existence seemed tentative and stagnant. Was I but a shadow in a plastic bubble hovering in a place outside mind and body? *Et in Utah ego.* I was slipping out of myself again, dissolving into a unicellular beginning, trying to locate the nucleus at the end of the spiral.[24]

This kind of absorptive immersion, in which the body of the artist (and, by extension, the viewer) becomes one with the body of the matter of the work, is also signified by the "with" of with/in. The human subject feels himself or herself to be very much *with* the work: at its level, living its way, feeling its textures and shapes. I become intimately close to the work—and it to me. The critical witness is two-way in character: I-with-it, it-with-me. An indicative relation, by contrast, is always one way, from the index to the indicatum; even the directionality of "in" signifies a movement of entering something from one area (designated as "outside") in such a way as to penetrate the area into which one wishes to move: a single directionality is entailed here. But when I am with something or someone in an immersed mode, each entity is qualified by the "with": each is with the other and on equal terms in this relational respect.

Such bilateral witness lies at the core of earth-mapping. Body and work coexist with each other in an interdynamic manner: each bringing out the potentiality in the other. The two form an intimate dyad of inseparable partners who, in their very interaction with each other, effect mapping of a special intensity. Each sets the other to work—the work of earth-mapping. Each draws the other into this enterprise.

(iv) *mapping out*. Each also draws the other out. This means extending beyond the usual limits within which bodies and matter operate: limits of substance (metaphysically regarded), limits of physicality (physically considered). To map out is to reach out beyond these limits, to extend them into another, unaccustomed order. It is the emergence of this new order—this novel cosmos—out of ordinary materials (mud, rocks, sand, etc.) that is of such significance in the works of earth artists. They have not merely built something striking that stands out on the land or in the sea. What they have really done is to transmute matter in its most mundane forms into works that rise organically and not artificially from certain natural milieux: an ingenious circle of sand set out in the pond of an old quarry in Holland, lights beaming upward through dark waters to suggest a constellation brought down upon earth, rainwater that is transformed into richly diverse etchings on plates onto which it has fallen day by day, leaves and soil brought bodily onto the very surface of the painting. These works map out in the precise sense that they take matter to its outer boundaries where it rejoins the artwork as its transmogrified material basis—thanks to the artist's active body as the indispensable mediatrix.

Mapping out in this expanded sense is not reducible to the tracing out of preexisting masses or structures. Such tracing out is merely a following of already determinate shapes, reproducing them as they stand—instead of experimenting with them, finding new forms within them, reconfiguring them. In tracing out, the settled habit of formulation, sticking to the given form, takes the place of the capacity to reformulate what already exists. The redundancies of tracing triumph over the newness of mapping out novel directions and discovering new worlds within the old.

To map out means to undertake a voyage in matter—a voyage into what is not yet the case. It is to chart out one's course not only in the known but over unknown waters; it is to move into the possible rather than clinging to the actual. Mapping out is moving out into *terra incognita*. It is to transport oneself with/in matter so as to move out of culturally conventional or physically given limits. Instead of reiterating or reinforcing these limits, it is to re-implace and re-embody them in such a way as to expand (and sometimes to undermine) them. It is to take them out of the arena of the commonplace and into new domains of possible experience.

Like walking on ordinary rocks out onto the Great Salt Lake on the Spiral Jetty. This is to move from an encounter with banal entities—with known quantities and given limits—to a genuinely new place that calls for a new sensibility: not just a new way of walking but a new way of feeling oneself, psychically and bodily, to be on earth.

> A dormant earthquake spread into the fluttering stillness, into a spinning sensation without movement. This site was a rotary that enclosed itself in an immense roundness. From that gyrating space emerged the possibility of the Spiral Jetty...the flaming reflection suggested the ion source of a cyclotron that extended into a spiral of collapsed matter. All sense of energy acceleration expired into a rippling stillness of reflected heat. A withering light swallowed the rocky particles of the spiral..."[25]

And what of Smithson's last question to himself: "Was I but a shadow in a plastic bubble hovering in a place outside mind and body? *Et in Utah ego?*" Thanks to his experiment of mapping out, Smithson answers his own question. Far from being a mere shadow somewhere outside mind and body, he is in a particular place, Utah, and he is there body and mind (*ego* in the richest sense) in a psychical-somatic *kinésis* that amounts to a moment of *ecstasis*. The artist is "standing out" (the literal sense of "ecstasy") from himself with/in his own production, his own performance: an unprecedented earth work that maps out land and sea in a new collaboration that brings about a new artwork, a new world for art. He is out there walking and mapping—and savoring the world he has brought into being in this immense, yet intensely intimate, way.

Notes

1. Margot McLean, in conversation, July 29, 2000.

2. My use of "ingress" is borrowed from A. N. Whitehead, who argues that feeling is a phase of concrescence that extends into the entire physical world. See his *Process and Reality: An Essay in Cosmology*, second edition, ed. D. R. Griffin and D. W. Sherburne (New York: Free Press, 1978). I am using "psychical" in a sense that is indebted to R. G. Collingwood's employment of this term in his *Principles of Art*, where he also distinguishes systematically between "feeling" and "emotion." See R. G. Collingswood, *Principles of Art* (Oxford: Oxford University Press, 1938), 157-171.

3. Valéry is cited to this effect by Merleau-Ponty in "Eye and Mind": "The painter 'takes

his body within,' says Valéry." (*The Primary of Perception*, ed. J. Idie, trans. C. Dallery [Evanston: Northwestern University Press, 1964], 162).

4. "I got interested in places by taking trips and just confronting the raw materials of the particular sectors before they were refined into steel or paint or anything else. My interest in the site [outside the gallery or studio] was really a return to the origins of material, sort of a dematerialization of refined matter." (Robert Smithson, *Collected Writings*, ed. Jack Flam [Berkeley: University of California Press, 1996], 192).

5. "You keep going from point to point," Robert Smithson, *Collected Writings*, 200.

6. I refer to Wallace Stevens's line "I was the world in which I walked" (from "Tea at the Palaz of Hoon") in *Wallace Stevens: Collected Poetry and Prose* (New York: Library of America, 1997), 51.

7. The term "coefficient of adversity" is Sartre's in *Being and Nothingness*, trans. H. Barnes (New York: Philosophical Library, 1956), 545.

8. James Corner, "The Agency of Mapping: Speculation, Critique and Invention," in *Mappings*, ed. D. Cosgrove (London: Reaktion Books, 1999), 225.

9. "Through rendering visible multiple and sometimes disparate field conditions, mapping allows for an understanding of terrin as only the surface expression of a complex and dynamic imbroglio of social and natural processes." (Corner, *Ibid.*, 214).

10. Lucy Lippard says this about Stuart: "All of Stuart's art is about digging—into the earth, into the past, into her personal history and psyche and those of native peoples." (Lucy R. Lippard, *Overlay: Contemporary Art History and the Art of Prehistory* [New York: Pantheon, 1983], 34).

11. Robert Smithson, *Collected Writings*, 60. His italics.

12. See, for example, Charles Simonds's miniature buildings in open landscapes, e.g., Figures 20A and B in Lippard, *Overlay*, 98. Sometimes the distinction between sculpture and architecture cannot be clearly drawn, as in Nancy Holt's "Sun Tunnels" (1973-1976), four large concrete cylinders set out in the Great Basin Desert, Utah, as reproduced in Figures 26A and B in Lippard, *Overlay*, 107.

13. *Ibid.*, 147.

14. *Ibid.*, 236.

15. Corner, *art. cit.*, 225.

16. Plato, *Phaedo*.

17. See Jorge Luis Borges.

18. "The distinction here [i.e., in Deleuze and Guattari's distinction between tracing and mapping] is between mapping as equal to what is ("tracing") and mapping as equal to what is and what is not yet. In other words, the unfolding agency of mapping is most effective when its capacity for description also sets the conditions for new eidetic and physical worlds to emerge. Unlike tracings, which propagate redundancies, mappings discover new worlds within past and present ones; they inaugurate new grounds upon the hidden traces of a living context. The capacity to reformulate what already exists is the important step." (James Corner, "The Agency of Mapping," *op. cit.*, 214).

19. For distinctions between "representation" and "re-presentation," see the Glossary of my *Representing Place in Landscape Painting and Maps* (Minneapolis: University of Minnesota Press, 2002).

20. These examples, and numerous others, are treated in my *Representing Place in Landscape Painting and Maps* (Minneapolis: University of Minnesota Press, 2002).

21. Smithson says of the Spiral Jetty that "My dialectics of site and non-site whirled into an indeterminate state, where solid and liquid lost themselves in each other" (*Collected Writings*, 146). But this same indeterminacy results from the ironic interplay of site and non-site in many of Smithson's earlier works.

22. The grid in Stuart's later paintings is "a set of co-ordinates for presenting the occurrences of both plan and infinite variable chance" (Patricia C. Phillips, "A Blossoming of Cells," *Artforum* [October 1986], 117).

23. On the work of art—especially the literary work—as an intransitive object, see Eliseo Vivas, *Artistic Transaction and Essays on Literature* (Columbus: Ohio State University Press, 1963).

24. Robert Smithson, *Collected Writings*, 149.

25. *Ibid.*, 146-149. His italics.

Chapter Thirteen

Grief Suspended: Lingis, Cavell, Emerson

Thomas L. Dumm

Sick World

In the spring of 1998, after a variety of tests and a first operation, my wife Brenda Bright was diagnosed as suffering from a terminal form of cancer, pleural mesothelioma. Experimental surgery that removed more of her insides than we thought it possible to remove, coupled with the most brutal of chemotherapy and radiation treatment over a period of six months, has extended her life indefinitely, and nowadays, self-conscious exemplars of Kurt Vonnegut's "nation of two," we live together in the light of death's presence, reminded, in all of our conversations with each other—a conversation resumed through, and by recovery, now moving to other places, hence a sense of remarriage at work—of the permanent debilites of medical treatment, of therapy's connection to life's fragility, and of the fateful contingencies that inevitably interrupt and hence shape quotidian existence. We celebrate days of energy and renewal, delighting in our still young children, happy to be burdened by the blessed thoughtlessness of everyday concerns. We enjoy as much as we can those many moments that have become more sharply focused as a consequence of this ongoing encounter with the pronounced possibility of a coming end. In other words, we remain (re)married to each other.

While attentive to the illness of my wife, the effects of this illness on the happiness of my children, and the concerns of those who love us, in quiet times, alone, I have experienced moments of startling pain, when a feeling bubbles up through my stomach to my chest and throat. A blind reflection about the prospect of her absence from my life takes hold of me, and sheer terror overwhelms me, a terror that I wish were not about love, but instead about death, knowing too well that this substitution can or will not work. This pain is only retrospectively explained with reasons. To raise our children without her; to fear I could never be loved by another, and to fear that I might; to be alone in an empty house; the cloying hurt of ordinary loss.

Running on a bicycle trail one morning last summer, I came to realize I was sobbing only after being stared at by others on the path, and so I slowed to a walk to catch my breath, tears running down my face. I was ashamed, realizing that I was grieving a loss that was not yet mine to grieve. I am still ashamed. She still lives.

I think that there are seasons when the journey to death seems more clearly pronounced as an event in one's life, if not only because one immediately senses one's own movement toward death, than because all around the atmosphere is charged with news of this movement as it occurs in others. On the first day of this year, 2001, my aged mother died. My father watched her final months of decline, caring for her, trying to help her, by her side and suffering with her. Like many old men long married, he will follow her to death sooner, rather than later, collapsing into his loneliness, a suddenly sweet and sad figure. His loneliness was already beginning as she slowly slipped away, moved from their apartment into a nursing home as he could no longer meet the physical demands of her illness, and as she, unhappy and frightened, slightly demented, shared her unhappiness in the bitter way of the unhappy old. Old, old, my parents in their eighties, bodies worn out by their lives, experiencing what many others of their age have experienced. I describe what has been happening to them with these common words and common descriptions. Do these words, these descriptions, do anything to help or hinder us children as we observe our parents in the time of their decline, even or despite the fact that we who are their children are verging on old age ourselves?

Do such encounters change us? How can they not? In my middle forties, I have found that I have become more comfortable in the company of older friends (both those who have aged before me and those who have aged with me), people who in the wake of my wife's diagnosis and treatment have shared with me information about the various stages of their decrepitude, their cautious checking of blood sugar, pressure, and cholesterol levels, the results of examinations for colon, breast, prostate cancer, progress reports on the declining state of hearts, lungs, livers, backs, and knees, questionable PAP smears, strange lumps, failing sight. The heightened awareness of death and the betrayals of the body that we have shared has also enabled my wife and me to notice how communities of the sick form around hospitals and their environments, extending their connections into homes and medicine cabinets and kitchens, how a heterotopia we have (sardonically) called "sick world" shadows the world of health and seems at times to overtake the concerns of "well world." It seems that sick world, like all other worlds, has various rules of membership, initiation, and resignation. But only with this new appreciation of death-boundedness have we begun to notice for ourselves what so many others have described in more rigorous and systematic ways, that modern sciences of medicine allow not only the extension of life but a segregation of sickness from wellness and sick people from well people. The community of those who have nothing in common is made common to us through these means of separation and uncommonness. Were we simply callous not to have noticed all of this before?

To be given more time to think about death as one anticipates its approach may likely be a more common experience than in the past—when infection could surely and swiftly take us away—for those of us who live in technologically dependent cultures.

Now the prophylactics of chemotherapy, coronary bypass surgery, and protease regimens have caught and restored, if in slightly or drastically diminished states, many who would have been gone to join the ranks of the dead sooner. This is a hint of historicity tracking through the experience of deathboundedness, an inauthenticizing gift of technology. I wonder how we might assess the difference this gift may make for a meditation of experience in this shadow. Does it offer up a hope that is false, and hence has it been one more means of preventing us from getting closer to that reality?

These questions of attention to and distraction from deathboundedness foreground one's experience in the temporary spaces of sick world. A hesitation, a suspension of the moment, a stretching out of time, an unease that is bound to boredom but is so different from it, is at play in the waiting rooms of hospitals, doctors' offices, psychotherapists' comfortingly darkened dens. We recreate the quiet of these places at home, the clash of life surrounding the paraphernalia of recovery and decline. In every home with a seriously sick person we find the debris of sickness—the clotted tissue, the bedpan, the medicine bottles, heating pads, pillows, and reclining chairs—residues of the specific technologies brought to bear against the foreign agent, the failing part. If we trace these quotidian objects to their sources, we will find a repetition of the divisions and differences announced by expressions of technology. Yet we refashion our objects into waste, and may find the waste more comforting, a way of healing of the wounds, covering over the constitutive divisions between our bodies and our minds.

What are we doing here, after all?

Grieving

In the history of thinking, some have commented upon a serious split between those who are affiliated with what is called the Continental tradition in philosophy and others who are affiliated with what is called the Anglo-American tradition. Stanley Cavell has written with passion in the face of and perhaps against this division, what could be called a mutual shunning.[1] He is profoundly informed by it. It has occupied his life's thinking both by the tragedy it lays out for us and by the energy it generates as a constitutive split in thought. This writing of philosophy in the context of American identity is shared by Alphonso Lingis, who, in claiming an inheritance of the Continental tradition in the United States, may choose to remain silent about a key incident in the turns of that thinking he has done so much to bring to this continent. But then again, he may not, for he likely knows and by his translations alone has helped so many of us be prepared to learn, that from Husserl to Heidegger, from Merleau-Ponty to Levinas, from Foucault to Derrida, there is a philosophical incident that may fictively reunite that which cannot be divided, namely, the occasion of Nietzsche's life embrace of that wanderingly wayward American, Ralph Waldo Emerson. I attach Lingis to Cavell for this reason, that for all the wonderful strangeness of his encounters, Lingis is no more a stranger to the thinking of this constitutive split than is Cavell, this philosopher of the ordinary.

Cavell's interested reading of Emerson as an underwriter of philosophical concern is linked by him to a fate of philosophy more generally, a fate that plays to the very idea that there may be a possibility of "doing Continental philosophy" in the United States. That a geographical division in the work of thinking is to be thought about in an age in which the overcoming and rearticulation of difference has become one of the key themes of political philosophy is perhaps ironical. But it may also be that the philosophy of mountaintops, for instance the Alleghenies of central Pennsylvania, and that of sea level, for instance the shores near Mahabalipuram, are but various expressions of the same imperative, a community with nothing in common, a community of grief. This is an experience written by Lingis, whom I permit myself to think of as a descendant of Emerson, standing in the light of this Cavellian conceit, but also standing well below the mountaintops Zarathustra strolled.

It seems to me that an element of Emerson's thought shared by Lingis is a concern with how the experience of deathboundedness isolates and unites us in a community of those who have nothing in common. In this specific sense I believe that the writings of Emerson and Lingis gesture toward each other and toward a reconciliation or a partial overcoming of the mutual shunning of two traditions in thinking, in acknowledgments of what may be their life's work out of school, even or especially if they do not reach the curriculum of schools of philosophy. The concern to illuminate as philosophical fragments key moments of the experience of deathboundedness is, in Lingis's work, an uncanny refraction of Emerson's struggle to recover from the experience of grief, to rise to an anticipation of something yet to be. This becoming, this enjoyment, this expression of an imperative that drives us, brings us to grief. And it is grief that brings these two thinkers together as it is grief that grounds the world they share as it is grief that marks the handsomeness or unhandsomeness of our condition, those of us who have not yet died.

Grief is a word rooted in injury, describing a response to a harm or wound or hurt (OED). But the description offered by Emerson early on in his essay of grief is both uncanny and somehow exactly the opposite of what etymology would suggest. Emerson records his sense of the death of his son, Waldo in what seems to be a denial of what grief is to be.

> The only thing grief has taught me is to know how shallow it is. That, like the rest, plays about the surface, and never introduces me into the reality, for contact with which, we would even pay the costly price of sons and lovers. Was it Boscovich who found out that bodies never come in contact? Well, souls never touch their objects. An innavigable sea washes with silent waves between us and the things we aim at and converse with. Grief too will make us idealists. In the death of my son, now more than two years ago, I seem to have lost a beautiful estate,—no more. I cannot get it nearer to me. If tomorrow I should be informed of the bankruptcy of my principle debtors, the loss of my property would be a great inconvenience to me, perhaps, for many years; but it would leave me as it found me,—neither better nor worse. So it is with this calamity: it does not touch me: some thing which I fancied was a part of me, which could not be torn away without tearing me, nor enlarged without enriching me, falls off from me, and leaves no scar. It was caducous. I grieve that grief can teach me nothing, nor carry me one step into real nature. The Indian who was laid under a curse, that the wind should not blow

on him, nor water flow to him, nor fire burn him, is a type of us all. The dearest events are summer-rain, and we the Para coats that shed every drop. Nothing is left us now but death. We look to that with a grim satisfaction, saying, there at least is reality that will not dodge us. (472-73)[2]

The caducous character of Emerson's grief—it leaves him unchanged, it does not touch him, it leaves no scar—culminates in the paradox of grieving that grief can teach him nothing. One may imagine that to be taught something one needs to be touched, that experience shapes one as it wounds one, that the hard lesson of life is the isolation of death, that the only school is the school of hard knocks. This dead end is real, the wound a doubting Thomas must touch. But also, alternatively or supplementarily, grief teaches us the lesson of nothingness, and we must appreciate that Emerson grieves this lesson of nothingness. He later writes, "It is very unhappy, but too late to be helped, the discovery we have made, that we exist" (487). That this grief does not lead us into nature, but elsewhere, to what is least of nature, and most of human, the anticipation of death, or deathbound subjectivity. Any claims we may make of experience are those that are oriented toward loss, and they must lead us away from anything but that reality that will not dodge us.

Emerson's calculation of the loss of an estate seems to echo the calculation made by King Lear in his division of his lands and what becomes of that division, compactly capitalizing the play of the loss of estate and the state of the debt. In reality, there is only death and nothing. ("Nothing is left us now but death" may be paired with Lear's famous warning to Cordelia, "Nothing will come of nothing.") In referring to the caducous character of the loss of his son he expresses the core paradox ("Para coats," he puns) of grief, that it is a wound that leaves us untouched, which is to say, still untaught. Grief teaches no lesson, and that is its lesson for us.

Emerson's confession may be paired with Lear's shame (and mine), in that there is no way any of us is able to face others in the face of the grief we feel. This is because the pathos of the self whose constitution is formed by an act of separation from all that is around itself experiences grief as the confrontation with nothing, and that confrontation reminds that self of the nothing that he is, when the other has been repelled or renounced as outside of the self. So while the demand of filial love as a return for the renunciation of power may be expressed as Lear's avoidance of love by Cavell,[3] it may also, as such, be an anticipation or prophecy of grief and the shame of the griever, whose grief is for himself and his loss. Waldo dies, and his father is devastated to realize that Waldo is not himself, that his own son is now nothing.

What enables Emerson to live with himself and with others? It is not only the waters of Lethe, that is, forgetfulness, that he claims instills in us a numbness that will anesthetize us from the pain. The wound itself is caducous, requiring no healing. The way is clear for our death. But for Emerson the fact that grief cannot carry him one step into real nature suggests that his grief prepares him "to die out of nature and to be born again into this new yet unapproachable America I have found in the West" (485). Cavell announces this insight in Emerson as a central element in his aversive thinking, "an Emersonian calculation of the unapproachable, a reckoning of it as the forbidding."[4] Aversion may be thought of as a turning around of what is not movable, a provisional (or providential) experience for that which is not yet experienced. While it is no wonder that this moment in Emerson can be interpreted as a resort to theistic belief, the rebirth through experience he offers may be considered alternatively as a phenomenology of deathbound subjectivity anticipating that provided by Lingis.

Lingis writes of the gradual withdrawal from the world of those who are dying, their function fading, vacating a space to be filled by others. The time of dying, he emphasizes, is like no other time. "Dying takes time; it extends a strange time that undermines the time one anticipates, a time without a future, without possibilities, where there is nothing to do but endure the presence of time. What is impending is absolutely out of reach..."[5] (174-75). When we get closer to our death the world begins to fall away, and becomes less intelligible to us. And yet we become more intelligible to ourselves because we come closer to experiencing that which is beyond experience, not something that is simply unknown, but beyond the pairing of known and unknown. Lingis teaches that we withdraw from the world and into the world as death approaches. This could be called the loss of self, except that it is the most self-aware, most personal, most individuating moment of life, in which we become a member of the community of those who have nothing in common. "The shadow of death circumscribes, in the unending array of possibilities that are possible for anyone, what alone is possible for me" (169).

Hence Lingis comprehends grief as Emerson does. When he writes as the last sentence of his book on nothing, "The grief, when the other has been taken and no medication or comfort were possible, understands that one has to grieve" (179). The nothing that grief teaches is this, that one has to grieve what is taken—not from me, or from you, only taken. The caregiver, soon to be the griever, goes toward the dying person to touch that person while that person is still touchable, while that person is still capable of the comfort a touch make bring, while that person is still alive. "The touch of consolation is not itself a medication or protection; it is a solicitude that has no idea of what to do or how to escape.... The touch of consolation is an accompaniment, by one mortal and susceptible to suffering, of the other as he sinks into the time that goes nowhere, not even into nothingness" (178). When that person is gone we grieve. But we no longer touch the person, because, as both Emerson and Lingis knows, the lost one is no longer touchable. Something has fallen off from me; it is caducous.

Was that person ever touched? How can any one of us know the answer to such a question? We can only offer our words to each other and it is better not to ask too much of that other, for then we are no longer concerned about that touch, but only looking into a mirror.

To experience the caducous character of the death of someone we have touched, who has touched us, is to experience the death of that someone who we have loved as an inverted sort of birth. That which we imagine as a part of us is separate now; the separation is occasioned by the sinking into nowhere of the other. For Lingis the imperative is found in the ethics of our responsible attention to the other in suffering and in enjoyment. For Emerson it is found in the aversion to conformity, a resistance to the forms into which we gradually sink as we slowly, infinitesimally, take steps toward that which we cannot reach and are always headed. For Emerson and Lingis, we may experience an enjoyment that is a consequence of how we embrace the imperative, how we trust ourselves, how we notice the other.

Living

So often our lives turn around in moments when we are inadequately aware of what we are doing. In this sense, more of life is retrospective than not. Shame comes to us when we reflect backward and see our failure to look forward. If the conditions of our possibility is known to us only retrospectively, then we are surely lost, and not to be found. To die out of nature, to enjoy ourselves, is to think forward, prospectively. Yet the final prospect for everyone of us, and those yet unborn, is the experience that leads us to not even nothingness. How are we to live? In conversation, in comity, in the comedy of our hopelessness. This is what I take to be a lesson that Cavell, Emerson, and Lingis share.

In lieu of a conclusion, here a memory I have of Al Lingis as a comedic storyteller may illustrate this complex adventure of the exoticism of the ordinary, a play of many acts, and the integrity of this philosopher. In the summer of 1986 I returned to central Pennsylvania from New England to introduce Brenda Bright to an old teacher, Jack Wikse, who had a cabin on the same road as where Al lived. I had not seen Al since I had defended a (miserable) master's thesis in political theory at Penn State in the spring 1978, in which he had, as a favor to Jack, agreed to participate. The meeting for the thesis defense had been my primary acquaintance with the philosopher, though I had audited some of his lectures on Heidegger and of course knew of his work and translations. On that warm summer evening eight years later, in a soft summer twilight of late June, we were sitting outside preparing a fire to cook dinner, and Al strolled up to Jack's house and said the following:

> Hello, Tom. I just returned from Bali yesterday, where I heard the most remarkable story about a young pearl diver. It seems he was diving for pearls and a giant sea turtle came up and, mistaking his penis for a fish, bit it off. The poor boy! He kept resurfacing, and diving, diving, looking for his penis. I guess it would be like looking for a needle in a hay stack!

I proceeded to introduce Al to Brenda, and we all laughed and laughed, with an undercurrent of sorrow for the poor pearl fisher. My astonishment at his recognition of a former student he barely had encountered eight years before, the way he resumed a conversation as though we had seen each other the previous day, the allegorical density of this little fable, the conversation, all combined for me to illustrate the perverse courage and consolation of philosophy. What is the truth of our grief?

To avert shame, we are compelled to touch each other while we live, unhappy to know that we exist, condemned to acknowledge that we will surely die some day, but laughing as well as crying, happy to hope, maybe not today.

Notes

1. Stanley Cavell, "Emerson's Constitutional Amending," in *Philosophical Passages: Wittgenstein, Emerson, Austin, Derrida* (Oxford: Blackwell, 1995).

2. Ralph Waldo Emerson, "Experience," in *Essays, Second Series*, in *Essays and Lectures*, ed. Joel Porte (New York: The Library of America, 1983).

3. Stanley Cavell, "The Avoidance of Love: A Reading of *King Lear*," in *Must We Mean What We Say?* (New York: Charles Scribner's Sons, 1969). For a more detailed reading of Cavell on Shakespeare's Lear, see Dumm, "Cordelia's Calculus: Love and Loneliness in Cavell's Reading of Lear," unpublished manuscript.

4. Stanley Cavell, "Finding as Founding: Taking Steps in Emerson's Experience," in *This New Yet Unapproachable America* (Alburquerque: Living Batch Press, 1989), 92.

5. Alphonso Lingis, "Community in Death," in *The Community of Those Who Have Nothing in Common* (Bloomington: University of Indiana Press, 1994).

III

THE RETURN HOME

The home base is a pole of repose and departure. The zone of the intimate is a pole of warmth and tranquility that we keep sight of as we advance into the stretches of the alien and that our nomadic wanderings gravitate back to.
—*"The Intimate and the Alien,"* The Imperative

But in most cases, we have to appeal to others to make ourselves at home. We appeal to the others to help us be at home in the desert, in the rain forest, in the tropics, in the tundra, and in the ocean. And in childhood, and in the strange nocturnal regions of the erotic, and in the shadow of death that advances.
—*"The Elemental That Faces,"*
The Community of Those Who Have Nothing in Common

Chapter Fourteen

Trust

Alphonso Lingis

The Jungle, the City

A friend invited me to come to Madagascar and join him on a walk into the jungle. He had chosen the zone of mountains and swamp most inaccessible to loggers. We left Antananaviro in a taxi-brousse, descended to the coast and then went to the end of the road, then by dugout canoe to the beginning of the river. We trudged through muck, then up and down rocky mountains in the rain. It was exhilarating, but I lagged behind my friend, he so full of vigor and determination. We crossed a young Malagasi of about twenty on the path; he looked at me and with a smile and a sign offered to carry my backpack. I accepted. After a couple of days of crotch rot I wimped out. As my friend continued into the jungle alone, I lingered at a hamlet we had come upon, dried my clothes, got fed. The next morning, the young man who had carried my backpack appeared again; I indicated I was going back. He reached again for my backpack and set out.

He spoke not a word of French; I could not, by nodding my head and appealing to him, even learn the Malagasy words for "yes" and "no." He wore second-hand runners' shorts distributed by some missionary; my coarse cotton pants, purchased to protect my legs from leaches, rasped against my thighs and left them raw. He strode barefoot up the rocks and through the rivers; my jungle boots blistered my feet and filled with muck. He was always well ahead of me, or behind me; he would put down the backpack and wait a half hour to let me get ahead or to catch up with me. When the path forked I could only wait for him to arrive, or come back, to indicate which branch of the path to take.

In my backpack I had an expensive camera and six hundred dollars in cash. Were I he, sitting somewhere ahead or behind with that backpack, I surely would not resist the temptation to look in it. He could do whatever he wanted with my backpack, and with me, with impunity. I knew his name was Javalson, but where he lived I had no idea.

When night fell he found an abandoned hut for us to sleep and produced some bananas found or purchased somewhere. The next day we reached the river and he found a dugout canoe to take me back down the river. Among the people gathered at the river's edge I found someone who spoke some French and asked him how much I should pay my guide and savior. Fifteen thousand francs, he pronounced, and indeed Javalson seemed pleased when I handed that to him: it's three dollars US. He was gazing at my backpack: I opened it and wondered miserably what gift I could give him: I had given away all my medicines on the way and the inadequate food I had brought was gone. He pointed to my extra socks, took them with a grin; we shook hands, he disappeared. Of course, without shoes, he would not wear those socks in the muck and on the rocks; I understood he would keep them as a bemused—and affectionate?—memory of my absurd outfitting.

A few weeks later I was in London. I explored its gracious streets, flabbergasted as one always is after a prolonged stay in destitute countries by the material abundance, in a spring sunshine that had not welcomed me there before. That night, a Saturday, before going to bed I turned on the television and learned that a bomb had exploded in a crowded street in a London district inhabited mostly by Blacks. A week later, again on early Saturday evening, a bomb exploded in a crowded street in a district inhabited mostly by Bangladeshis. The police determined that the bombs were simple explosives packed with nails that tore into and maimed people across the street, and that the bombs had been brought to these locations and left in a gym bag. The television did specials on skinhead and neo-Nazi gangs, showed Internet sites of hate groups, reported police investigations of linkages with American Militia organizations and Serbian agents. Newspapers received letters claiming responsibility for the bombings from an organization called Commando 18 (cipher for Adolph Hitler). But the police revealed they had infiltrated that organization, and instead suspected a break-off sect that called themselves White Wolves. The television showed repeatedly a film from a street surveillance camera that had recorded a young man circling the area of the bomb the hour before it exploded. Hundreds of undercover police were assigned to Jewish and Muslim areas, awaiting the following Saturday. But on Friday early evening, a bomb exploded instead inside a gay pub in a crowded street in Soho. The three nail bombs had killed seven people and injured more than three hundred, some now in critical condition, others with amputated limbs and destroyed eyes.

Whenever I went out I found my eyes scanning the curtained windows of brick apartment blocks, behind which people conduct their business shut from prying eyes. As evening fell it was not in the empty side streets but in the crowded streets that I began to feel the pervasive fear.

Two days later the police, tipped off by neighbors who thought they recognized the young man in the film, raided an apartment and found bombs made with materials that could be purchased in any hardware store, and packed with nails. They arrested the tenant, a young engineer of twenty-three, and the next day reported they were confident that he had acted alone.

For three weeks the media had run specials by criminologists, sociologists, and culture-critics analyzing the skinhead, hooligan, and neo-Nazi subcultures in democratic and prosperous Britain, specials on immigrants and racism, on the culture of violence on television and in pop, punk, and rap music. Civic leaders, beginning with the Prime Minister, called for a national examination of conscience on the pervasive and unremarked racism of everyday life and attitudes and for a national commitment to the rule of law and to multiculturalism. Now the newspapers and television channels ran specials on the genetic, biochemical, and social causes of criminal psychopathology.

"He was a good neighbor, didn't bother anybody, always polite," the neighbors said of the London bomber—neighbors say each time a monster is identified in their midst. Someone you trusted to rent that spare room to, you trusted to keep an eye on the baby while you went down a few blocks to get some groceries, turns out to have been making bombs to kill innocent strangers indiscriminately.

A cause, an ideology, a group marginalized in the dominant society, a vendetta do not explain the solitary bomber. He was not a member of the White Wolves. Because the police suspected he was, because they saw racism in the first bomb in the Black neighborhood and the second in the Bangladeshi, they did not foresee the third would explode in a gay pub.

The psychologists and criminologists look for reasons for a hate that first flared in the infancy or adolescence of the young bomber. Was he abandoned or abused as a child? Traumatized as a pubescent adolescent? But hatred is not the direct reaction to someone or something detestable. The young engineer who still hated his father who had sought to socialize him could have despised him instead or now consign him to insignificance. He who loathed his father who had sexually molested him could have instead used his father's libido as the excuse to liberate himself from parental authority and affirm his own virility. If hatred arises, it goes beyond reasons to despise or condemn. Before the father's order, hatred pushes aside the inclination to explain and justify oneself, to acquiesce or evade. Hatred is a force that breaks loose. It has its own momentum. It seeks out reasons or excuses to hate on. When the father is just chatting amicably with his friends or just dozing in the sofa, hatred feels the more free to intensify its force and indulge its virulence.

That is why the one that one hates, even if he is one's father or she one's ex-lover, becomes someone generic and anonymous. I hate my spouse for her castrating words, but at the moment she is visibly someone just making our evening meal; to sustain my hatred is to dissolve this image of someone who enjoys cooking. Before hatred, she becomes more and more "a bitch," "*the* bitch." For this young engineer, those before whom his hatred first arose had inexorably become "the others." Thus it could seem to him that his hatred acted effectively in wiping out strangers in a Black neighborhood. Once he heard the indignant television reports lament that the dead and injured were random strangers, his hatred could find in random strangers in any London district its target.

Opposition can be measured and counteracted, but hatred is feared. Fear is fear of what is unknown; it is not simply a reaction to the manifestly dangerous. Before a mountain path one knows will give way if one steps on it one either refuses to advance on it or else feels a resigned acceptance of death; it is before the mountain path whose stability is unsure that one feels fear. It is not the Commando 18 agent known and identified by the police who spread fear across all London's neighborhoods but someone possibly acting alone and without ideology who might explode a bomb anywhere, or who might stop his activities and live somewhere in London without those three bombs ever being attributed to him. Because the unknown is without mappable boundaries, there is also an inner spiral in fear, which suspects in the unknown yet ever further circles of the unknown.

The one who hates feels the force of his hatred in the waves of fear that spread about it. And those who become ever more fearful and irresolute intensify the hatred of the bomber, whose hatred extends to ever more indeterminate others.

Fear in turn flows into, becomes, hatred. The hatred of the solitary bomber ignites the hatred of millions against him and against any polite young engineer who keeps to himself. Were it not for the fact that only the laboratory staff studying videos from the street cameras and the desk staff in the police stations studying their files could identify and locate the bomber, and the police officers arrived by stealth in the neighborhood and sped him away in an armed vehicle, he would have been lynched by his neighbors. The specials the television featured with psychologists and criminal pathologists were not only broadcast in order to satisfy the public craving for understanding; they were also broadcast in an effort to smother the flames of public hatred. Human rights organizations warned the public against antiterrorism legislation that would curtail their own liberties. They fear that the police equipped with forensic and detective science and rigorously controlled by Parliamentary legislation are themselves instruments of terror. The citizens come to fear, and thus to hate, their own terror.

Trust, Confidence, Faith

Although we do rather improperly speak of trusting a set of knowledge-claims, or distrusting them, more properly let us say that we *believe* statements, believe them to be true, or probably true, or doubt them, do not believe them to be true. What we trust is someone. We trust someone who affirms something though we do not see or cannot understand the evidence or the proof he or she may have. We trust someone in action: we trust someone to do what he or she says or to do what is best. Trust is not based on what we think we know about human causality; we trust someone to help us, guide us, save us, though we and he know that to do so is not in his self-interest.

We do also speak of trusting things: trusting the mechanical condition of the car, trusting the solidity of a scaffolding we set out to climb. More properly it would be better to say that we *expect* or *believe* that the car will make the trip to the West Coast, that the iron-pipe scaffolding is solid. Here our expectation is attached to the laws of nature.

Let us use the word *confidence* and not trust where we count on someone not as an individual agent but as occupying a role in an established social system where behaviors are socially defined and sanctioned. We rely on the bus driver following the scheduled route, we count on the bank teller giving us proper credit for our mortgage payment. Here our expectation about the action of the individual is based on our knowledge of how the transportation or commercial system works. We would have to have a reason to suspect a specific individual might not behave as expected. Similarly our expectations about our doctor, our teachers, and our parents are confidences in these socially defined roles and not trust in individual agents.

There is another form of confidence, in which we count of an individual acting in certain ways because of the value he puts on kinship, shared circumstances, or shared religious belief. When the value he puts on these things is tied up with what for him is his very identity, it becomes a strong determinant of his action.

Our trust, in someone to speak truthfully or to act as she says she will, is akin to the *faith* invoked in some religions in that it is an attachment to an individual subject as a locus of insight and initiative. Since that speaking and acting subject is singular, what he or she will say and do cannot be predicted from general laws, and is unknowable by me. Religious faith is attached to a personal deity whose mind and will are unknowable, but who, one claims to know, is omniscient, truthful, and unfailingly benevolent. Trust differs from faith in that it is attached to someone whose words or whose movements one does not understand, whose reasons or motives one does not see, and who is capable of ignorance and incompetence, mendacity and malevolence.

Knowledge induces belief, belief in what one sees clearly or in a coherent and consistent account that supplies evidence or proof. Trust, which is as compelling as belief, is not produced by knowledge. In trust one adheres to something one sees only partially or unclearly or understands only vaguely or ambiguously. One attaches to someone whose words or whose movements one does not understand, whose reasons or motives one does not see.

Is it all the things that are known that encourage the leap, in this one instance, to adhere to something unknown as though it were known? Is it not because of a long past tried and true that someone becomes a trusted advisor? But the more one knows about a tried and true advisor the more clearly one sees that every act of loyalty opens an opportunity for disloyalty. Those who most selflessly fought in the war of liberation have found, twenty years later, how to enrich themselves in public office. Is it all that one knows about the laws, the institutions, the policing, and all that one knows about the values, the education, the peer pressure of individuals in a society that induce one to trust this individual met at random on a jungle path? The more one understands about the laws and programming of a culture the more clearly one understands how they exist in a struggle with impulses contrary to them. To be sure we extend our trust to someone when we see how last week, yesterday, the last hour what he said turned out to be true, he did what he said he would do. But of course it is by thus eliciting our trust that he will able to betray us.

Trust was not a human impulse favored in modern philosophy. What trauma, what great deception did René Descartes suffer that made him look with consternation upon all that, in his education and in his travels, he had taken on trust? What crisis of faith made him seriously invoke the possibility that he was a plaything of an Evil Genius? Descartes set out to replace all that he had held to be true through trusting others with his own direct intuition of realities: of his own existence, of the existence and nature of his mind, of the fundamental truths of mathematics and logic, of the existence and nature of things outside of his mind. It is striking, however, that in order to ensure himself of the real existence of things external to himself he was only able to replace the trust in other men with faith in a God he has to believe is not an Evil Genius.

Today philosophers understand that truth cannot be determined by an individual thinker for himself. What can be true is a statement that can be integrated into the common discourse. Statements can be true, and first meaningful, only in the discourse of an established community that determines what could count as observations, what standards of accuracy in determining observations are possible, how the words of common language are restricted and refined for use in different scientific disciplines and practical or technological uses. Further, the discourse of our community determines what could count as an argument—in logic, in physics, in history, in economics, in penology, jurisprudence and military strategy, in medical treatment, in automotive repair, in agriculture. Establishing what can and must be said about things requires a community with institutions, which set up and finance research teams and laboratories to gather information and observations according to community standards of accuracy and repeatability, institutions which select and train researchers, and certify and evaluate the researchers and technicians. Establishing what can and must be said about things requires institutions which select what research is to be published, and how it is to be judged.

The institutions in which a people have confidence were themselves built on trust. Every kind of social organization for the production and distribution of knowledge, as well as of wealth, power, and prestige, while it may have been set up by coercion can be maintained only through a combination of coercion and consent. Emile Durkheim spoke of a "precontractual" element in all social organization: prior to the explicit consent a multiplicity of humans can give to a specific social organization, there is a fundamental level where individuals are individual agents each with his own motivations—and where bonds of trust can be formed among them.

What first and continually installs each of us in the common discourse and the common scientific endeavor are multiple bonds of trust: trust in those who determine what can count as an observation in a branch of empirical or practical knowledge, what can count as an argument, as evidence, what can count as reliable and accurate language in which to report observations.

An individual who inquires after what is known inquires of an individual who responds, in person or in writing, as a representative of the current state of particle physics, meteorology, genetics, or neuropathology. We accept what he or she says because we have confidence in the practices, methods, and institutions of community knowledge and confidence in him or her as a representative of an established discipline.

Yet the one who speaks or writes as a representative of an established discipline is also an individual seat of vision, insight, understanding, and conviction who can deceive himself and deceive others. Each time we address a licensed electrical engineer or veterinarian, in taking what they say as credible we extend our confidence in the established discipline and institutions of engineering or veterinary science. At the same time since we do not really know that he is not deceiving himself or deceiving us, in following his instructions we trust *him* or *her*.

There is always the necessary question: Is trust here warranted? Since trust is an attachment to something that is not known, there never is a demonstration of trustworthiness. All there can be are evidences of untrustworthiness. But just as in the experimental sciences there is no crucial experiment in which a hypothesis is falsified, so there is no crucial evidence that consigns any given informant, or any ethnographic report, any book by Margaret Mead or Edward Evan Evans-Pritchard, to the outer darkness of fiction.

Anthropology is the study of human nature. It is said that what makes anthropologists different from all other kinds of social scientists is the fieldwork experience. Government officials, traders, explorers, missionaries are also in the field, and longer. Is it not the heady, intoxicating, unforgettable abandon to trust that makes the anthropologist's experience so distinctive?

Ethnographers singlemindedly set out to produce the most credible possible report of how the people they observe live and what they think. The ethnographer's observations cannot be separated from her interviewing, for what the people are doing is shaped by what they believe and what they feel. Then the credibility of the ethnographer's report is generated by trust in her informants. To be sure, the ethnographer scrupulously sets out to check on this trustworthiness—but can do so only by appealing to more trust. It is by trusting not only the cognitive competence but the veracity of other informants that she confirms or negates the trustworthiness of any given informant.

Every anthropologist working in the field has known such times when trust emerges alone, the sole force holding one from the abysses of death, trust in someone as far as possible from oneself in culture, education, and age, someone with whom one has no kinship or ethnic or national or religious bonds. Indeed, upon arriving at his or her field, every anthropologist recognizes that his or her lodging, food, very survival there will depend on trusting these strangers whose very language he or she barely understands.

Immediacy

When we set out to know a mineral or a salt, we isolate a pure sample of it and peer at it with naked eyes and with all our instruments of enlargement and testing. But when we have the evidence of someone of our own kind in front of us, speaking directly to us, our understanding seems to be multiply mediated: He is not speaking his own language but the language of his gender, his family, his class, his education, his culture, his economic and political interests, his unconscious drives, indeed his state of physical health and alertness. The effort to know him gets detoured across all these layers. There then does not seem to be any place in our current epistemologies for trust—trusting a stranger, trusting someone whose words we do not understand. Yet each of us who have felt the force and the effects of trust cannot doubt that trust is a movement that short-circuits across all the mediations, that makes immediate contact with the real individual agent there.

For some time now I have been struck by this really amazing fact: it happens every day that someone exterior to me approaches and makes contact with *me*—the real me, the core me, whatever I can take to be *me*. To be sure so often others are only addressing some role I occupy in a society, some pantomime I am performing, some set of clothes and haircut I am wearing: they see and address the American, the professor, or the decently dressed restaurant client. And I—this individual me—thinks for himself and acts on his own, behind that image they see. But then it happens that I feel a force that plunges out of the passing forms and clamps on to me: "Hey you!" "Hey Al!" Isn't it quite striking—really our theories do not account for it—that I feel these words coming straight at me, hitting me, clamping on to *me*? An appeal is being addressed to *me*, a demand put on *me*. I feel someone has not taken hold simply of the American, the professor, or the guy in the way, the words have penetrated right through the role, the social identity, the visible and interpretable form, to the very core that is *me*. Each time I do answer on my own, I have found it undeniable that that is what has happened.

The movement of trust is that kind of movement. It holds on to the other as a real and individual seat of insight, an individual agent. In listening to the several surgeons I consult about my condition, I become confident that the one and the other speaks as a representative of the state of the art of surgical methods and techniques. But the trust I extend to one I choose to do the surgery is a bond with the real individual she is, whose insights and motives I do not see and who is capable of ignorance and incompetence, mendacity and malevolence. Upon watching Javalson leaving me at the edge of the river, I could not deny that the one I had been with those days and nights is the real Javalson, even though I could not formulate intelligibly to myself or to anyone what he said, what were his family, clan, and village coordinates, the categories with which he represented for himself society, nature, and the cosmos.

Two skydivers leap from a plane flying 500 mph at an altitude of 20,000 feet; the first spreads his arms and freefalls with nothing; the second leaping a few seconds after him has the two parachutes. They are both very experienced and very skilled, but the one does not know what dreams pestered the other last night, the other himself may not know. So many things unknowable to themselves can vitiate that skill—for in the love between the closest of buddies there is also rivalry, jealousy, resentment: wherever there is love for someone, there is also somewhere hatred of him. If despite all that could go wrong the second does deliver his parachute to the first, will there not clamp a bond between these two men such that all the other kinds of bondings others, even wives and children, could have with them could not disconnect that bond?

Immediacy: Courage, Laughter, Lust

It takes courage to trust someone you do not know. One attaches to someone whose words or whose movements one does not understand, whose reasons or motives one does not see. Courage is the force that does not banish fears but endures them. Courage is the force to stand firm in the face of danger, in the end: mortal danger.

If philosophers have avoided speaking of trust, preferring to generalize and universalize distrust, courage was a central topic for philosophy when it started up. Socrates, at his trial, claimed no intellectual virtues, save the negative one of knowing he knows nothing, but he affirmed his courage, proven three times in battle. Aristotle in his *Nichomachean Ethics*, listing the virtues, puts courage first. It is not simply first in a list, it is the transcendental virtue, the virtue without which the other virtues—truthfulness, friendship, magnanimity, even wit in conversation—are not possible. If we recognize courage in the force that makes us steadfast in the face of small and great dangers, courage is what makes men and women steadfast in the face of death.

Aristotle did maintain courage as a military virtue, denying that those who confront death by drowning or disease can really be said to be courageous. Though

Socrates reminded his fellow citizens of his courage in battle, he asserted that philosophers alone are truly courageous, for men who prove themselves fearless in battle are so because they fear something more—the death or capture of their families and fellow citizens, whereas philosophers know how to overcome all fear of death.

Socrates set out to demonstrate that courage could be produced only by philosophy, that is, by critical examination of knowledge claims. He argues that those who fear death claim to know what in fact they do not know: what death is, that death is evil, is the ultimate evil. But then Socrates demonstrates, with his arguments in the *Phaedo* and with his own calm drinking of the hemlock poison, that he knows what death is: that it is nothing. What is called death is the liberation of the immortal soul, the passage to pure life. What then is called death, what is experienced as death, is unreal.

Subsequent social and military history seems to demonstrate that indeed philosophy, that is, ideas, are necessary to produce courage. Socrates's idea later produced Christian martyrs and crusaders, as well as missionaries in hostile lands and in leper colonies. There is the same intellectual act of denial of the reality of death in the idea of the mystical body of the nation: the soldier is said to give his life so that the community, the nation may live. The soldier is seen not really to die at all, because the society to which he belongs, of which he is a member, lives on.

But there is another courage that can arise when the ideas one has fashioned about death, about the unreality of death, break up and one is faced with death itself. What does one see when one faces death? Death will be the extinction of the whole landscape about one, the irreversible extinction of one's individual existence. One sees nothingness itself, gaping open, the indeterminate and interminable abysss, awaiting one. One feels death lurking everywhere, lurking in the next moment, imminent, and what feels its reality is the anxiety that shudders in the very core of what one is. As death closes in, courage can arise from some unknown core of oneself. Courage is a force that can hold one steadfast as death itself approaches. Courage rises up and takes hold and builds on itself.

Courage and trust have this is common: they are not attitudes with regard to images and representations. Courage is a force that can arise and hold steadfast before the devastating force of death itself. Trust is a force that can arise and hold on to someone whose motivations are as unknown as those of death.

Laughter and sexual attraction are also forces that break through images and representations. Laughter is released by the outbreak of incoherence in discourse, the break up of meaning, by awkward, bungling efforts, and by goals that collapse when one has laboriously reached them. The peals of laughter hold on to the moment when the past that gave drive and skill to movements disconnects, when the future that gave sense and purpose to words and actions breaks off. There is just left the present, the raw and meaningless things, the thrashings of bodies—and the excess energies of the one who laughs. The energies ricocheting off the raw things fuel the peals of laughter.

At the same time laughter is contagious, a force that passes through the boundaries of individual identities. The anthropologist, who had worked out in a fitness club for a year in preparation for the rigors of the field, advances with bold steps over the log fallen over the river; halfway across he slips, tries to grab the log as he holds on to his video camera, lurches into the muddy river. Still holding high his mud-splattered video camera, he looks up and sees laughter spreading in waves across the locals he had come to ingratiate and study. He feels the immediacy and the reality of their presence in the force of the shared laugher.

Erotic excitement is aroused by all the artifices of imagery and pantomime; it is attracted to sumptuous garments and intense colors, to jewelry whose metal and crystal glitter across the billowing softness of flesh, it is mesmerized by the dances of seductive eyes, gracefully pirouetting fingers and hands, provocative and gamey words. But erotic excitement, *pace* Baudrillard, is not held in the fascination with images and simulacra; it unleashes lustful desires which crave to break through the images to palpate and penetrate the anonymous animal body behind them. And while the sexual craving that torments us shuts us off to the projects and solicitations of the common and practicable world, it is also anonymous and spreads by contagion making us transparent to one another. A very pregnant woman is dancing voluptuously in the street in Salvador de Bahia during Carnaval; we fix our fevered eyes on her and feel a current of complicity with the men and women about us, white or black, adolescent or aged.

In the way that laughter and sexual craving break through the images and representations and labeling of things and make contact with the singular reality, they have a kinship with courage and with trust. Indeed, just as there is courage in trust, so there is pleasure, exhilaration in trust: trust laughs at dangers. And sexual attraction is so like trust: it careens toward sexual surrender to another as into an ultimate trust. Conversely, there is something erotic in trust, for trust is not a bare thrust of will holding on to the unintelligible core of another; it is holding on to the sensibility and forces of another. There is something erotic in the trust that a skydiver extends to his buddy leaping into the air after him with his parachute, as in the trust that an individual lost in the jungle extends to a native youth. Trust is courageous, giddy, and lustful.

Typhoon

Trust is a break, a cut made in the extending map of certainties and probabilities. The force which breaks with the cohesion of doubts and deliberations is an upsurge, a birth, a commencement. It has its own momentum, and builds on itself. How one feels this force! Before these strangers in whom one's suspicious and anxious mind elaborates so many scheming motivations, abruptly one fixes on this one, at random, and one feels trust, like a river released from a lock, swelling one's mind and launching one on the way.

I determined, at a glance at this young man whose words I could not understand, to trust him to guide me out of the jungle. To have put trust in him is to have to put still further trust in him, each time he was a half hour ahead or a half hour behind me with my bag. Once trust takes hold, it compounds itself.

The one who finds himself trusted knows the path because he has trekked it regularly, come by this way just yesterday, but he knows that in this rain mountain paths collapse, rivers crossed yesterday may be untraversable today. He knows there is much he does not know; he trusts himself to be able to deal with the unknown when it shows itself. He then counts on his trust of himself more than on his knowledge. Once one puts one's trust in him, this trust can only generate yet more trust. The force of the trust one puts in him makes his trust in himself the dominant force in him, dissipating his anxieties and vacillations.

Trust binds one ever more deeply to another; it is an energy that becomes ever stronger and more intoxicated. Upon watching Javalson leaving me at the edge of the river, how I felt I had known him so much more deeply than if I had listened to someone who had, the length of an evening, recounted his life to me in a language I could understand!

Bibliography

Alphonso Lingis

Separately Bound Publications

Trans. and Introduction, *The Visible and the Invisible* by Maurice Merleau-Ponty. Evanston, IL: Northwestern University Press, 1968.

Trans., *Totality and Infinity* by Emmanuel Levinas. Pittsburgh, PA: Duquesne University Press, 1969.

Trans. and Introduction, *Existence and Existents* by Emmanuel Levinas. The Hague and Boston: Martinus Nijhoff, 1978.

Trans., *Images Poems* by Nicole Janicaud. Vence: Pierre Chave, 1980.

Trans. and Introduction, *Otherwise than Being or Beyond Essence* by Emmanuel Levinas. The Hague: Martinus Nijhoff, 1981.

Excesses: Eros and Culture. Albany, NY: State University of New York Press, 1984.

Libido: The French Existential Theories. Bloomington, IN: Indiana University Press, 1985.

Phenomenological Explanations. Dordrecht, The Netherlands: Martinus Nijhoff, 1986.

Ed., Trans., and Introduction, *Collected Philosophical Papers of Emmanuel Levinas*. Dordrecht, The Netherlands: Martinus Nijhoff, 1987.

Deathbound Subjectivity. Bloomington, IN: Indiana University Press, 1989.

Trans. and Introduction, *Sade My Neighbor* by Pierre Klossowski. Evanston, IL: Northwestern University Press, 1991.

The Community of Those Who Have Nothing in Common. Bloomington and Indianapolis, IN: Indiana University Press, 1994.

Abuses. Berkeley/Los Angeles/London: University of California Press, 1994.

Foreign Bodies. New York and London: Routledge, 1994.

Sensation: Intelligibility in Sensibility. New York: Humanities, 1996.

Ortak bir Seyleri Olmayanlarin Ortakligi. Trans. of *The Community of Those Who Have Nothing in Common*, into Turkish by Tuncay Birkan. Istanbul: Ayrinti Yayinlari, 1997.

N ieko bendra neturinciuju bendrija. Trans. into Lithuanian of *The Community of Those Who Have Nothing in Common*. Baltos Lankos, Vilnius, Lithuania, 1997.

Abusi, Viaggio tra i dannati della Terra. Trans. into Italian of *Abuses* by Roberto Festa Milan. Paratiche Peditrice, 1997.

L'ivresse des profondeurs et autres excès. Trans. by Dominique and Nicole Janicaud of Excesses. Paris: Belin, 1997.

The Imperative. Bloomington: Indiana University Press, 1998.

Dangerous Emotions. Berkeley: University of California Press, 2000.

The Community of Those Who Have Nothing in Common. Trans. into Japanese, 2002.

Susturulmuslar. Ankara: Dost, 2002. Trans. into Turkish of *Abuses* by Figon Dereli. Berkeley: University of California Press, 1994.

Pavojingos Emocijos, Kaunas: Poligrafija ir Informatika, 2002. Trans. into Lithuanian of *Dangerous Emotions* by Ieva Skarzinskaité. Berkeley: University of California, 2000.

Contributions to Books

"On the Essence of Technique," in *Heidegger and the Quest for Truth*. Ed. Manfred S. Frings. Chicago, IL: Quadrangle Books (1968), pp. 126-138.

"Non-Violence as Historical Action," in *Violence in Contemporary American Society*. Eds. Hale B. Harris and John A. Sample. University Park, PA: Pennsylvania State University Press (1960), pp. 231-237.

"The Elemental Background," in *New Essays in Phenomenology*. Chicago, IL: Quadrangle Books (1969), pp. 24-38.

"Intentionality and Corporeity," in *Analecta Husserliana*, Vol. I. Ed. A.-T. Tymieniecka. Dordrecht, The Netherlands and New York, NY: D. Reidel (1970), pp. 75-90.

"Hyletic Data," in *Analecta Husserliana, The Later Husserl and the Idea of Phenomenology*, Vol. II. Ed. A.-T. Tymieniecka. Dordrecht, The Netherlands and New York, NY: D. Reidel (1972), pp. 96-101.

Trans. of J. Taminiaux, "Phenomenology in Merleau-Ponty's Late Work," in *Life-World and Consciousness*. Ed. L. E. Embree. Evanston, IL: Northwestern University Press (1972), pp. 370-322.

"Being in the Interrogative Mood," in *The Horizons of the Flesh*. Ed. Garth Gillan. Carbondale and Edwardsville, IL: Southern Illinois University Press (1973), pp. 78-91. Also published by Feffer & Simons, Inc., London and Amsterdam.

"The Will to Power," in *The New Nietzsche—Contemporary Styles of Interpretation*. Ed. David Allison. New York, NY: Dell Publishing Co. (1977), pp. 37-63.

Translation of Henri Birault, "Beatitude in Nietzsche," in *The New Nietzsche—Contemporary Styles of Interpretation*. Ed. David Allison. New York, NY: Dell Publishing Co. (1977), pp. 219-231.

"A Time to Exist on One's Own," in *The Self and the Other. Analecta Husserliana*, Vol. VI. Ed. A.-T. Tymieniecka. Dordrecht, The Netherlands and New York, NY: D. Reidel (1977), pp. 31-40.

"Association," in *Analecta Husserliana, The Human Being in Action, The Irreducible Element in Man, Part II, Investigations at the Intersection of Philosophy and Psychiatry*, Vol. VII. Ed. A.-T. Tymieniecka. Dordrecht, The Netherlands, Boston, MA and London, England: D. Reidel (1978), pp. 215-234.

"Authentic Time," in *Crosscurrents in Phenomenology*. Eds. Ronald Bruzina and Bruce Wilshire. The Hague, Boston, MA and London, England: Martinus Nijhoff (1978), pp. 276-296.

"Old and New Forms of the Will to Power," in *Philosophy of the Humanistic Society*. Ed. Alfred E. Loenig. Washington, DC: University Press of America (1981), pp. 39-40.

"Abject Communication," in *Interpersonal Communication: Essays in Phenomenology and Hermeneutics*. Ed. Joseph J. Pilotta. Washington, DC: Center for Advanced Research in Phenomenology and University Press of America (1982), pp. 161-171.

"The Language of the Gay Science," in *The Philosophical Reflection of Man in Literature, Analecta Husserliana,* Vol. XI. Ed. A.-T. Tymieniecka. Boston, MA: D. Reidel (1982), pp. 313-319.

"Theory and Idealization in Nietzsche," in *The Great Year of Zarathustra (1881-1981).* Ed. David Goicolchea. Lanham, MD: University Press of America (1983), pp. 257-278.

"The Pleasure in Postcards," in *Hermeneutics and Deconstruction.* Eds. Hugh J. Silverman and Don Idhe. Albany, NY: SUNY Press (1985), pp. 152-164.

"The Sensuality and the Sensitivity," in *Face to Face with Levinas.* Ed. Richard Cohen. Albany, NY: SUNY Press (1986), pp. 219-230.

"Mastery in Eternal Recurrence," in *Analecta Husserliana.* vol. xxi *The Phenomenology of Man and of the Human Condition, Part II. The Meeting Point Between Occidental and Oriental Philosophies.* Ed. A.-T. Tymieniecka. Dordrecht, The Netherlands: D. Reidel (1986), pp. 89-101.

"A Phenomenological Approach," in *Theories of Human Sexuality. Perspectives in Sexuality.* Eds. James H. Geer and William R. O'Donohue. New York, NY and London, England: Plenum Press (1987), pp. 127-161.

"Effets de language," in *Nouvelles lectures de Nietzsche.* Ed. Dominique Janicaud. Lausanne, Switzerland: l'Age d'Homme (1985), pp. 50-57.

Trans. of Emmanuel Levinas, "The Trace of the Other," in *Deconstruction in Context.* Ed. Mark C. Taylor. Chicago, IL: University of Chicago Press (1986), pp. 345-359.

"Deleuze on a Deserted Island," in *Philosophy and Non-Philosophy Since Merleau-Ponty.* Ed. Hugh J. Silverman. New York, NY and London, England: Routledge (1988), pp. 152-173.

"The Sensitive Flesh," in *The Collegium Phaenomenologicum. The First Ten Years.* Eds. J. C. Sallis, G. Monetz, and J. Taminiaux. Dordrecht, The Netherlands, Boston, MA, and London: Kluwer Academic Publishers (1988), pp. 225-240.

"The Din of the Celestial Birds or Why I Crave to Become a Woman," in *Psychosis and Sexual Identity.* Eds. David Allison, Pardo de Oliveira, Mark Roberts, and Allen Weiss. Albany, NY: SUNY Press (1988), pp. 130-142.

"Substitution," in *Postmodernism and Continental Philosophy*. Eds. Hugh Silverman and Donn Welton. Albany, NY: SUNY Press (1988), pp. 26-33.

"Self-Presentation," in *American Phenomenology: Origins and Developments*. Vol. XXVI. Eds. Eugene F. Kaelin and Calvin O. Schrag. Dordrecht, The Netherlands: Kluwer Academic Publishers (1989), pp. 252-256.

"The Final Kingdom," in *Phenomenology and Beyond: The Self and Its Language*. Eds. H. A. Durfee and D. F. Rodier. Dordrecht, The Netherlands: Kluwer Academic Publishers (1989), pp. 11-25.

"Morele vaarden. Over het eerste hoofdstuk van 'Zur Genealogie der Moral,'" in *Nietzsche als Arts van de Cultuur*. Ed. Paul van Tongeren. Kampen, The Netherlands: Kok Agora (1990), pp.185-215.

"Being Elsewhere," in *Falling in Love with Wisdom*. Ed. David D. Karnos and Robert G. Shoemaker. New York and Oxford: Oxford University Press (1993), pp. 256-261.

"The Society of Dismembered Body Parts," in *Gilles Deleuze and the Theater of Philosophy*. Eds. Constantin V. Boundas and Dorothea Olkowski. New York and London: Routledge (1994), pp. 289-303.

"The Destination," in *Eros and Eris: Contributions to a Hermeneutical Phenomenology Liber Amicorum for Adriaan Peperzak*. Eds. Paul van Tongeren, Paul Sars, Chris Bremmers, and Koen Boey. Dordrecht, The Netherlands: Kluwer Academic Publishers (1992), pp. 263-272.

"Extremities," in *Being Human in the Ultimate: Studies in the Thought of John M. Anderson*. Eds. N. Geogopoulos and Michael Heim. Amsterdam, The Netherlands: Rodopi (1995), pp. 189-206.

"Hands Detach Themselves," in *And Yet*. Ed. Russell Dumas. Sydney, Australia: Dance Exchange Incorporated (1995), pp. 11-13.

"Heidegger's Conception of the Technological Imperative: A Critique," in *Continental and Postmodern Perspectives in the Philosophy of Science*. Eds. Babette Babich, Debra Bergoffen, and Simon Glynn Brookfield. Hong Kong and Singapore: John Avebury Press (1995), pp. 227-245.

"Intentionnalité et impératif," in *L'intentionnalité en question*. Ed. Dominique Janicaud. Paris: Vrin (1995), pp. 367-382.

"Levinas and the Elemental Response," in *Joyful Wisdom, Glory and the Ethics of Joy, Studies in Postmodern Ethics*, Vol. 3. Ed. David Goicoechea. Ottawa: Thought House Publishing Group (1994), pp. 42-51.

"The Society of the Friends of Crime," in *Sade and the Narrative of Transgression*. Eds. David B. Allison, Mark S. Roberts, and Allen S. Weiss. Cambridge: Cambridge University Press (1995), pp. 100-121.

"The Body Postured and Dissolute," in *Merleau-Ponty: Difference, Materiality, Painting*. Ed. Véronique Foti. New Jersey: Humanities Press (1996), pp. 60-71.

"Wonders Seen in Forsaken Places," CD-Rom. State College, PA.: Chester Perkowski (1996).

"Anger," in *On Jean-Luc Nancy: The Sense of Philosophy*. Eds. Darren Sheppard, Simon Sparks, and Colin Thomas. London and New York: Routledge (1997), pp. 197-215.

"Autrement qu'être," in *Emmanuel Levinas*. Eds. Catherine Chalier and Miguel Abensour. Paris: Cahiers de l'Herne (1991), pp. 163-184.

"Autrement qu'être," in *Emmanuel Levinas*, Cahiers de l'Herne. Ed. Jacques Rolland. Paris: Livre de Poche (1996).

"Appetite," in *Eating Culture*. Eds. Ron Scapp and Brian Seitz. Albany: State University of New York Press (1998), pp. 121-131.

"Love Song," in *Articulations of Difference*. Eds. Dominique D. Fisher and Lawrence R. Schehr. Stanford: Stanford University Press (1997), pp. 167-184.

Trans. into Japanese of "Pura Dalem," in *Tabi no hazama*. Ed. Keijiro Suga. Tokyo: Iaanami Shoten, Toyko (1997), pp. 38-56.

"The Sovereign's Table," in *Taste Nostalgia*. Ed. Allen S. Weiss. New York: Lusitania Press (1997), pp. 111-116.

"What is at Stake in Conversation," in *Interkulturelle Philosophie und Phanomenologie in Japan*. Eds. Tadashi Ogawa, Michael Lazarin, and Guido Rappe. Munchen: Iudicium (1998), pp. 139-152.

"Schizoanalysis of Race," in *The Psychoanalysis of Race*. Ed. Christopher Lane. New York: Columbia University Press (1998), pp. 176-189.

"Naked Eyes, Stained Surfaces," in Clark Lunberry, *Naked Eyes Stained Surfaces, Photographs in the Philosophy of Alphonso Lingis*, a Website text, 142 pp.

"Black Stars: The Pedigree of the Evaluators," in *Critical Assessments: Friedrich Nietzsche*, Ed. Daniel Conway. London and New York: Routledge (1998).

"The Unlived Life Is Not Worth Examining," in *Portraits of American Continental Philosophers*. Ed. James R. Watson. Bloomington: Indiana University Press (1999), pp. 119-25. Trans. in *Neue amerikanische Philosophinnen in Selbstdarsteelungen*. Ed. James R. Watson. Wien: Verlag Turia and Kant (1998).

"Innocence," in *Becomings, Explorations in Time, Memory, and Futures*. Ed. Elizabeth Grosz. Ithaca: Cornell University Press (1999), pp. 201-216.

"Segmented Organisms," in *Merleau-Ponty, Interiority and Exteriority, Psychic Life and the World*, Eds. Dorothea Olkowski and James Morley. Albany: State University of New York Press (1999), pp. 167-182.

"Bestiality," in *Animal Others: On Ethics, Ontology, and Animal Life*. Ed. H. Peter Steeves. Albany: State University of New York Press (1999), pp. 37-54.

Trans. of Emmanuel Levinas "Reality and Its Shadow," in *A Continental Aesthetics Reader*, Ed. Clive Cazeau. London and New York: Routledge, (1999).

"Foreign Bodies," in *Foreign Dialogues*. Ed. Mary Zournazi. Anandale, Australia: Pluto Press (1998), pp. 169-188.

"Deadly Pleasures," in *Must We Burn Sade?* Ed. Deepak Narang Sawhney. New York: Humanity Books (1999), pp. 31-49.

"Ecological Emotions," in *Earth Matters*. Ed. Robert Frodeman. Upper Saddle River, NJ: Prentice-Hall (1999), pp. 175-187.

"Satyrs and Centaurs: Miscegenation and the Master race," in *Why Nietzsche Still?* Ed. Alan Schrift. Berkeley: University of California Press (2000), pp. 154-169.

"The Last Hours," in *The Limits of Death*. Eds. Joanne Morra, Mark Robson, and Marquard Smith. Manchester: Manchester University Press (2000), pp. 144-163.

"The Elemental Imperative," in *Rereading Merleau-Ponty*. Eds. Lawrence Hass and Dorothea Olkowski. Amherst: Humanity Books (2000), pp. 209-232.

"The God of Evil," in *Evil Spirits: Nihilism and the Fate of Modernity*. Eds. Gary Banham and Charlie Blake. Manchester: Manchester University Press (2000), pp. 40-51.

"Cues, Watchwords, Passwords," in *The Politics of Community*. Ed. Michael Strysick. Aurora, Colorado: The Davies Group (2002), pp. 15-30.

"Eye on the Killer," Preface to Brian Evenson, *Altman's Tongue*, University of Nebraska Press (2002).

"Armed Assault," in *Aesthetic Subjects*. Eds. Pam Matthews and David McWhirter. University of Minnesota Press (2001).

"Obstacles to Dialogue Today," in *Dialogue Among Civilizations*. Paris: United Nations Educational, Scientific, and Cultural Organization (2002), pp. 81-86.

"Love Junkies," in *High Culture: Reflections on Addiction and Modernity*. Eds. Alexander and Mark S. Roberts. Albany, State University of New York Press (2003), pp. 279-296.

"Language and Persecution," in *Between Deleuze and Derrida*. Eds. Paul Patton and Johyn Protevi. London, Continuum (2003), pp. 169-182.

Contributions to Periodicals

"The Aesthetic as Aesthetic." *Duquesne Review* (Spring, 1963), pp. 22-25.

Translation of Paul Ricoeur, "The Historical Presence of Non-Violence." *Cross Currents* 14:2 (1964), pp. 15-23.

Trans. of Jacques Sarano, "The Spirit, Sexuality and the Beast." *Cross Currents* 14:2 (1964), pp. 214-227.

"Sensation and Sentiment: On the Meaning of Immanence." *Proceedings of the American Catholic Philosophical Association* 41 (1967), pp. 69-75.

"Man as a Symbol Maker: The Face and the Things." *Worship* 44:8 (1970), pp. 475- 487.

"The Perception of Others." *Research in Phenomenology* 2 (1972), pp. 47-62.

"Truth and Art, Heidegger and the Temples of Constantinople." *Philosophy Today* 16:2/4 (1972), pp. 122-134.

"The Perception of Others." *The Philosophical Forum* 5:3 (1974), pp. 460-474.

"The Void that Waits. The Force of Anxiety." *Journal of Phenomenological Psychology* 6:2 (1976), pp. 153-162.

"Sense and Non-Sense in the Sexed Body." *Cultural Hermeneutics* 4 (1977), pp. 345- 365.

"L'Origine de l'infini." *Le Savior Philosophique, Annales de la Faculte des Lettres et Sciences Humaines de Nice* 32 (1977), pp. 59-72.

"A Time of One's Own." *Dialogos* 11:29/30 (1977), pp. 113-122.

"The Last Form of the Will to Power." *Philosophy Today* 22:3/4 (1978), pp. 193-205.

"Difference in the Eternal Return of the Same." *Research in Phenomenology* 8 (1978), pp. 77-91.

"Emmanuel Levinas and the Intentional Analysis of the Libido." *Philosophy in Context* (1978), pp. 60-69.

Trans. of Jacques Derrida, "Speech and Writing According to Hegel." *Man and World* 2:1/2 (1978), pp. 107-130.

"Phenomenology in Middle Age." *Human Studies* 2 (1979), pp. 77-85.

"Face to Face, A Phenomenological Meditation." *International Philosophical Quarterly* 19:2 (1979), pp. 151-163.

"The Difficulties of a Phenomenological Investigation of Language." *The Modern Schoolman* 57:1 (1979), pp. 56-64.

"An Infinite Time of One's Own." *Eidos* 1:2 (1979), pp. 180-197.

"A New Philosophical Interpretation of the Libido." *SubStance* 25 (1980), pp. 87-97.

"Rangda." *Metmenys* 39 (1980), pp. 10-27. Translation into Lithuanian by Algis Mickunas.

"The Imperative to be Master." *The Southwestern Journal of Philosophy* 11:2 (1980), pp. 95-107.

"On Phenomenological Explanation." *The Journal of the British Society for Phenomenology* 11:1 (1980), pp. 54-68.

"Sensations." *Philosophy and Phenomenological Research* 42:2 (1981), pp. 60-70.

"Intuition of Freedom, Intuition of Law." *The Journal of Philosophy* 79:10 (1982), pp. 558-596.

"Intentional Libido, Impulsive Libido." *Journal of Phenomenological Psychology* 12:1 (1982), pp. 51-62.

"The Fatality of Consciousness." *Philosophy Today* 27:3/4 (1983), pp. 247-257.

"In This Country Called El Salvador, War of Rich, Poor." *The Daily Collegian* 84:47 (1983), p. 8.

"The Signs of Consciousness." *SubStance* 42, 13:1 (1984), pp. 3-14.

"The Truth Imperative." *Auslegung* 2:1 (1984), pp. 317-339.

"Oedipus Rex: The Oedipus Rule and Its Subversion." *Human Studies* 7 (1984), pp. 91-100.

"The Visible and the Vision." *Journal of the British Society for Phenomenology* 15:2 (1984), pp. 155-163.

"The Assignation." *Philosophy in Context* 14 (1984), pp. 70-79.

"The Incommunicable." *Art & Text* 18 (1984), pp. 108-113.

"The Imperative to be Master." *Cogito* 111:3 (1985), pp. 69-82.

"Sade or the Philosopher-Villain by Pierre Klossowski." *SubStance* 15:2 (1986), pp. 5-15.

"The Other Death." *Phenomenological Inquiry* 10 (1986), pp. 92-108.

"The Elemental Imperative." *Research and Phenomenology* vol. xviii (1988), pp. 3-21.

"L'ivresse des profondeurs." *Poësie* (Paris), 51 (1989), pp. 85-94.

"Painted Faces." *Art & Text*, Special Issue: Art Brut (Paddington, NWS, Australia), 27 (1989), pp. 80-92.

"The Irrecuperable." *International Studies in Philosophy* 23:2 (1991), pp. 65-74.

"From Under Dismembered Bodies." *The Review of Contemporary Fiction* 11:1 (Spring, 1991), pp. 289-297.

"Black Stars: The Pedigree of the Evaluators." *Graduate Faculty Philosophy Journal* 15:2 (1991), pp. 67-91.

"La vérité qui babille." *LeCOQ - HéRON* 124 (March 1992), pp. 39-43.

"The Mortals." *Dialogos* 59 (1992), pp. 7-18.

"The Society of Dismembered Body Parts." *PLI Warwick Journal in Philosophy* 4:182 (Oct. 1992), pp. 1-19.

Trans. of Henri Birault, "Nihilism and Beatitude." *Epoché* 1:1 (1993), pp. 65-76.

"Some Questions about Lyotard's Postmodern Legitimation Narrative." *Philosophy and Social Criticism* 20:1/2 (1994), pp. 1-12.

"Henrykkelsen ved dybet." (Trans. by Claus Bech.) *Den Blå Port* 25-26 (1993), pp. 57-66.

"Intentionality and the Imperative," *International Philosophical Quarterly* (1994), vol. xxxiv:3, pp. 289-300.

"The Postmodern Economic High-Growth Society," *Theory, Culture & Society*, 11:1 (February 1994), pp. 171-187.

"Bodies That Touch Us." *Thesis* 11:36 (1993), pp. 159-167.

"Carnaval in Rio," in *Vulvamorphia*, Lusitania 6, pp. 59-63.

"Death Drive." *The Journal of Value Inquiry* 29 (1995), pp. 217-229.

"Sex Objects." *SubStance* 75, 22:3 (1994), pp. 30-45.

"The Real Haiti." *The Daily Collegian* 95:74 (Oct. 24, 1994), p. 8.

"The State of the World," *Al-Ahram* (Cairo), 13-19 (April 1995), p. 14.

"The World as a Whole," *Research in Phenomenology.* 25 (1995), pp. 142-159.

"Hands Detach Themselves..." *Writings on Dance* 15 (Winter, 1996), pp. 68-70.

"The Misunderstanding." *Parallax* 4:97, pp. 79-88.

"Juodieji dievai." *Baltos Lankos* 7 (1996).

"Travelling with Lingis," An Interview with Alphonso Lingis, by D. J. Huppatz, Ananda Rubens, and Sarah Tutton, in *Melbourne Journal of Politics* (Melbourne, Australia) 24 (1997), pp. 26-40.

"Animal Body, Inhuman Face." *Social Semiotics* 7:1 (August 1997), pp. 113-126.

"Practical Necessity." *Graduate Faculty Philosophy Journal* 20: 2 and 21:1 (1997), pp. 71-82.

"A Phenomenology of Substances." *American Catholic Philosophical Quarterly* 71:4 (1998), pp. 505-522.

"Fateful Images." *Research in Phenomenology* 28 (1998), pp. 55-71.

"Animal Bodies." *Discourse* 20:3 (Fall, 1998), pp. 194-203.

"Word of Honor." *Paragraph* 22: 2 (July 1999), pp. 146-163.

"Reply to Peter Jackson," in *Intersections: Gender, History and Culture in the Asian Context*, (Dec. 1999).

"The Private Myth of Dignity." *The Journal of the British Society for Phenomenology* 31:1 (Jan. 2000), pp. 4-20.

"Objectivity and Justice." *Continental Philosophy Review* 32:4 (Oct. 1999), pp. 395-407.

"Flesh Trade." *Parallax* 18 (Jan.-Mar. 2001), pp. 48-63.

"Quadrille." *Performance Research* 5:2 (Summer, 2000), pp. 5-14.

"The Return to, the Return of Peoples of Long Ago and Far Away." *Angelaki* 6:2 (2001).

"Fantasy Space, Private Myths, Visions." *Journal of Phenomenological Psychology* 30:2 (Fall, 1999), pp. 94-108.

"The Dreadful Mystic Banquet." *Janus Head* (Fall, 2000), pp. 192-212.

"Ecological Consciousness." *Budhi* 4:2 and 3 (2000), pp. 1-16.

"The Return of Extinct Religions." *Budhi* 4:2 and 3 (2000), pp. 17-31.

"Vakarieti_k_ mit_ era pasaulyje gali greitai baigtis," in *Lietuvos rytas/* 2001 m. gegu_es 19d, Nr. 116.

"Ecological Consciousness: Reflections on Hominids and Other Thinking Animals." *Critical Horizons* 2:2 (2001), pp. 282-300.

"The Return of Extinct Religions." *New Nietzsche Studies* 4:3/4 (2000), pp. 15-28.

"Arouane." *Antioch Review* 60:1 (Winter, 2000), pp. 87-93.

"The Song of the Norias." *Sandwich* A (Autumn, 2001), pp. 1-6.

"Recalling Lacan: The Unstamped Letter." *The Semiotic Review of Books* 13:1 (2002), p.16.

"AsmensTapatumas," *Problemos* 61 (2002), pp. 9-17.

"Petra," *The Journal of Visual Culture* 1:1 (April 2002), pp. 47-55.

Index

Ackerman, Diane, xiii
anger, 40, 68
animals, 26, 36, 55-56, 61n4, 66, 84-85, 92-93, 96, 133
Aristotle, 21, 23, 25, 52, 53, 141, 153, 156, 182
art, 120, 123-130, 132n14, 146, 148, 153-155, 157, 194
Augustine, xv, 47, 59
Austin, xiv, 37, 172
authentic, 28, 32, 189

Bacon, 127
Bataille, George, ix, xiii, xiv, 7, 20, 36, 40, 69, 96, 104, 124
Baudrillard, 6, 9, 184
beauty, xi, xii, 88, 94, 126
Bergson, 36
Blake, 44, 46, 48
Blanchot, Maurice, 11, 12
body, xvi, xvii, 26-27, 37, 46-47, 91-93, 97, 120-127, 130, 143-144, 150-151, 153, 160, 191, 192, 197
Borges, Jorge Luis, 65, 66, 153, 162
brave, 95-96
bravery, 95-96

Cavell, Stanley, xvii, 165, 167, 168, 169, 171, 172
certainty, 21, 23
character, 52, 94-95, 169, 170
Collingwood, R. G., 161
communication, 7-8, 11, 56-58, 67-68, 71, 74, 76, 117, 189
communities, 24, 69, 93, 96
community, 12, 27, 32n8, 33n17, 62n7, 68, 71, 72, 73, 76, 80n18, 93-94, 140, 145n16, 168, 172n5, 180, 187
consciousness, 23, 47, 52, 85, 113, 189, 196, 198, 199
courage, 68, 73, 94-96, 182-184

Dante, xv, 44, 47
Darwin, 120
Dasein, 52, 101
de Certeau, Michel, ix, 93
de Sade, 39
death, xvii, 7, 26, 27, 28, 80n19, 96-97, 113, 145n6, 166, 168-170, 172n5, 182-183, 201
Defoe, Daniel, 135, 137, 144, 145, 146
Deleuze, Gilles, ix, xiii, xiv, 20, 36, 37, 78, 147, 152, 153, 162, 190, 191, 194
Derrida, Jacques, 12, 78, 130, 132, 167, 172, 194, 195, 201
Descartes, René 23, 59, 101, 179
desire, 89, 107, 110, 129, 139
distrust, 38, 182
dream, xvi, 110-113, 116-118
Durkheim, Emile, 78, 180

Emerson, Ralph Waldo, xiv, xvii, 16, 165, 167, 168, 169, 170, 171, 172
emotions, 39, 40, 67-68, 69, 76
enlightenment, xiv, 23, 66, 78
erotic, 54, 57, 62n7, 89, 110, 125, 126, 127, 130, 131n10, 184
Evans-Pritchard, Edward Evan, 180

face, xiii, 11, 23, 24, 42, 55-57, 59, 88-90, 111-112, 131n4, 194
faith, 179
fear, 85, 131n10, 177-178, 183
feeling, 68, 149, 160, 161n2
Feyerabend, Paul, xiii
finitude, 102-103, 105, 107, 115
force, 68, 105, 106, 116, 117, 121,

177, 178, 181, 182, 183, 184, 185, 195
Foucault, Michel, ix, x, xi, xii, xiii, xv, 20, 27, 36, 63, 64, 65, 66, 67, 68, 69, 70, 71, 72, 74, 75, 77, 78, 79, 80, 81, 93, 130, 132, 167, 201
Freud, Sigmund, 5, 6, 8, 9, 20, 22, 46, 117, 118, 121, 123, 131, 137, 138, 141
friend, 85, 139, 141, 175
friendship, xi, 38, 53, 54, 57, 85

Gadamer, 154
generosity, 53-54
globalism, 39
God, 6, 38, 44, 46, 48, 53, 79, 93, 179, 194, 201
grief, xvii, 41, 68, 168-171

Hacking, Ian, 79
hate, 177-178
health, 166
Hegel, 10, 20, 48
Heidegger, Martin, ix, x, xiv, 4, 20, 21, 22, 27, 28, 31, 32, 35, 36, 37, 52, 96, 102, 167, 171, 188, 191, 194
Helmslef, 36
honor, 41, 53, 77, 79, 198
Hume, David, 28, 29, 30
Husserl, Edmund, ix, 20, 21, 23, 27, 32, 37, 48, 52, 138, 159, 167, 189, 190

immediate, 24, 25, 76, 181
imperative, 7, 8, 11, 12, 24-26, 28-32, 44, 47, 56, 58, 60, 116, 168, 170, 195, 196

jealousy, 182
joy, xii, 28, 39
Joyce, xv, 17, 44, 45, 46, 47, 48, 49, 156
joyous, 68, 76
justice, 42, 110

Kant, Immanuel, 20, 24, 29, 30, 31, 64, 78, 193
Kierkegaard, Soren, xv, 59
Klossowski, Pierre, 37, 187, 196

Lacan, Jacques, 7, 44, 93, 126
Lakoff, George, 36, 91
language, xvii, 35-36, 44, 45, 63, 68, 71, 75, 77, 84, 86, 90, 91, 93-94, 180-181, 185, 190, 194, 195
laughter, 7, 57-58, 66-69, 76, 182-184
Lawrence, D. H., xiv, 4, 17, 80, 192, 193, 202
Lévi-Strauss, Claude, 25, 93, 137
Levinas, Emmanuel, ix, x, xiii, xiv, 20, 22, 23, 24, 25, 28, 32, 36, 37, 44, 47, 52, 60, 64, 88, 91, 123, 128, 131, 138, 167, 187, 190, 192, 193, 195
love, 16, 25, 46, 131n10, 169, 172n3, 182
lust, 5-6, 9-10, 184

mapping, 148-162
Margulis, 36, 131, 132
Mauss, 25
Mead, 180
meaning, 117, 183, 194
Melville, 149
Merleau-Ponty, ix, x, xiii, xiv, 7, 20, 21, 25, 26, 27, 30, 32, 37, 52, 61, 64, 91, 138, 161, 167, 187, 189, 190, 192, 193
Montaigne, xiii
mortality, x, xvii, 12, 28

naked, 97, 119, 123-128, 131
nakedness, 89, 97, 125-128
Nancy, Jean-Luc, xvi, 11, 80, 90, 101, 118, 162, 192, 202
necessity, 29-30, 32
Nietzsche, Friedrich, ix, xiii, xiv, xv, 7, 13, 19, 20, 25, 27, 31, 32, 36, 37, 39, 45, 46, 48, 59, 61, 67, 68, 73,

76, 79, 80, 81, 84, 92, 93, 96, 103, 120, 122, 123, 124, 130, 131, 138, 140, 167, 189, 190, 191, 193, 199, 201
nobility, 53, 92-93, 96, 127
noble, 92-94, 96
nude, 126, 127, 130
nudity, 119, 125-128

obligation, 12, 24, 89
ontology, 124, 193
original, 19, 46
originality, 19
other, xiii, 11, 12, 22-25, 28, 30, 47, 55-58, 72, 74, 86, 91, 116, 117, 122, 123, 124, 125, 127, 128, 135, 136, 137, 139, 140, 142
otherness, xiv, 11, 22, 23, 24, 25, 83, 85, 96, 116, 136, 140, 143

pain, 12, 27, 29, 40, 53, 57-59
passions, 64-70
perception, xiii, 21, 22, 23, 29-32, 37, 54, 61n3, 86, 88, 90-92, 128, 194
phenomenology, xiii, 20, 21, 26, 35, 51-52, 54-55, 64, 77, 170, 188, 189, 190, 191, 194, 195, 196, 197, 198, 201
philosophy, ix-xv, 16, 19, 20-25, 28, 35-37, 40, 43, 44, 46, 48, 52, 55, 56, 58, 59, 61n2, 61n6, 62n7, 63, 64, 75, 78, 79, 119, 167, 168, 171, 182, 183
Piaget, Jean, 147
place, 35, 87, 101-102, 105-107, 139, 149, 157-161, 162n4
Plato, 9, 19, 59, 62, 73, 74, 127, 152, 162
pleasure, 9, 27, 40, 57, 59, 67, 190
Putnam, Hillary, xiii

rage, 39
reconciliation, 41
resentment, 39, 41, 42,

respect, 22, 24, 56-57, 68, 74, 96
responsibility, 47-49, 55-56
Rilke, 108
Rousseau, Jean-Jacques, 136, 145

sacred, 14-16, 43
sacrifice, 43-49
Sartre, Jean-Paul, ix, x, 7, 20, 52, 145, 162
Schneewind, J. B., 78, 81
sex, 123, 197
sexual, 57, 70, 75, 86-87, 122, 123, 125, 126, 127, 132n13, 183-184
singular, xiv, xvi, 28, 68, 69, 101-107
singularity, xvi, 101-105
Socrates, 62, 73, 74, 182, 183
Sontag, Susan, 93
spectacle, xi, 127, 130
Stevens, Wallace, 162
subjectivity, 27, 68, 156
suffering, 84-85, 90, 95-96, 166, 170

tears, 15, 57, 67, 68, 117
Tournier, Michel, xii, xvi, xvii, 133, 134, 136, 137, 138, 140, 141, 143, 144, 145, 146
transgress, 69
trust, xvii, 38, 40, 178-185
truth, 21, 27, 45, 53, 56, 57-58, 67, 68, 74, 76, 77, 179

violation, 58
violence, 23, 38, 45-46, 57, 94
Vonnegut, Kurt, 165
vulnerability, 7, 119, 124-126, 128, 131n9

Whitehead, Alfred North, 19, 161
Whitman, Walt, xiv, 4, 5, 17
Williams, Bernard, xiii, xiv, 37
Wittgenstein, xiv, 37, 172
wonder, 21-22, 84

Zizek, Slavoj, 9, 96

Contributors

Thomas J. Altizer is the author of twelve books including: *The Gospel of Christian Atheism* (1966), *The New Apocalypse* (1967), *The Self-Embodiment of God* (1977), *History as Apocalypse* (1985), *Genesis and Apocalypse* (1990), *The Genesis of God* (1993), and *The Contemporary Jesus* (1997).

Edward S. Casey is a professor at Stony Brook University. Some of his publications are *Remembering: A Phenomenological Study* (1987), *Getting Back into Place* (1993), and *The Fate of Place: A Philosophical History* (1996).

Thomas L. Dumm is a professor of political science at Amherst College. He is the author of *Democracy and Punishment* (1987), *United States* (1994), *Michael Foucault and the Politics of Freedom* (1996, second ed., 2001) and *A Politics of the Ordinary* (1999). He is the founder of the journal *Theory & Event* and served as its coeditor from 1996 to 2001. He is a Guggenheim fellow for the 2001-2002 academic year, and is writing a book on loneliness and experience.

Wolfgang Fuchs is professor of philosophy at Towson University. He has published articles on a variety of contemporary topics, including deconstruction, pragmatism, phenomenology, and semiotics. He is the author of *The Metaphysics of Presence*.

Elizabeth Grosz teaches in Women's and Gender Studies at Rutgers University. She is the author of *Architecture from the Outside: Essays on Virtual and Real Space* (The MIT Press, 2001) and has published widely in the area of feminist theory.

Alexander E. Hooke teaches philosophy at Villa Julie College. He has published articles on Nietzsche, Foucault, Lingis, criminal justice, informal logic, and is editor of *Virtuous Persons, Vicious Deeds*, an ethics anthology.

David Karnos teaches philosophy in Montana. Otherwise, he fishes. He first took courses from Alphonso Lingis at the Pennsylvania State University in 1970. He is coeditor with Robert Shoemaker of *Falling in Love with Wisdom: American Philosophers Talk About Their Calling*.

David Farrell Krell is professor of philosophy and founding director of the Humanities Center at DePaul University in Chicago. He is the author of *The Purest of Bastards: Works of Mourning, Art, and Affirmation in the Thought of Jacques Derrida* (Penn State, 2000), *Contagion: Sexuality, Disease, and Death in German Idealism and Romanticism* (Indiana University Press, 1998), and other scholarly books. He has also written three works of fiction, published by SUNY Press: *The Recalcitrant Art: Diotima's Letters to Holderlin and Related Missives* (2000), *Son of Spirit* (1997), and *Nietzsche: A Novel* (1996).

Gerald Majer teaches literature and writing at Villa Julie College. His essays and poems have been published in numerous journals, including *Georgia Review*, *Western Humanities Review*, and *Yale Review*. He is currently completing a book of essays titled *Jazzed*.

Janice McLane is assistant professor of philosophy at Morgan State University. Her research is on philosophical perspectives on feminism, literature, and the body. She is currently working on a book, *Red Rose of Passion: Women and Internalized Oppression*.

Jean-Luc Nancy is professor of philosophy at the University of Strausborg, France. He is the author of *Being Singular Plural*, *Gravity of Thought*, *Hegel: The Restlessness of the Negative*, and *Birth to Presence*.

Mary Zournazi is a writer, philosopher, and radio producer. Her books include *Foreign Dialogues, After the Revolution—On Kristeva* (with John Lechte). She has forthcoming books, *Hope* (Pluto Press, Lawrence and Wishart)—a book which explores the philosophy and politics of hope, and *Julia Kristeva—A Critical Reader* (Edinburgh Press).